THE BIBLE IN AMERICAN EDUCATION

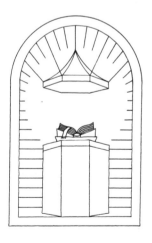

SOCIETY OF BIBLICAL LITERATURE

The Bible in American Culture

General Editors:

Edwin S. Gaustad
Professor of History
University of California, Riverside

Walter Harrelson
Distinguished Professor of Old Testament
Vanderbilt University

1. *The Bible and Bibles in America*
   Edited by Ernest S. Frerichs

2. *The Bible and Popular Culture in America*
   Edited by Allene S. Phy

3. *The Bible in Letters and the Arts*
   Edited by Giles Gunn

4. *The Bible in American Law, Politics, and Rhetoric*
   Edited by James T. Johnson

5. *The Bible in American Education*
   Edited by David Barr and Nicholas Piediscalzi

6. *The Bible and Social Reform*
   Edited by Ernest R. Sandeen

THE BIBLE IN AMERICAN EDUCATION:
From Source Book to Textbook

edited by

DAVID L. BARR
and
NICHOLAS PIEDISCALZI

FORTRESS PRESS
Philadelphia, Pennsylvania

SCHOLARS PRESS
Chico, California

SOCIETY OF BIBLICAL LITERATURE

CENTENNIAL PUBLICATIONS

Editorial Board

© 1982
Society of Biblical Literature

Library of Congress Cataloging in Publication Data

Main entry under title:

The Bible in American education.

(The Bible in American culture)
Includes index.
1. Bible—Study—United States—History—Addresses,
essays, lectures. 2. Bible—Criticism, interpretation,
etc.—United States—History—Addresses, essays,
lectures. 3. Church and education—United States—
History—Addresses, essays, lectures. 4. Religious
education—United States—History—Addresses, essays,
lectures. 5. United States—Religion—Addresses,
essays, lectures. I. Barr, David L. II. Piediscalzi,
Nicholas. III. Series.
BS586.U6B53   1982   220'.07'1073   81-71385
ISBN 0-8006-0612-4   AACR2

34,764

9413E82   Printed in the United States of America   1-612

CONTENTS

Editors and Contributors vii

Preface to the Series ix

Acknowledgments x

Introduction
  David L. Barr & Nicholas Piediscalzi 1

 I. The Creation of a New Order:
   Colonial Education and the Bible
   W. Clark Gilpin 5

 II. The Struggle for a Common Culture: Biblical
   Images in Nineteenth-Century Schoolbooks
   John H. Westerhoff III 25

 III. The Public Schools Are Not Enough: The Bible
   and Private Schools
   Virginia L. Brereton 41

 IV. Stabilizing a Changing Culture: The Bible and the
   Sunday School in the Late Nineteenth Century
   William L. Sachs 77

 V. Intellectual Ferment and Instruction in the
   Scriptures: The Bible in Higher Education
   Thomas H. Olbricht 97

 VI. New Attitudes and New Curricula: The Changing Role
   of the Bible in Protestant Education, 1880–1920
   Charles R. Kniker 121

 VII. New Interest in the Bible: The Contexts of Bible
   Study Today
   Boardman W. Kathan 143

 VIII. The Bible is Worthy of Secular Study: The Bible in
   Public Education Today
   Peter S. Bracher and David L. Barr 165

Index 199

Editors and Contributors

DAVID L. BARR is Associate Professor and Chairperson of the Department of Religion and Co-director of the Public Education Religion Studies Center at Wright State University. He is co-author of *Religion Goes to School.*

PETER S. BRACHER is Professor of English at Wright State University. He is co-editor of *Public Education Religion Studies: Questions and Answers* (PERSC Handbook) and *Religion Studies in the Curriculum: Retrospect and Prospect, 1963–83.*

VIRGINIA L. BRERETON earned her doctorate at Columbia University in 1981. Her dissertation examines the history of Protestant fundamentalist education. She is an author of the collaborative Auburn History of Protestant Theological Education in America (in progress) and has published essays on the history of American Protestant women.

W. CLARK GILPIN is Associate Dean and Associate Professor of Church History at the Graduate Seminary, Phillips University. He is the author of *The Millenarian Piety of Roger Williams.*

BOARDMAN W. KATHAN is Executive Secretary of the Religious Education Association of the U.S. and Canada and a doctoral candidate at New York University. He is co-author of *Youth—Where the Action is.*

CHARLES R. KNIKER is Professor of Education at Iowa State University. He is co-editor of *Myth and Reality,* author of *You and Values Education,* and senior author of *Teaching Today and Tomorrow.*

THOMAS H. OLBRICHT is Dean of the College of Liberal and Fine Arts and Professor of Religion at Abilene Christian University. He is also chairman of the Board of Directors of *The Second Century: A Journal of Early Christian Studies.* He is currently working on a book on the history of biblical studies in America, a subject on which he has published several essays in scholarly books and journals.

NICHOLAS PIEDISCALZI is Professor of Religion and co-director of the Public Education Religion Studies Center at Wright State University. He is co-editor of *Teaching About Religion in Public Schools, Public Education Religion Studies: An Overview; Contemporary Religion and Social Responsibility* and *From Hope to Liberation: Towards a New Marxist-Christian Dialogue.*

WILLIAM L. SACHS recently completed his doctoral studies at the University of Chicago. His dissertation analyzed the relationship between English Evangelicalism and social reform in the early nineteenth century. He is assistant Rector at St. Stephen's Episcopal Church in Richmond, Virginia.

JOHN H. WESTERHOFF III is Professor of Religion and Education at Duke University Divinity School. He is author of *McGuffey and His Readers: Piety, Morality, and Education in Nineteenth Century America*, and current editor of *Religious Education*.

Preface to the Series

To what extent are Americans a "people of the book"? To what degree is the history of their nation intermixt with the theology and story and imagery of the Bible? These and other questions are addressed in the several volumes of our series, The Bible in American Culture.

Initially conceived as part of the 1980 centennial celebration of the Society of Biblical Literature, this series explores the biblical influence—for good or ill—in the arts, music, literature, politics, law, education, ethnicity and many other facets of American civilization in general. It is the task of other series to examine biblical scholarship per se; these books, in contrast, search out the way in which the Bible permeates, subtly or powerfully, the very fabric of life within the United States.

The undersigned heartily commend the individual editors of each volume. They have persisted and pursued until all authors finally entered the fold. We also gladly acknowledge the wise counsel of Samuel Sandmel in an earlier stage of our planning, regretting only that he is not with us at the end.

Finally, we express our deep appreciation to the Lilly Endowment for its generous assistance in bringing this entire series to publication and wider dissemination.

EDWIN S. GAUSTAD
WALTER HARRELSON

Acknowledgments

The editors express appreciation to the following individuals who offered constructive criticism of the early formulations of the thesis and contents of this volume and who suggested individuals who might serve as authors of specific chapters: James S. Ackerman, Peter S. Bracher, Jacob H. Dorn, Robert W. Lynn, Martin E. Marty, the late Samuel Sandmel and Thayer S. Warshaw. The editors made all final decisions, however, and are wholly responsible for the thesis, the topics, and the selection of authors.

Gratitude is offered also to Mrs. Veda Horton, Secretary of the Department of Religion at Wright State University, for her patient and careful typing of manuscripts.

D.L.B.
N.P.

FOR OUR WIVES,

Judy
and
Sibyl

Introduction

David L. Barr and Nicholas Piediscalzi

Intimately related to the origins and development of American educational institutions, the Bible was taught by both clergy and laity in the churches, homes, and schools of colonial America. In 1647 the Massachusetts Bay Colony adopted "Ye olde deluder Satan Act," which called for the establishment of schools to help children develop the "ability to read and understand the principles of religion and the capital lawes of this country" and thereby frustrate "one chiefe project of ye olde deluder, Satan, to keepe men from the knowledge of ye Scriptures." The Bible was viewed as the foundation of true religion and piety, the source of morality and law, and the handbook on social and political order.

Three hundred and sixteen years later the Supreme Court ruled that devotional readings from the Bible in the public schools of Pennsylvania and Maryland at the beginning of each day were unconstitutional. It appeared to many that a radical cultural shift had taken place, and in many ways it had, though not in the way usually suggested. The Court did not banish the Bible from public education, for it continues to play a significant role even today in both public and private education in America. This role, however, is very different from that imagined by the Puritan ancestors.

As long as the colonies remained small and fairly homogeneous the Bible served as a source of unity and harmony. However, as soon as they began to grow and include different Protestant and non-Protestant groups, theological controversies over correct interpretation of the Scriptures arose and the Bible became a source of conflict and divisiveness. These conflicts in turn influenced the educational institutions of the society. In some places these conflicts led to the establishment of new private schools based upon specific theological traditions and interpretations of the Bible, while in public schools controversy became so severe that the Bible was reduced to being read without comment in the vain hope that conflicting interpretations could be avoided.

Many other factors contributed to the changing role of the Bible in American life, including new developments in science and in historiography that seemed to question the accuracy and authority of the Bible. Religious communions reacted to these changes in a variety of ways. Many accepted in varying degrees the new knowledge and incorporated it into their study and use of the Bible; others rejected it and devoted themselves to regaining the Bible's hegemony over the society. But whether open to these new ideas or trying to reclaim a lost heritage, each group's views and actions had profound effects upon the structure and curricula of both public and private educational institutions.

These conflicts and changes reveal the constant interaction between the Bible, the religious organizations, the educational institutions, and other cultural forces in American society. At times the Bible has been used to shape the culture and at times its interpretation has been shaped by cultural changes. This book endeavors to trace the long, complex, and often confused interaction between the Bible and education in America. These chapters show the impact of the Bible as a powerful force in education in the seventeenth and eighteenth centuries and reveal the gradual decline of that force in the nineteenth and twentieth centuries. But it is not a case of simple decline in influence, for the Bible remains an immensely popular and widely studied book—both in private and public education. These essays illuminate the sources of the present paradoxical situation in which the Bible has no official standing in our public life and yet remains the most widely studied book in America. Each chapter attempts to trace the relationship between the Bible and education in a specific historical period, often focusing on only one type of educational institution or activity.

W. Clark Gilpin reviews the complex relation between the Bible and the origin and development of elementary, secondary, and higher education in the American colonies. He shows how the Bible and the schools were viewed as the major sources of reformation of church and society, while at the same time they were used to justify and reinforce existing values and social structures. Even though the Bible was interpreted at first according to assumptions transmitted from European institutions, it eventually was used to challenge them and became a source for new assumptions and new institutional structures.

John H. Westerhoff III traces the use of the Bible in the textbooks of the nineteenth century. By a careful examination of the various editions of McGuffey's *Eclectic Readers*, he demonstrates how, owing to radical changes in America, the biblical content and Calvinist theology which dominated textbooks during the first fifty years of that century gradually disappeared and were replaced by the tenets and values of a newly forged "civil religion." This was no simple process but represented a confluence of the growing pluralism, the increase in government control over education, the growth of a rationalistic ideal, and the need to enhance national unity.

Virginia L. Brereton explores how disputes over the Bible and its gradual removal from the public schools led several religious bodies to establish alternative school systems and supplemental religious education programs. She also examines the problems these innovations raised for the religious institutions and parents who wanted their children to receive an education equal to that provided by the public schools so that they would not be put at a financial and social disadvantage. Despite these obstacles, the impetus toward alternative schools continues strong into the current century.

William L. Sachs analyzes the American Sunday school movement and describes how the Bible, originally used in the nineteenth century to "civilize" the children of immigrant laborers and to preserve a Protestant social order, gradually came to be treated as a primer for salvation. In the process he shows how the Sunday school movement became more sophisticated in its teaching methods and traces the conflicts between the interdenominational Sunday school societies and denominational churches.

Thomas H. Olbricht reviews the major works of six prominent biblical scholars—William H. Green (Princeton), Joseph Henry Thayer (Andover and Harvard), Crawford H. Toy (Harvard), Charles A. Briggs (Union Theological Seminary), Benjamin W. Bacon (Yale) and Shailer Mathews (Chicago) in order to delineate the influence of late nineteenth-century intellectual and cultural perspectives upon biblical pedagogy. Olbricht discovers that, even though these six scholars differ in their approaches and conclusions, all of them share a single cultural expectation—that a historical study of the Bible would enable them and others to attain a new identity and a viable faith in a changing world.

Charles R. Kniker traces a similar shift in the popular literature of American Protestant education at the beginning of the twentieth century. Controversies over the use of the Bible in public education and the development of new study methods in denominational curricula are examined as Kniker investigates the cultural factors that led most Protestants to shift from presenting the Bible as the undisputed source of God's infallible revelation to calling for a scholarly analysis of the Bible and religious questions in general. "Scientific reasoning" became the hallmark of Protestant leaders: they strove to establish an educated piety as a foundation for the new world emerging in their midst.

Boardman W. Kathan surveys the many and diverse Bible study programs and resource materials available in contemporary churches and synagogues and other religious agencies. He sets these study materials in the context of a cultural search for meaning, trying to provide biblical solutions for contemporary problems. He shows clearly that there is no dearth of interest in studying the Bible; in divergent traditions, in divergent ways, the Bible continues to make a major impact on contemporary education.

In the final chapter Peter S. Bracher and David L. Barr analyze how the 1963 *Schempp* decision of the United States Supreme Court served as a catalyst for introducing the study of the Bible in public schools. They survey the various developments of the past two decades, giving special emphasis to the different ways in which the Bible is studied in the English, humanities, and social science curricula. Focusing on the Bible as literature, they show the various ways the Bible is properly studied in the public school context, pointing out the resources available and discussing the special problems raised by introducing an academic study of the Bible into public education. They analyze such problems as objectivity, sensitivity, teacher competency, appropriate methods, and adequate study materials.

Taken together these essays alert us to the diversity of times, places, and educational issues that have been shaped by the Bible and demonstrate how those events have shaped our own perceptions of the Bible. This dialectical relationship between the Bible and the various educational and cultural forces examined in these essays is the primary focus of this volume. It is an ongoing dialectic of which we must be continually cognizant. Neither the present intense interest in the Bible nor its lack of authority in our public life can be adequately understood until we see from whence we have come. The editors hope that the reader who carefully explores the specific educational and historical vignettes of these various chapters will gain some perspective on the present interaction between the Bible and American education.

I

The Creation of a New Order:
Colonial Education and the Bible

W. Clark Gilpin

From the reign of Henry VIII to that of James I the great venture of English education was the translation of the Bible. Contemporary tradition held that William Tyndale had embarked upon his career as a biblical translator with the vow that "if God spare my life, ere many years I will cause a boy that driveth the plough shall know more of the Scripture" than the reputedly learned person of the day (Bruce: 29). With a similarly broad audience in mind, Richard Cox, Bishop of Ely, gave the terse injunction "ink-horn terms to be avoided" to the translators preparing the Bishop's Bible of 1568 (Pollard: 291). "All manner of persons, of what estate or condition soever they be," wrote Archbishop Thomas Cranmer in his preface to the Great Bible of 1539, would learn from this book "what they ought to believe, what they ought to do, and what they should not do, as well concerning Almighty God, as also concerning themselves, and all others" (Bruce: 71). It was a formula that would be frequently repeated: knowledge of one's duties to God, to self, and to others has its foundation in a genuine knowledge of Scripture. To the widest limits of the literate public the vernacular Bible was to educate the English character, to form its habits of mind and of conduct (Bruce: 29).

In the first half of the seventeenth century, this sense of the educative potency of the English Bible played a major role in establishing the methods and goals of colonial education. During those years the European colonies in America were transformed from unstable mercantile outposts into settlements that were rapidly developing the institutions of a permanent society: households, churches, schools, governments, and a network of merchants supplying the needs of daily living. With this developing permanence came the necessity for education—the selective but systematic transmission of European culture to the American colonies and its adaptation there to meet the new environment. The magnitude of this task accentuated the educational responsibilities of virtually every social institution, and modern historians of colonial education have rightly stressed that a wide variety of social agencies—not simply schools—were engaged in the educational "effort to transmit or evoke knowledge, attitudes, values, skills, and sensibilities"

(Bailyn; Cremin: xiii). This broader perspective is especially appropriate for understanding the educational roles of the Bible, which were as vigorously pursued in the church and household as in the school or college.

The transit of culture from old world to new was of course no simple process. In the first place, the European settlements in America were not simply English; the Spanish, French, Dutch, and Swedes established colonies as an aspect of governmental and economic policy, while French Huguenots, Sephardic Jews, Scottish Presbyterians, and a variety of German sectarians migrated for less "official" personal, economic, and religious reasons. But despite this colonial pluralism it was the English who most clearly understood their colonies as "permanent, self-sustaining communities," who pursued that vision in the greatest numbers and with the most methodical vigor, and who successfully defended it during the colonial wars of the eighteenth century (Cremin: 22–23). It was thus the case that English culture, including English patterns of education, ordered the diversities of life in the thirteen colonies. By the middle of the eighteenth century, for example, the Dutch Reformed Church in New York City was seeking an English-speaking pastor, Swedes were neglecting their native tongue in favor of English, and Huguenots in South Carolina were affiliating with the Church of England (Wright: 49–54). Not every group or individual sought such thorough assimilation to English ways, but the prevalence of this pattern suggests the extent to which English customs and institutions prevailed throughout the colonial period.

In large measure, the English cultural hegemony was rendered possible by those who were placed beyond the boundaries of the consensus. Although the thirteen colonies contained a variety of nationalities, they were overwhelmingly Protestant. By the 1780s there were only fifty-six Roman Catholic churches, and Bishop John Carroll of Baltimore would report only 24,500 communicants in 1785, at which time the total white population of the United States exceeded 3,000,000 (Gaustad: 4–5, 36). The native Americans and the Africans imported as slaves were also on the margins of this white and Protestant society, and as will be seen the ambivalent attitudes of whites toward them profoundly affected colonial educational efforts.

All of these factors—the effort to bring European culture to a new environment, the steady expansion of colonial society, and the relative diversity of the population—demanded that sustained attention be given not only to the "content" of education but to its broad social aims. Its preeminent task was the formation of character, equipping the person with the skills and virtues appropriate for life at his or her station in society. And its cardinal objectives were epitomized in three attributes: piety, civility, and learning.

The Bible and the Ends of Education

In the pursuit of piety, civility, and learning, knowledge of the Bible was in no small measure an educational end in itself. Throughout the colonial period, the Protestant majority fiercely insisted that the ability and the liberty to read the Bible were essential to their faith. It was further assumed that freedom to study Scripture was a right that had to be defended from the encroachments of Catholic nations, and in 1754 at the beginning of the French and Indian War the Boston parson Jonathan Mayhew sounded this alarm:

> Do I behold these territories of freedom, become the prey of arbitrary power? . . . Do I see the slaves of Lewis with their Indian allies, dispossessing the free-born subjects of King George, of the inheritance received from their forefathers, and purchased at the expense of their ease, their treasure, their blood! . . . Do I see a protestant, there taking a look at his Bible, and being taken in the fact and punished like a felon! (Sweet: 11–12)

Development of the ability to read the Bible and know its contents, therefore, represented a duty to be pursued in a host of formal and informal settings. One sees it not only in the catechizing of Henry Muhlenberg among Lutherans on the Pennsylvania frontier but also in the personal discipline of Virginia aristocrat William Byrd, arising at six to breakfast upon a bowl of warm milk and two chapters from the Bible, one in Hebrew and one in Greek. It appears as well in the rearing of young Benjamin Franklin, whose father "had a clear and pleasing voice, so that when he played psalm tunes on his violin and sung withal, as he sometimes did in an evening after the business of the day was over, it was extremely agreeable to hear" (Franklin: 13–14). And it is clearly evident in the labors of Anglican missionaries of the Society for the Propagation of the Gospel, who taught slaves in Virginia and North Carolina to read the Bible and the Book of Common Prayer with sufficient skill to participate regularly in public worship. But to regard knowledge of the Bible simply as one among the several aims of colonial education would be to neglect the more formative influence it had upon colonial ideas about the very nature and purpose of education. It would also obscure important changes that occurred over the seventeenth and eighteenth centuries in the relation between the Bible and the ends of education.

The seventeenth-century founders of American society discerned in Scripture the patterns by which God directed the whole of human destiny, and they were convinced that all true knowledge was ordered by its relation to that divine plan. Hence, the methods and aims of education were finally to be governed by the biblical revelation, and in the most fundamental way God was the one true teacher. This view of education was particularly evident among the Puritans who settled New England in the decades following 1630. Having arisen as a movement of dissent against the English religious establishment, the Puritans were stimulated by a rigorous religious discipline to strive for a thorough reformation of church and society. They believed that the divine pattern for that reformation was revealed in Scripture, and they hoped to order all elements of social life in accordance with its rule.

The Puritans carried this reforming zeal with them to New England, where they sought to make "godly" citizens the foundation for what Massachusetts Governor John Winthrop called "a due form of Government both civill and ecclesiasticall." Following this principle, in 1631 Massachusetts Bay Colony restricted citizenship through legislation that declared "noe man shalbe admitted to the freedome of this body polliticke, but such as are members of some of the churches within the lymitts of the same" (Forbes: 2:293; Shurtleff: 1:87). From this perspective the Puritans, more than any other group within seventeenth-century colonial society, succeeded in institutionalizing the Bible's influence upon the basic goals of education.

This Puritan vision of the relation between the Bible and the ends of education may be said to have begun with their assessment of what actually was entailed in the phrase *knowledge of the Bible*. It could not mean, they were convinced, simply an objective knowledge of the contents of the Bible. Genuine knowledge must also include acknowledgment of the authority of Scripture in one's life and the redirection of life and conduct upon the basis of that authority. Further, they agreed with John Calvin that this capacity to know and apply the truth of Scripture was not within the unaided power of human reason or will. Rather, said Calvin, the believer's conviction that the Bible was in fact the word of truth was an assurance granted by the immediate testimony of the Spirit of God.

> For as God alone is a suitable witness for his own word, so also the word will never gain credit in the hearts of men until it is sealed by the internal testimony of the Spirit. It is necessary that the same Spirit who spoke by the mouth of the prophets should penetrate our hearts in order to convince us that they delivered faithfully the message that was divinely given. (Dowey: 106)

The Puritans redirected and elaborated Calvin's position by connecting the Holy Spirit's immediate verification of Scripture's authority with the experience of conversion. In conversion, the Puritans argued, the believer was granted a new capacity of discernment, a new "taste" or "relish" for God and his creation as Jonathan Edwards would later put it. This new gift of discernment enabled the person to see and act upon what "natural man" could not see: the unitary meaning of Scripture, which ordered one's duties to God, to self, and to neighbor. They would have agreed enthusiastically with the English divine John Preston, when he said that in conversion "there is a sagacitie given to the Saints, a certaine new qualitie, that others want, by which they are able to finde out the steppes of *Gods* way" (192).

Clearly, then, Puritan theology placed the ends of education—piety, civility, and learning—within a definite hierarchy. Civility, in the sense of a capacity for responsible leadership within society, was impossible apart from genuine piety; again, in early Massachusetts only church members, "visible saints," were eligible for citizenship. Likewise, learning, whether it be the classical scholarship of the gentility or the utilitarian skills of the artisans, was vain without religious virtue; in regard to classical literature, for instance, the Puritans were virtually unanimous in their agreement with Augustine that it was fruitless and misleading when read uninformed by the Spirit of God. M. M. Knappen has observed, therefore, that "the Puritan enthusiasm for learning was thus a strictly limited zeal, confined to those branches which were of direct assistance in building up the Puritan commonwealth, but it was inspired by the glory of the millennial vision to which it opened the way, and it flamed with corresponding vigor" (468).

The educational influences of the conversion experience were far-reaching. According to Puritan divines on both sides of the Atlantic, the process of conversion was the means by which God rescued the elect from the sinful mass of humanity, redirected their vision toward the divine glory, and empowered them to pursue a life of obedience to the divine will. As such, it inculcated lasting habits of personal religious discipline, initiated believers into the Puritan community's devotion to "Root and Branch" reformation, and incorporated them into a view of the world founded upon a searching study of Scripture. Thus, as Jerald C. Brauer has observed, conversion represented the motivating center of the Puritan movement: "Almost every Puritan of stature appears to have had a profound conversion experience. They preached for it, they sought it, they recounted it in spiritual biographies and in hagiographies, they checked its authenticity with those already converted, and they disdained those who had not experienced it" (230).

Although conversions were occasionally recounted as "instantaneous" events, they were more usually described as processes drawn out over several years. In these spiritual journeys the Bible had several important functions, and the account set forth in 1637 by Governor John Winthrop of Massachusetts is illustrative of their basic features (Forbes: 3:338–44). Winthrop recalled his youth as amply illustrating the ill-effects of original sin; he was often "very lewdly disposed," and his interest in religion was ephemeral and selfishly motivated. At eighteen he married into a family under the care of a Puritan pastor and found that his conscience would no longer allow him to "dally with religion." During this time he began to reform his manners, would travel many miles to hear a sermon which "did search deep into the Conscience," and took some pride in the admiration that others had of his piety. But looking back, Winthrop recognized that these changes were only external, a legalistic "Covenant of workes," while his actual "affections" toward God "were not constant but very unsettled." He continued in this troubled state for some time, all the while reading and hearing Puritan sermons, studying the Bible, "opening" his case to his minister, and leading his family in regular devotions. In so doing "the difference between the Covenant of Grace, and the Covenant of workes . . . began to take great impression" upon him. Finally, when he was about thirty years of age, the long struggle of introspection, testing, and doubt was resolved in an experience of assurance in which Winthrop realized that the promises of the gospel were made to him: "Now could my soule close with Christ, and rest there with sweet content." From that state of spiritual contentment and sense of unity with Christ, Winthrop was launched upon the journey of sanctification, still experiencing "conflicts between the flesh and the spirit," yet never losing the vision of the divinely revealed destiny and meaning of his life.

As Winthrop's narration indicates, the total resources of the Puritan community were brought to bear upon the conversion experience. Sermons, manuals of piety, the counsel of pastors, and the concern of family were among the "means" used by God in this transformation of character. But the Bible was the preeminent authority. Again and again the spiritual itinerary of conversion was checked against Scripture; it was the sure guide to one's spiritual state; to search its pages was to search one's heart. In this sense, the Puritans again agreed with Calvin that knowledge of God and a true knowledge of self existed in the closest conjunction. Hence, the pattern of Winthrop's conversion—youthful depravity, legalistic reform, conviction of the need for grace, and sense of assurance—stood parallel to what the Puritans conceived to be the scriptural history of redemption: the Adamic fall, the Old Testament covenant of works, and the New Testament covenant of grace prefigured in Abraham and realized in Christ. One thus entered the biblical world by conversion. The Spirit which had inspired the writers of Scripture now enlightened its godly readers, and this spiritual continuity enabled the Bible to be illuminated by present experience and to act as a criterion for testing that experience (see Nuttall).

The significance that these views attached to a serious study of the Bible is apparent in the daily conduct of personal and public life. Massachusetts law, for example, required a strict observance of the Sabbath and called for the selectmen of every town to inquire into the ability of children and apprentices to read and to understand the basic principles of religion. Personal Bible reading was urged and guided by a host of devotional manuals. Merely to list some titles indicates the context of piety within which the Bible was to be read: *The Whole Duty of Man, A Guide to Godlynesse*, or *The Plaine Mans Path-Way to Heaven*. Best loved among these manuals throughout the seventeenth century was *The Practise of Pietie* (1612) by Lewis Bayly. The educational message of Bayly's work was that the cultivation of piety ordered all learning, and he presented a clear daily discipline of prayer, meditation, and reading by which that goal might be pursued. He gave instructions for a program of morning and evening Bible reading that would take the reader through the Scriptures once each year. And he gave particular advice upon how this reading might be done with most profit: "Apply these things to thine owne heart, and reade not these Chapters as matters of *Historicall* discourse; but as if they were so many *Letters* or *Epistles* sent downe from God out of *heaven* unto thee" (245–46).

This sense of the direct applicability of Scripture to present experience was also evident in Puritan exegetical methods. For example, they shared with such Dutch reformed theologians as Johannes Cocceius a devotion to the typological interpretation of Scripture. By this method events of the Old Testament were understood to be the "types" by which God prefigured the events of the New Testament, and a single narrative significance was thereby given to the whole of Scripture. Further, the Bible was believed to contain types or prefigurements of later, contemporary, and future history until the end of the world. Thus, there was revealed in Scripture, for discerning eyes, the single total pattern of history, and present experience was literally included in that scriptural narrative (see Frei: 1–50). The significance of this for Puritan social views is clearly illustrated in the famous controversy of the 1640s between John Cotton and Roger Williams over religious liberty and the separation of church and state. In large measure, the debate was conducted in terms of differing typological interpretations of ancient Israel. Cotton and Williams agreed that the Bible revealed normative patterns for the social order. But Cotton argued that ancient Israel prefigured a holy commonwealth such as Massachusetts Bay in which church and state were coordinate and mutually supporting powers. Williams asserted in opposition that Israel prefigured separated congregations of the faithful, free to pursue true religion without benefit or hindrance from the coercive power of the state.

Puritan conceptions of the authority of the Bible were also evident in their propensity for millenarian exegesis. In this case the conviction that the Bible revealed the whole order of history was coupled with speculation about the one thousand year reign of the saints foretold in Revelation. From John Cotton in the 1630s to Jonathan Edwards in the 1730s, the effort to perceive the relation between the present and that promised age of glory was a regular concern of colonial divines. Interest in such speculation had considerable effect upon Indian missions, for instance. Since the earliest days of American colonization, theories had been propounded about the identity of the native Americans which would locate them within the Genesis account of the population of the earth. By the seventeenth century such missionaries to the Indians as John Eliot of Roxbury were identifying them with the ten lost tribes of Israel. The prevalent belief among pious English folk that the conversion of those tribes was part of the biblical calendar of events anticipating the millennium stirred interest in and financial support for Eliot's missionary ventures. Once again, the effort was to place each new experience or encounter within the biblical order.

Genuinely to know the Bible, then, meant being enabled to discern through its revelation the providential order which governed the whole creation. More than any other colonial thinker, Jonathan Edwards was able to capture and express brilliantly this Puritan understanding of true religious knowledge. Apart from the revelation of Scripture, Edwards wrote in 1739, life's episodes "will all look like confusion, like a number of jumbled events coming to pass without any order or method, like the tossing of the waves of the sea." But when one considers these events in the light of Scripture, "they appear far from being jumbled and confused, an orderly series of events, all wisely ordered and directed in excellent harmony and consistence, tending all to one end." Hence, human knowledge of the order and significance of existence depends upon the biblical revelation:

> Now there is nothing else that informs us what this scheme and design of God in his works is, but only the Holy Scriptures. Nothing else pretends to set in view the whole series of God's works of providence from beginning to end, and to inform us how all things were from God at first, and for what end they are, and how they are ordered from the beginning, and how they will proceed to the end of the world. (Heimert: 30–33)

As these quotations from Edwards suggest, Puritan conceptions of the relation between the Bible and the aims of education prevailed well into the eighteenth century. Further, despite hearty disagreement with Puritan insistence upon the conversion experience, other Protestant educators in the colonies shared these general views. Fruitful learning and the proper conduct of civil life depended upon a vital piety, and piety in turn depended upon the revealed truths of Scripture. The duties of social life were grounded in the prior covenant of God. In 1706, for instance, Anglican schoolteachers employed by the Society for the Propagation of the Gospel were told that their primary objective was "instructing and disposing Children to believe and live as Christians." They were to teach children to read in order "that they may be capable of reading the Holy Scriptures, and other pious and useful Books, for informing their Understandings, and regulating their Manners" (Knight: 1:75–77).

Indeed, the middle decades of the eighteenth century witnessed a revitalization and extension of Puritan educational theory in the religious revival known as the Great Awakening. Throughout the colonies and in most of the denominations, advocates of the Awakening insisted that the fruitful exercise of learning was dependent upon the grace of God and the disciplines of pious living. The revivalist position was particularly evident in debates among the Presbyterians regarding ministerial training. Gilbert Tennent's polemical sermon "The Danger of an Unconverted Ministry" (1740), for example, argued that theological education was of no avail to ministers "ignorant of the New-Birth." Pastors "having no Experience of a special Work of the Holy Ghost, upon their own Souls" would likely be guilty of faulty exegesis, of "misapplying the Word" in their sermons, and hence of misleading their congregations (H. S. Smith: 1:324–35). This zeal for piety as the foundation of learning would make the revivalistic Presbyterians leaders in ministerial education and the founding of colleges over the remainder of the century.

But over the course of the eighteenth century a variety of social and intellectual changes were serving to shift the balance in the traditional hierarchy of the aims of education. First, continued immigration, the need for able colonists, and the lure of American space were rapidly breaking down illusions of uniformity in the colonies. German Lutheran and Reformed were arriving in significant numbers, and a major immigration from the north of Ireland was spreading Scotch-Irish Presbyterianism throughout the colonies. This diversity was especially evident in New York and Pennsylvania, and William Warren Sweet has stated that "in 1776 there were in Pennsylvania 403 different congregations. Of these 106 were German Reformed; 68 were Presbyterian; 63 Lutheran; 61 Quaker; 33 Episcopalian; 27 Baptist; 14 Moravian; 13 Mennonite; 13 Dunker or German Baptist Brethren; 9 Catholic and 1 Dutch Reformed" (163). Furthermore, there was a dramatic increase in the black slave population during this period. In 1715, 58,850 black slaves were registered in the colonies; on the eve of the Revolution that number had risen to 409,145 (H. S. Smith: 1:190).

Second, Enlightenment rationalism was making its appearance (albeit sometimes timidly) upon the American scene. In various ways such colonial thinkers as John Wise, Samuel Quincy, and Benjamin Franklin were reasserting the integrity of human reason and rethinking its relation to revelation. And the educational views of John Locke, especially as popularized in such works as Isaac Watts's *Improvement of the Mind* (1751), were suggesting new methods in formal education.

This increased social and intellectual diversity of the eighteenth century tested the ability of educational institutions to succeed at their traditional task of promoting social harmony and order. Merle Curti has argued persuasively that in the colonial period, "religious conformity and the maintenance of existing authority characterized educational efforts" (4). However, the reasons advanced in support of social order shifted perceptibly as the colonial period progressed. Perhaps too simply put, the authority of reason as well as revelation began to be cited in justification of the order of colonial institutions; and civility—the qualities of responsible citizenship—began to challenge, or at least redefine, piety in its place as the chief aim of education.

In 1717, for example, John Wise's *Vindication of the Government of New-England Churches* added the "light of reason" to that of special revelation in arguing the rightness of congregational polity. His observations in the same tract upon the basis of civil government took a similar direction:

> It is certain civil government in general, is a very admirable result of providence, and an incomparable benefit to mankind, yet must needs be acknowledged to be the effect of human free-compacts and not of divine institution; it is the produce of mans reason, of human rational combinations, and not from any direct orders of infinite wisdom, in any positive law wherein is drawn up this or that scheme of civil government. (H. S. Smith: 1:385).

Both of Wise's arguments were at variance with the earlier Puritan view that Scripture propounded what John Winthrop had called a "due form of Goverment" in church and state. These differences have been called a "unique feature" of Wise's *Vindication*, for which he "may therefore well be called the Morning Light of the American Age of Reason" (H. S. Smith: 1:384).

Benjamin Franklin is another notable example of this rationalistic trend among some eighteenth-century colonial thinkers. Having read the literature of the English Deists as a young man, in later life he reached the conclusion that their doctrine, "tho' it might be true," was not useful in promoting good character. Despite this caveat, he did not turn to the revealed authority of Scripture as a sanction for morality:

> Revelation had indeed no weight with me as such; but I entertain'd an opinion that, though certain actions might not be bad because they were forbidden by it, or good because it commanded them, yet probably these actions might be forbidden because they were bad for us, or commanded because they were beneficial to us, in their own natures, all the circumstances of things considered. (Franklin: 71–73)

In this brief statement, Franklin had summarily reversed the relation between reason and revelation that had been developed in the Puritan tradition. Whereas for Puritanism the divine order discerned in the Scriptures by faith had been determinative of truth and goodness, Franklin now argued that the relations among things "in their own natures, all the circumstances of things considered" determined good and bad. Revelation, he added, "probably" conformed to this criterion of reasonable observation.

In a similar manner, the conception of religion held by such persons as Franklin and Thomas Jefferson shifted the essence of religion from divinely inspired piety to moral virtue, the personal integrity and public spirit that made one a responsible citizen. Religious belief in turn was evaluated in terms of its "tendency to inspire, promote, or confirm morality" (Franklin: 100). The broad effect of these changes upon the aims of education was to redefine religion in such a way that civility became the primary virtue to be pursued through education. Piety, meanwhile, came to be associated with the particularities of doctrine, worship, or behavior that characterized the separate denominations; as such it was no longer the prior necessity for sound citizenship or true learning. Education, in sum, was here portrayed as an activity in which the human person, not God, was the principal actor.

The Bible and the Institutions of Education

The development of the social institutions within which the Bible played an educational role was gradual and uneven in the colonial period. Household and church had particularly large educational responsibilities in the early decades, while the influence of missions, schools, and colleges remained quite limited until the eighteenth century. The shapes that these institutions took were affected not only be the broad goals of education discussed above but also by a number of social and environmental factors.

During the seventeenth century geography placed severe limits upon the development of schools and colleges, especially outside New England. The widely separated plantations of Virginia, for example, made it very difficult to establish schools there. Thus, although as early as 1619 attempts were made to raise funds for a "college" at Henrico for native American and white children, no college would actually exist in Virginia until the founding of William and Mary in 1693. By contrast, New England was blessed with what Louis B. Wright has called "the great advantage of a compact town life, which more than any other factor made possible its educational progress" (99). Largely as a consequence, Massachusetts successfully set up three important educational institutions—the Boston Latin School, Harvard College, and a printing press—during the first decade of its existence.

Another important factor for education in the seventeenth century was the degree to which the colonies depended upon European governments and churches for educational leadership. Among the Dutch Reformed, the Lutherans, and the Anglicans, efforts to obtain adequate supplies of Bibles or hymnals, to produce their own catechetical materials, and especially to obtain trained and competent ministers were a regular source of friction between the colonies and ecclesiastical authorities at home. Yet another factor that influenced institutional development was the degree to which education was controlled by the clergy. Whether as private tutors, college faculty, or local pastors, the clergy largely controlled education in the colonies; and, as is well known, preparation of a learned clergy was a primary stimulus to the establishment of America's two colleges of the seventeenth century, Harvard and William and Mary.

These factors underwent partial change in the eighteenth century. As the population increased and settlements were extended, geography became less of an impediment to the development of schools and colleges, although the South still progressed more slowly than New England and the Middle Colonies. This development of American educational institutions in turn made the churches somewhat less dependent upon Europe for educated leadership, although at mid-century there were acerbic debates within the Dutch Reformed and Presbyterian churches over the necessity of a degree from a European university as a qualification for ministry.

During the eighteenth century clerical and religious influences on education remained quite strong. Teachers in New England, for example, were generally "required throughout the eighteenth century to secure clerical approval before assuming their functions" (Curti: 12). Schoolteachers representing the Society for the Propagation of the Gospel were expected to consult frequently with the parish minister "about the Methods of managing their Schools, and be ready to be advised by him" (Knight: 1:76–77). And in 1785 the Presbyterian Synod of New York and Pennsylvania emphasized the connection between the education of children and the advancement of religion and morality; churches were to make the establishment and care of schools "a part of their congregational business" and to solicit contributions supporting such schools (Gewehr: 220–21).

Of the social factors affecting education in the colonial period, perhaps the most resistant to change was the anti-Catholic sentiment of the Protestant majority. Among the colonial colleges, only the College of Philadelphia and the College of Rhode Island admitted Catholics, while Catholic schools were prohibited (Sweet: 181–82). In sum, two factors shaped the way in which most people studied the Bible in the colonial era. First, the study of the Bible was often pursued in the informal settings of homes, churches, or schools without trained leaders. Second, most people maintained a strong sense of affiliation with specific denominations, which provided their own resources for interpreting the Bible.

The vernacular Bibles that had begun to be produced in the sixteenth century already contained significant study helps. Among English translations, for example, Coverdale's Bible (1535) was the first to introduce chapter summaries; the Geneva Bible (1560) became famous for its marginal notes; and no translation, including the Authorized Version of 1611, was presented to the public without explanatory prefaces. Similar study aids appeared in other vernacular Bibles brought to America such as the Swedish version of 1702–3 known as Charles XII's Bible. To these helps were added the innumerable manuals of piety that directed disciplined study and the commentaries upon Scripture that regularly came from the pens of local pastors as well as university fellows.

This churchly context for colonial education and the study of the Bible was also evident in the educational uses made of catechisms, psalters, and liturgies. They served as reading primers and thereby provided instruction in the interpretation of the Bible and familiarity with its contents. So, for example, generations of colonial Anglicans learned the Psalms in the version of the Great Bible through their use of the Book of Common Prayer. Such aids to the study of Scripture were particularly useful for the Bible's least formal but most prevalent educational setting—the household. In colonial society with its paucity of more specialized educational institutions, the household by necessity was a center of learning. Its educational responsibilities had been delineated in a number of popular tracts on "household government," and these typically defined "a network of mutual responsibilities and obligations that pertain within the family, viewing education as a primary duty parents owe their children and, by extension, their wards, servants, and apprentices" (Cremin: 50–51). In *Bonifacius: An Essay upon the Good*, the Puritan divine Cotton Mather (1663–1728) drew together this advice on family education in a way that throws useful light upon the role of the Bible. Mather proposed a number of methods that were designed simply to teach children the contents of the Bible: stories from the Bible at the dinner table or rewards for the memorization of verses. And he advised that these stories and verses be selected to match the age, interests, and abilities of the individual child. But Mather insisted that such teaching must be combined with observations upon "some *lessons* of piety, to be inferred" from the story or verse. He suggested that fathers teach children to pray, for example, by directing the children "that every morning they shall take one text or two out of the *Sacred Scripture*, and shape it into a *desire*, which they shall add unto their *usual prayer*" (44, 46). Mather extended these educational responsibilities to include the servants of the household, advocating that they not only be furnished with Bibles but also be allowed specific time for reading them.

Like the family, the church had very extensive educational tasks during the colonial period. The pastor in particular was understood to be the chief educator of many communities, and this responsibility was fulfilled in a variety of ways in addition to preaching. One noteworthy instance was the minister's role as lender of books. This had been a typical practice among both Anglican and Puritan ministers of the seventeenth century, and it was widely used as an educational device by the ministers of various communions who participated in the Great Awakening of the eighteenth century. But it was raised to a high calling by the Anglican Society for the Propagation of the Gospel. Founded in 1701 by Thomas Bray, the S.P.G. printed a full library of books for lending and distribution, including not only devotional works but also volumes on utilitarian topics such as agriculture and gardening. By the end of the century the Methodists had similarly established their own book concern and were distributing denominational tracts and sermons, which provided a common literature binding together the Methodist societies and educating them in Methodist principles (Gewehr: 165–66). The usefulness of such book lending was limited by the inability of many people to read. Cotton Mather suggested that the prudent pastor in parish calls would seek to discover such problems: "Some of the *lesser folks*, you may order, to bring their *Bibles* unto you, and read unto you from thence two or three verses, whereto you may turn them. This will *try*, whether they can *read well*, or no" (76). Similar problems with literacy in North Carolina led S.P.G. missionaries there to recommend that

> If the Society would send . . . as many well-bound bibles and prayer-books for the ministers desks as there are parishes, it would have a better effect than a ship load of small books recommending the duty of a christian. The ignorant would hear their duty delivered out of the former, when they would not instruct themselves in the latter. (Knight: 1:92–93)

Not only ministers and missionaries but also the laity had significant educational responsibilities in the colonial churches. Prominent among the institutions promoting this responsibility were the study and devotional groups that were a common feature of congregational life from the Bible

study group attended by Judge Samuel Sewall of Massachusetts in the 1690s
to the disciplined Methodist classes a century later. A noteworthy instance of
such meetings was the group that introduced the Great Awakening to Hanover County, Virginia. In the early 1740s one Samuel Morris and a few
neighbors began gathering to read from a tiny collection of religious books,
including Luther's *Commentary on Galatians*. The reading had remarkable
spiritual effects, the meetings grew in size, and Morris "was invited to travel
long distances in order to read to congregations who desired his services."
Soon regular "reading houses" were built for this purpose as other capable
readers were enlisted in the work. The Presbyterian revivalists William
Robinson, John Blair, and John Roan drew the movement into the Presbyterian fold, but the lay readers continued to be highly esteemed among the
churches (Gewehr: 46–52).

In the educational settings of household and church, then, study of the
Bible was decisively guided by Protestant religious perspectives, which
increasingly flowed in denominational channels established by catechisms,
liturgies, and tractarian literature. In no small measure this was also true of
more formal education in schools and colleges. The Great Awakening, for
instance, stimulated the founding of numerous denominational academies
and colleges by Presbyterians, Baptists, and Methodists; and these schools, in
turn, were themselves settings for the inauguration of later revivals.

But it must also be said that a number of factors already discussed were
at work in school and college to enlarge this denominational context of colonial education. First, the increasing religious diversity of the colonies meant
that schools were attended and supported by constituencies representing
more than one Protestant tradition. Further, eighteenth-century revivalists
increasingly found common cause with fellow revivalists in other communions. At the same time rationalists like Benjamin Franklin were appealing
to a common reason that transcended denominational doctrines in their
efforts toward the founding of schools and colleges. Whether the justification
came, therefore, from the pious "heart" or the reasoning "head," the cause of
formal education was one that extended beyond denominational loyalties.
Piety, civility, and learning were broad educational aims that could be
embraced by diverse colonies moving toward their place as an independent
nation (see Mead; Cremin: 331).

The relation of minority groups to the institutions that pursued these
European and Protestant objectives of course constituted a major problem.
For example, one of the most significant educational efforts of the eighteenth century was the mission of S.P.G. missionaries and revivalistic
preachers to the slaves. In this venture, however, there were numerous
ambiguities. On the one hand, it had been generally assumed that
Christianity served to bring civility to all those whom it influenced. But in
the case of the slaves there was fear on the part of the owners that
knowledge of Christianity and the ability to read would lead to desires for

freedom. For this reason, the missionaries among the blacks throughout the century spent much time attempting to quell the misgivings of the slaveholders. The slave who could read, and especially the slave who could teach others to read, was an object of fear and suspicion. Further, it was generally the case among the missionaries themselves that, although they took pride in their students' abilities to read the Bible or recite the catechism, they rarely questioned the institution of slavery itself.

The dilemmas that slavery posed for these ecclesiastical educators well illustrate the central issues within the colonial legacy to American education. First, throughout the colonial period both the Bible and education had been called upon to perform two different and at times conflicting social functions. They were viewed as powerful engines for the renovation of church and society, but they were also used to justify and instill the values of the standing order. Through the Revolution to the Civil War and beyond, the Bible and education were to be the rightful possessions of every person, and they were to sustain cultural privilege. They were to challenge economic and political power, and they were to advance it. They were to authorize change, and they were to protect the inherited ways. Although the language of evolution and progress was often able to suggest continuities between these two functions, the Bible and education have nonetheless remained the "classic" foci for controversies over change in American society.

Second, the role that colonial educators gave to the Bible in delineating the proper ends of education persisted in American understandings of the religious and moral objectives of education. In some sense, schooling was not merely to convey knowledge but to inculcate the duties of the student to self, to others, and to God. Education was, in other words, to establish and to perpetuate the civic virtues, and these virtues were long considered to have a religious foundation.

But the colonial period reveals the initial struggles over the educational role of the Bible within a society of increasing social and religious pluralism. To be sure, the largely Protestant leadership of colonial education shared a reverence for the authority of Scripture and a commitment to its use in education. But they also had sharp differences over the interpretation and ethical applications of Scripture, as controversy over the education of slaves suggests. Admitting these differences, how was education, especially formal education, to succeed in instilling a coherent set of public values and duties, which was agreed to be its ultimate objective?

WORKS CONSULTED

Bailyn, Bernard
1960   *Education in the Forming of American Society: Needs and Opportunities for Study*. Chapel Hill: University of North Carolina Press.

Baxter, Richard
1656   *Gildas Salvianus: The Reformed Pastor*. London: By Robert White for Nevil Simmons.

Bayly, Lewis
1620   *The Practise of Pietie, Directing a Christian How to Walk That He May Please God*. 12th ed. London: For John Hodgetts.

Brauer, Jerald C.
1978   "Conversion: From Puritanism to Revivalism." *Journal of Religion* 58: 227–43.

Bruce, F. F.
1961   *The English Bible: A History of Translations*. New York: Oxford University Press.

Cherry, Conrad, ed.
1971   *God's New Israel: Religious Interpretations of American Destiny*. Englewood Cliffs, NJ: Prentice-Hall.

Cremin, Lawrence A.
1970   *American Education: The Colonial Experience, 1607–1783*. New York: Harper and Row.

Curti, Merle
1935   *The Social Ideas of American Educators*. New York: Charles Scribner's Sons.

Dell, William
1653   *The Tryal of Spirits Both in Teachers & Hearers*. London: For Giles Calvert.

Dowey, Edward A.
1952   *The Knowledge of God in Calvin's Theology.*
                New York: Columbia University Press.

Franklin, Benjamin
1940   *The Autobiography of Benjamin Franklin.* New
                York: Washington Square Press.

Forbes, Allyn B., and Mitchell, Stewart, eds.
1929–47   *Winthrop Papers.* 5 vols. Boston: Massachusetts
                Historical Society.

Frei, Hans W.
1974   *The Eclipse of Biblical Narrative: A Study of
                Eighteenth and Nineteenth Century Hermeneu-
                tics.* New Haven: Yale University Press.

Gaustad, Edwin Scott
1976   *Historical Atlas of Religion in America.* Rev. ed.
                New York: Harper and Row.

Gewehr, Wesley M.
1930   *The Great Awakening in Virginia, 1740–1790.*
                Durham, NC: Duke University Press.

Haroutunian, Joseph
1932   *Piety Versus Moralism: The Passing of the New
                England Theology.* New York: Henry Holt.

Heimert, Alan, and Miller, Perry, eds.
1967   *The Great Awakening: Documents Illustrating
                the Crisis and Its Consequences.* Indianapolis:
                Bobbs-Merrill.

Herbert, George
1652   *Herbert's Remains.* 2 vols. London: For Timothy
                Garthwait.

Huit, Ephraim
1643   *The Whole Prophecie of Daniel Explained.* Lon-
                don: For Henry Overton.

Knappen, M. M.
1966   *Tudor Puritanism.* Chicago: University of Chicago
                Press, Phoenix edition.

Knight, Edward W., ed.
1949–53   *A Documentary History of Education in the South before 1860*. 5 vols. Chapel Hill: University of North Carolina Press.

Mather, Cotton
1966   *Bonifacius: An Essay upon the Good*. Ed. David Levin. Cambridge: Belknap Press of Harvard University Press.

[Mather, Richard]
1643   *Church-Government and Church-Covenant Discussed*. London: By R. O. and G. D. for Benjamin Allen.

Maxson, Charles H.
1920   *The Great Awakening in the Middle Colonies*. Chicago: University of Chicago Press.

Mead, Sidney E.
1963   *The Lively Experiment: The Shaping of Christianity in America*. New York: Harper and Row.

Morison, Samuel Eliot
1936   *The Puritan Pronaos*. New York: New York University Press.

Murdock, Kenneth B.
1949   *Literature and Theology in Colonial New England*. Cambridge: Harvard University Press.

New Englands First Fruits
1643   London: By R. O. and G. D. For Henry Overton.

Nuttall, Geoffrey F.
1946   *The Holy Spirit in Puritan Faith and Experience*. Oxford: Basil Blackwell.

Pollard, Alfred W., ed.
1911   *Records of the English Bible*. London: Oxford University Press.

Preston, John
1629   *The New Covenant*. 3d ed. London: By I. D. for Nicolas Bourne.

Shurtleff, Nathaniel B., ed.
1853–54   *Records of the Governor and Company of the Massachusetts Bay in New England (1628–1686)*. Boston: Commonwealth of Massachusetts.

Simms, P. Marion
1936   *The Bible in America: Versions that Have Played Their Part in the Making of the Republic*. New York: Wilson-Erickson.

Smith, H. Shelton, Handy, Robert T., and Loetscher, Lefferts A., eds.
1960–63   *American Christianity: An Historical Interpretation with Representative Documents*. New York: Charles Scribner's Sons.

Smith, Wilson, ed.
1973   *Theories of Education in Early America, 1655–1819*. Indianapolis: Bobbs-Merrill.

Sweet, William Warren
1942   *Religion in Colonial America*. New York: Charles Scribner's Sons.

Trinterud, Leonard J.
1949   *The Forming of an American Tradition: A Reexamination of Colonial Presbyterianism*. Philadelphia: Westminster Press.

Wright, Louis B.
1957   *The Cultural Life of the American Colonies, 1607–1763*. New York: Harper and Brothers.

II

The Struggle for a Common Culture:
Biblical Images in Nineteenth-Century Schoolbooks

John H. Westerhoff III

Tremendous changes in the character of the United States and a revolution in education occurred during the nineteenth century. It was a century in which the nation doubled in population and expanded to the Pacific shoreline. And it was a century in which the existing educational configuration of family, church, and school made significant shifts. While the family and church were the principal agencies of education in the seventeenth and eighteenth centuries, the school became the dominant educational institution in the nineteenth. By mid-century, a common school system had taken shape and assumed the responsibility for providing free, publicly subsidized and controlled, formal instruction and also moral education.

The history of education in the nineteenth century is a history of the extraordinary influence of the public school, especially in small-town, rural America west of the Alleghenies. Through its schools, a new nation—still predominantly white, Anglo-Saxon, and Protestant—sought to provide a sense of unity and national identity for a population that was increasing in numbers and becoming more diversified in nationality, race, and religion. It is the story of how this new immature institution assumed the essential tasks of instilling patriotism, developing civic responsibility, assimilating newcomers into the majority culture, providing occupational training, and producing the educated citizenry that is essential to a democratic society; and it is the story of how a changing American society influenced the character of its schools.

It would be a mistake, however, to ignore other influential educational institutions. The home, church, and community still made major contributions to the education of the nation's children. The public school in its earliest years was understood only as supplemental to the education provided by home and church. Nevertheless, what quickly developed was the dominance of the school. This shift in influence signaled the end of the church's control of the people's education and the assumption of that responsibility by the state. Some feared a resultant secularization, while others—the new immigrants to the United States—experienced the continuing dominance of Protestant influence in the public schools. As a result, Roman Catholics and a few Protestants advocated and supported a system of parochial schools, while the majority sought to create a parallel educational ecology comprised of public schools for "general" religious education and Sunday schools for conversion and denominational instruction.

At this point it is important to note that the Sunday school was the forerunner of the common school. As such, the Sunday school provided general elementary education for many—particularly the poor—especially during the first quarter of the century. Indeed such schools continued to serve this function until mid-century in many rural and urban areas of the country. Typically they were nonsectarian, held on Sunday, and taught by untrained volunteers. The two dominant texts used in these schools were *The Union Spelling Book* published by the American Sunday School Union in 1838 and *The Sunday School Spelling Book* published by the Episcopal Sunday and Adult School Union of Philadelphia in 1822 for "the use of schools in general." On the title page of the latter text are these words: "[This text has been] compiled with a view as well to teach children to spell and read as to contribute to their moral and religious instruction." Here was a small 150-page collection of words, biblical texts, and other materials in the form of progressively more difficult lessons. The passages quoted from the Bible are not identified, but they represent sentences taken from the Old and New Testaments and united into lessons whose dominant themes are judgment, repentance, and salvation. The second lesson is typical:

1.	What shall I do to be saved?
2.	Believe on the Lord Jesus Christ and thou shalt be saved.
3.	By grace ye are saved through faith and that not of yourselves, it is the gift of God not works lest any man should boast.
4.	Repent and believe the Gospel.
5.	God be merciful to me a sinner. (*Sunday School Spelling Book:* 5)

Other lessons, while not from the Bible, used biblical language and for the student were probably indistinguishable from biblical passages. The subjects of these lessons were lying, industry, covetousness, temperance, honesty, modesty, prayer, and the like. About one-third of the way through the book a more systematic presentation of solely biblical material is presented—beginning with the story of creation and proceeding through Adam and Eve, Noah, Abraham, Isaac, Jacob, Joseph, Moses and the Ten Commandments, to the life of Jesus and the reception of the Holy Spirit by the Apostles. The last third of the book is a catechism made up of theological and moral questions whose answers are identified biblical passages and whose themes are almost identical to those in the first third of the text: judgment, repentance, and salvation.

In spite of the Sunday school's significant contribution to the education of the public, it was agreed by most citizens and especially the nation's educated leaders that the Sunday school could not provide the education required for the nation's children. A common or public school system controlled by the state seemed desirable. The leaders of the public school movement were willing to assume continuing responsibility for some religious education. Horace Mann, for example, asserted that the fundamental principles of Christianity should be inculcated in the public school, even as each denomination through its Sunday schools must be responsible for inculcating its own faith and creed. Almost everyone expected the public schools to teach religion, but there was little agreement on what that implied. In most places the public schools taught the predominant religious beliefs of the community (particularly where there was religious homogeneity) and typically ruled out anything not believed in common. Since the Bible was the one item on which Protestants could agree, the reading of the Bible became a regular aspect of the public school curriculum. Generally, public school teachers reflected the predominant Protestant piety. It is probable that teachers accepted the church teaching about the truths of the Bible and its relevance to everyday life and used the Bible in their teaching; however, in this essay we shall explore the images of the Bible only in the school books used in the public schools during the nineteenth century.

In the early days of the century, teachers compiled their own reading manuals. Among the earliest nineteenth-century texts compiled by clergy were Samuel Wood's *New York Readers* (1820) and Lyman Cobb's *Juvenile Reader* (1830). Neither gained general acceptance. It was not until after 1830 that it was common for printers to publish and promote a series of readers to be used in numerous schools. Among the most popular textbooks of the nineteenth century were those compiled by Charles Sanders, George Hillard, Lindley Murry, Salem Town, and William Holmes McGuffey, the last being clearly the most representative and influential. First published in 1836, McGuffey's *Eclectic Readers* became by mid-century the basic school reader in thirty-seven states. Indeed, for seventy-five years they were the textbooks used by four-fifths of the nation's school children.

An Overview

Before describing the images of the Bible found in nineteenth-century school books, it is important to have a general sense of these texts and their changing contents during the century. But first, some popular impressions about textbooks in this century should be dispelled. For example, no less a historian than Henry Steele Commager writes that "the Readers were filled with stories of the Bible and tributes to its truth and beauty" (1968:96). It would be more accurate to comment on how few stories from the Bible are found in nineteenth-century school readers. Some readers, even in the early years, contained only the Beatitudes, the Ten Commandments, and the Lord's Prayer. Even the first edition of McGuffey's *Readers*, which contain the greatest amount of biblical material, had only about 10 percent of its lessons taken from Scripture. A careful examination of school books published and used in the common schools of the United States before 1850 reveals minimal references to the Bible, while those published or revised after 1850 contain almost none at all. The history of McGuffey's *Readers* is characteristic of the history of all nineteenth-century readers.

The first edition of McGuffey's *Eclectic Readers* appeared in 1836. While nonbiblical material predominated, a significant amount of biblical content was found within the pages of these six readers. However, there were two major revisions of the *Readers*—the first in 1857 and the second, more drastic, in 1879. Each revision eliminated some of the biblical material. Of the 120 million copies of this reader sold, more than half were of the 1879 edition; only seven million copies of the first, most biblically-oriented edition were sold. The 1879 revision of McGuffey's *Eclectic Readers* represented the most popular readers used in the last quarter of the century and those that contained the least amount of biblical content. By 1879 there was no biblical material in McGuffey's first and second readers, and only the Lord's Prayer was found in the third. The fourth reader contained the Sermon on the Mount; the fifth reader, two selections from Psalms; and the sixth, the story of the death of Absalom (2 Samuel 18), Paul's speech on the Areopagus (Acts 17), and Psalm 37. The lack of biblical content, however, did not imply a negative attitude toward the Bible. In the 1879 edition, the Bible was typically referred to as "the Book of God," "a source of inspiration," "an important basis for life," and it was cited in support of particular moral issues. Nevertheless, such references were scarce, and there was only one lesson on the Bible in the *Eclectic Fifth Reader*—"The Bible: the Best of the Classics."

In addition to school readers, texts on geography, science, and history on rare occasions appealed to the Scriptures but almost never quoted them. Most spellers, while they did not contain Scripture passages, did contain words and names of persons found in the Bible, but such references were few by the end of the century. The diminishing attention to the Bible through the century is not easily explained. There is much about the place of the Bible in nineteenth-century schools that is not known. Teachers may have used the Bible as a supplemental text, reading a passage at the beginning of each day and perhaps using the content of this reading in their classes. In any case the lack of biblical content did not mean the absence of religion. A brief summary of the world view and value system found in McGuffey's *Eclectic Readers* can serve as an example, though it must be noted again, that other school books published at the same time were more secular, and by the end of the century the world view and value system in McGuffey's *Readers* were radically secularized.

In the first editions of McGuffey's *Eclectic Readers*, belief in the God of the Old and New Testaments was assumed. All true knowledge of God was believed to be dependent upon "God's book, the Bible." According to this view, God sent his Word for the eternal benefit of humanity; God reveals himself within the pages of the Bible, along with the mystery of creation, the nature of human life and death, and all that is required of humans; God uniquely reveals himself in the life, death, and resurrection of Jesus Christ, without whom life has no meaning or purpose. Three dominant images of God emerge: God as creator, preserver, and governor. God is the creator of heaven and earth, the ultimate source of the universe and the preserver of life and human lives. God continues to act in the world to govern and preserve creation, providing humanity with every necessity, guiding personal and social life. Nothing in life or history can be understood without God. Like a human parent, God loves, watches, listens, ministers to the needs of humans and guides their lives; humanity is totally dependent upon God. God is omnipresent, omnipotent, and omniscient, a heavenly monarch who sees all and knows all and has all power, clearly inspiring gratitude and obedience. God wishes to keep human beings from sin and hell. God judges, rewards, and punishes. Humans are to fear, obey, and be grateful to God for all his goodness.

The natural world can be properly understood only in relationship to God. Everything in creation is grounded in and expressive of God's purposes. Humans are called to be stewards of God's creation; they are not to misuse nature for their own benefit. Respect, not control, is the proper relationship, and they depart from stewardship at their own peril. This is a cause-and-effect universe. Evil acts result in punishment, and good acts are rewarded. Evil never pays. If the wicked are not punished in this world, they will be in the next. In any case people get what they deserve; they reap what they sow. God works out his purposes in and through the natural world. Nothing is without purpose or use; indeed, everything in creation has a benevolent purpose. Further, God reveals himself in nature. Still this world is not humanity's home. The purpose of life is to prepare for another world. Immortality is assured. People will be rewarded or punished in the next life according to their behavior in this. Each person faces a day of judgment when God decides who will enter heaven and who will enter hell, both of which were envisioned as real places. The vanity of the present world is assumed and true joy is reserved in a future state for the pious servants of God.

God creates persons and sets before them the ways of life and death. Humans are born in a state of sin and are destined for eternal damnation, but God has not abandoned them in their misery. There is hope for all those who repent of their sin and turn to God in faith, for God is willing and able to save all who seek forgiveness. Christ the Savior has suffered and died for humanity. If people have faith in Christ their lives will be blessed.

Such is the world view presented in the first editions of McGuffey's *Readers;* the dominant terminal values are salvation and righteousness and the dominant instrumental value is piety. But this theistic, Calvinist perspective and its resultant values disappeared by the time of the 1879 editions. All that remained were the morality and life styles of the emerging middle class and the cultural values of American civil religion. The history of the *Readers* over the century provides a mirror for changes occurring in the history of American public education. While it appears that the Bible was still devotionally read in nineteenth-century schools, the content of the textbooks was secularized and religious instruction was turned over to the churches and their Sunday schools. Education in morality and values remained but without theological foundations. Thus, the history of the changing content of nineteenth-century American public school textbooks is the history of a gradual elimination of biblical material from these books.

Biblical Attitudes

During the first half of the nineteenth century the most popular school books made some allusions to the Bible. One of the first lessons in McGuffey's first reader for elementary school children states: "The Bible says that you must not use bad words; and you must mind what the Bible says, for it is God's Book" (1836a:17). An edition of a more advanced reader in a series compiled by Samuel Goodrich and published at mid-century summarized the basic attitude of the century's school books to the Bible: "Of all the books you will read, the Bible is the most interesting and useful, to those who read it attentively. It recounts the true story of creation, the first human family and clearly unfolds our duty and destiny" (1857:21). Other readers of the period testified to the Bible's value. In one, Dr. Spring contended that there is no poetry to compare with the Song of Moses, the Psalms of David, and the Song of Solomon. He further argued that all good English literature is in debt to the Bible and that without a knowledge of the Bible it is meaningless to read and impossible to understand adequately most of English literature (McGuffey, 1866:294–97). In another reader North Carolina lawyer Thomas Grimkee defended a similar position: "The Bible [is] the Best of the Classics" (McGuffey, 1837b:164–65). Following Grimkee's essay is a poem by G. P. Morris, editor of the *New York Mirror*, entitled "My Mother's Bible." Morris reminisced that his father read the Bible regularly and that his mother before she died gave him her "most valued possession," her Bible, explaining that it should become his truest friend for it is the best way to learn how to live and die (McGuffey, 1866:351).

Another reader in the McGuffey series contains a short essay by the French philosopher Rousseau. In this work, "The Scripture and the Saviour," Rousseau asserted that the Bible is not fiction but is a work of God without which human beings would not know about the superior characteristics of Jesus Christ essential for salvation (1837b:64–65). In another reader compiled by McGuffey, a second essay by Thomas Grimkee, "The Bible," argued that the Bible is of value to all humankind. "The Bible," he wrote "is the only book which God has ever sent, the only one he will send into this world" (1836b:

159). Grimkee explained that among the Bible's most remarkable attributes is its teaching on justice. It "looks with impartial eyes on kings and slaves, heroes and soldiers, philosophers and peasants, the eloquent and the dumb. . . . From all, it exacts the same obedience to its commands and promises to the good the fruits of his labors; to the evil the reward of his hands" (160).

Two essays in a third grade reader come from the pen of S. H. Tyng. The first is entitled "The Bible" and the second, "More About the Bible" (McGuffey, 1837a:52–61). Tyng contended that the Bible has been preserved through the years by God's providence and that the only possible errors—in spite of numerous copies, translations, and printings—are omissions or alterations of some letters, syllables, or words. But no important doctrine, precept, or passage of history has been corrupted in any way (52). Tyng explained that the Bible was penned at different times by different writers—"the Old Testament before the coming of Christ and the New Testament after his death" (56), but God is the true author of every word. "All Scripture is given us by the inspiration of God" (58), and its writers were "supernaturally influenced by God's holy spirit" (59). Further, each translation is made infallible by God's providence. The Bible is a "sanctifying and transforming influence upon the minds of all who read it with proper spirit. . . . [It is] the only book which teaches everything that our creator requires of us either to know, or believe, or do, that we may escape his deserved displeasure, obtain his sovereign favor and dwell forever in the bliss of his immediate presence" (56). The Bible, continued Tyng, teaches the mystery of creation; the nature of God, angels, humanity; the immortality of the soul; the end for which humans were created; the origin of evil; the connection between sin and misery; the vanity of the present world; and the glory reserved for the pious servants of God in their future state. The Bible is "especially designed to make us wise unto salvation through faith in Jesus Christ" (60).

Throughout the various readers of the period anti-Jewish attitudes were common. The value of the Old Testament is seen in its predictive nature, especially those "extraordinary predictions concerning the infidelity of the [Jews] and the rise, progress and extensive prevalence of Christianity" (McGuffey, 1837a:61). Anti–Roman Catholic attitudes were also prevalent. For example, a geography text states that true religion is limited to Protestants who "take the Bible only for their guide on religious matters" while Catholics are guided by the Pope (Goodrich, 1827:19–20).

The Bible was used in early nineteenth-century school books also to defend nationalism and ethnocentrism. Another geography text declares: "Those nations are most distinguished for justice and kindness in which the Bible is best known and Christianity most pure" (Woodbridge: 326). Further, the Bible was used to explain and defend slavery: "the wretched condition of the African Negroes proves them to be the descendents of Ham in whom the curse of his father was denounced. In every portion of the earth, where their lot may have fallen, they are literally the servants of servants" (Blake: 33). The injustice committed against Native Americans was also sanctioned: "God in his wise providence has permitted the white man to take the Indians' land from him. The Indian would not cut down the trees and raise grain, except here and there a little patch, but the white man, as the Bible says has made 'the wilderness to blossom as the rose'" (Lossing: 10).

In spite of contemporary science, Charles Darwin, and evolutionary thought, the textbooks of the period portrayed the biblical story of creation and the history of the world as literally true: "The Bible contains the only rational and authentic history of the creation of the world which took place, as we are there informed 4004 years before the commencement of the Christian era. At that point the visible universe was called into being by the word and power of God" (Blake: 10). Only a few authors mentioned the new scientific hypothesis of Darwin. S. C. Goodrich, in *A Comprehensive Geography*, refuted evolutionary theory and defended the biblical account of creation, explaining that the world was created by God as "a training ground for souls of men" (1853:42).

Biblical Content

McGuffey's *Eclectic Readers* contain the greatest amount of biblical material—more than three times as much as any other text of the period; no other text contains biblical material not included in McGuffey's books. (All references in this section are to McGuffey's readers.) Interestingly, there is four times as much Old Testament material included in these textbooks as there is New Testament material. However, in most cases the Old Testament material is understood typologically—as corresponding to and informed by New Testament content. The only biblical accounts found generally throughout all the popular texts during the first half of the century are the story of Joseph (Genesis), the Ten Commandments (Exodus), David's lament over Absalom (2 Samuel), the story of King Solomon (1 Kings), assorted poems of praise and thanksgiving (Psalms), the Sermon on the Mount (Matthew), and Paul's address to Agrippa (Acts).

Old Testament

Genesis

While the biblical accounts of creation and the fall are assumed to be true and frequent allusion is made to them, the two stories from Genesis included in nineteenth-century school books are the story of Noah (Gen 7:1–24) and the story of Joseph (Genesis 37–45). In the story of Noah God is described in anthropomorphic terms. Because of humanity's wickedness God punishes every human being; indeed, God destroys everything he has created. It is only Noah's high character that induces God to warn and save him, his family, and a male/female pair of all the animal kingdom. While it is the story of humanity's new beginning with the righteous Noah, the questions included at the end of the story reveal the educational aims intended: "1. What evidence is there in nature of the Flood? 2. What does this confirm? 3. Why was the flood sent? 4. Who was saved and why?" (1837b:114–15).

The story about Joseph is made up of excerpts from eight chapters of Genesis, beginning with Joseph's being sold into slavery and ending with his father Jacob's death. Following the story is this moral: "In this world our friends and parents die and we all suffer much pain and trouble. But there is a land where there is no affliction, where no one is sick or dies. Our best friend—the Lord Jesus—who died for us on the cross lives there. He is the Lord and ruler of that happy land. He will send his holy angels to bring all those who love him to live with him forever" (1836b:42).

Exodus

Two stories from Exodus are included in nineteenth-century school books: Moses' song of deliverance (Exodus 15) and the Ten Commandments (Exodus 20). In one reader the biblical commandments are prefaced by these comments:

> Every little boy and girl should know the Ten Commandments and be careful to obey them. They were written by God himself on tablets of stone. They are the laws of God and all sin consists in breaking this law. Unfortunately we have all broken it and have thus become exposed to the penalty which says "the soul that sinneth, it shall die." But there is a way to escape from the punishment we all deserve. The savior has died and suffered with us. He is able and willing to save all who seek the forgiveness of God through him. (1836b:59–60)

1 and 2 Samuel

The call of Samuel (1 Sam 3:2–10), which emphasizes God's personal call to service, is found in two popular readers of the period, and most of the textbooks of the first half of the century contain the story of the death of Absalom (2 Sam 18:1–33). This story recounts the meeting of the armies of David and Absalom. David remained in a place of safety, charging his officers to deal gently with Absalom, but Absalom was slain and his army defeated (1837b:40–47). In the providence of God, Absalom's rebellion ended in disaster, and God avenged his faithful people and gave the victory to David. "Blessed be the Lord thy God, which has delivered up the men that lifted up their hands against my Lord and king" (18:28). The king wept for his son; David's affection is touching and reveals his noble character. While David could not kill his rebellious son, he put himself unreservedly in God's hands and God gave him the victory. It is a story about a world in which God rules, in which God rewards and punishes his children, in which parents cannot save their children nor protect them by faithfulness. Each must live a faithful life or be punished by God.

Another story from 2 Samuel that is found is the account of the lament of Saul for Jonathan (1:17–27). This story is understood to convey the message that faithfulness is rewarded and faithlessness is not. In this case Saul is unable to distinguish between his own will and God's; acting on his own desires Saul incurs God's rejection and punishment.

1 Kings

The story of Elijah (1 Kgs 19:1–18) found in one reader tells how God protected his true prophet from the people who despised him because of his judgment of their lives. The lesson is that, like Elijah, others called to speak for God may fear how people will react, but God will save all those who are faithful (1866:157).

A more popular story is that of King Solomon. Even in the same series, this story is repeated in more than one reader (1836b:52–54; 1837a:95–96). In McGuffey's second reader this biblical story is rewritten emphasizing that Solomon's prosperity, wisdom, and power are all rewards from God. The lesson begins: "Those whom God blesses, they are indeed blessed" (1836b:52) and ends: "It would be a great thing to be as fine and wise, and rich and glorious as Solomon, would it not? Indeed it would. Yet we might have all these fine things and not be happy. Fine clothes and fine things cannot make the mind of anyone happy. We must have favor with God and love and serve him, or we shall never gain what we are seeking" (54). The moral is clear: people who seek God first will be rewarded with power and wealth. Those who seek power and wealth may gain them, but they will never be happy.

In McGuffey's *Eclectic Fourth Reader* is a composite, "Solomon's Wise Choice," from 1 Kgs 3:5–15; 4:29–31; 10:1–8. God asks Solomon what gift he desires. Solomon acknowledges all that he has as a gift of God and expresses his gratitude. He then asks for wisdom, an understanding heart that can discern good and evil. Since Solomon asks for wisdom rather than long life, riches, or power, God gave him wisdom, wealth, and power explaining that if he would walk in God's ways and keep God's laws as faithfully as David, God would give him also long life. At the close of the lesson is the account of the Queen of Sheba's letter to Solomon in which she expresses her amazement at his wisdom; the lesson closes with her words: "Blessed be the Lord thy God which delights in thee" (1837a:96).

Psalms

Ten psalms appear in the period's textbooks. Most of these are songs of praise and thanksgiving, but one nature psalm (Psalm 19) was quite popular. In one reader it is entitled "The Voice of Nature" but speaks of the revelation of God in nature and in the law (1837a:146–47). Law and nature go together in the school books of the period. God gives the gift of law, and this is a law-and-order universe. People are to love the law and obey it, to love the natural world and protect it. In another textbook the same psalm is entitled "Nature and Revelation" (1837b:63–69). At the close of the lesson are these questions: "1. What is the character of God exhibited by works of nature? 2. What is the character and influence of the laws of God? 3. How can we be kept from sin?" (69).

Psalm 100, an exhortation to thank and praise God, was popular. Also included in numerous school books was Psalm 104, which reminded people always to be thankful to God—even when they cannot understand what is happening in their lives. Psalm 103, "The Goodness of God," was taken as a reminder of God's mercy explaining how God forgives and restores, how God can change sorrow into joy, and how God will always keep his promises to the faithful (1837a:113–14). Psalm 37, "God's Goodness To Such As Fear Him," was viewed as a song of lament containing a similar message (1866:479). People should be patient even in distress. The wicked will not last; God will destroy the sinful. The prosperity of the sinful is an illusion. The righteous will end their lives in peace; God cares for the faithful. Psalm 23 offered a reminder that God is provider, guardian, and guide. Psalm 115, entitled in a textbook "The God of the Heathen," provided testimony that "our" God is greater than other gods; people should trust him, for in God's good time he will bless them (1837b:256–57). In Psalm 42 was a reminder that humanity is to thirst for righteousness, while Psalm 129 called to mind the omnipresence of God who orders human lives and will not tolerate wickedness. At the close of this lesson are these questions: "1. Can you do anything without God seeing and knowing it? 2. How should the sentiments of this Psalm influence your conduct?" (1837b:199). Finally, Psalm 148 appears in two texts as a song of praise for God's chosen people (obviously the readers of the lesson), who have special reason to praise God (1837b:101).

Proverbs

In one text a lesson entitled "The Proverbs of Solomon" includes Prov 10:1–32 (1837b:316–17). This lesson teaches that God will take care of the righteous and destroy the wicked. People should, therefore, be diligent, hard working, caring of others, and fearful of God; that is what it means to be righteous. Those who live accordingly will be rewarded with riches.

Job

The book of Job was very popular. McGuffey assigned five lessons to material from this book. McGuffey's first choice was Job 4:1–21, which was taken as testimony that God is just and that affliction is not causeless; indeed affliction is best understood as punishment. The righteous are always secure, for finally all reap what they sow (1837b:122–23). In a lesson entitled "Divine Providence" (Job 5:1–27) suffering is viewed as a result of sin rather than chance (1837b:140–41). Suffering should be both accepted and welcomed for it is the way God converts people. After the price of the sin is paid, God will deliver and save those who turn to him in their suffering. "True Wisdom" (Job 28:12–28) contends that God alone has true wisdom (1837b:221). People should fear God, depart from evil, and pursue God's wisdom. A paraphrase of Job 36:26 and 37:24 entitled "Justice and Power of God" teaches that affliction is a warning (1866:211–16). Even the good do wrong and need to be corrected. People are exhorted to fear God and to submit to suffering with patient hope. In a lengthy lesson that includes Job 38:1–27 and Job 39:19–25, God answers Job's challenge (1837b:315–16). In the end Job confesses his insignificance, his helplessness, and the absurdity of his questioning and submits to God. The only adequate response to human suffering is patient endurance and faith which will bring God's peace.

Isaiah

Isaiah was the most popular of the prophets in nineteenth-century school books. One of the most frequently cited passages is Isa 29:1–14, a parable in which Jerusalem is addressed under the mystical name Ariel (which means "place of bloody sacrifice") (1837b:150–51). God is not satisfied with the lip service of his people. Only righteous life is acceptable to him. Yet God spares the city; there is hope for those who repent. The rest of the passages taken from Isaiah have traditionally been understood by Christians as predictions of Christ's coming. Isa 40:1–31 tells of God's deliverance of those who trust in him (1837b:317–23). For those who pay the price of their sin and wait on the Lord justice will be done, and through them God will establish his kingdom (Isa 52:1–12; 1837a:156–57). The rule of God is coming. People need to wake up, prepare themselves, and live accordingly. Or as Isa 55:1–13 ("Gospel Invitation"; 1837a:161–62) puts it: God offers a new life. Let people repent and be restored. Let people change their lives and live as new people for then God will grant mercy and pardon.

Joel

For those who may not be motivated to repent, there was a lesson taken from Joel 2, with its vivid description of the coming judgment and a reminder that it is not too late to repent; what is required is a genuine conversion, a total change of life.

New Testament

Matthew

Two lessons from Matthew's Gospel are found in nineteenth-century school books: the parable of the sower (Matt 13:18–23), which reminds people that they reap what they sow; and the first section of the Sermon on the Mount (Matt 5:1–48), which contains the Beatitudes (1837a:80–83).

Luke

From Luke's Gospel the story of the Good Samaritan (Luke 10:29–37) is taken as a reminder that God desires good deeds as acts of mercy and that one's neighbors are everyone and anyone in need.

John

Two stories from John's Gospel can be found in textbooks of the period. (1) The account of Jesus talking to the women of Samaria (John 4:1:26), which teaches that Jesus offers what humanity truly needs—salvation. (2) The story about "Christ and the Blind Man" (John 9:1–34) ends with these questions: "What is a miracle? Who performs miracles? Was Christ a mere man? Why were the Jews not convinced? How did the Jews treat the man whose sight was restored?" (1837b:153–58).

Acts

Paul's defense before Agrippa (Acts 26:1–32) and his speech on the Areopagus (Acts 17:22–31) recount his conversion and his evangelical witness that Jesus is the Messiah who has come to save humans from their sins.

Revelation

Revelation was another popular book. While "The New Song" (Rev 5:9–13) appears only once, "The Celestial City" (Rev 21:1–8) was quite popular. It contains an eschatological vision of the world's end, the last judgment, the kingdom of God, and the establishment of a new heaven and earth (1836b:320–23).

A Biblical Theology

The theology that emerges from the biblical images found in nineteenth-century school books is based upon the worship of the one true God (the God who reveals himself in Jesus Christ) whose ways are made known in the Bible and whose faithfulness is eternal to those who fear him. God is always personal and anthropomorphic. At the same time, a distinct contrast between humanity and God is emphasized. God is independent of human existence and beyond human comprehension, though never separated from his creation. God is a distinct and real person who created the world and is still at work in it. God is in control of the universe; humanity is never at the mercy of unpredictable forces; indeed, it is impossible to escape his presence and power. The most fundamental expressions of piety are fear and love. God has power and majesty. God is sovereign. God knows what is good for humanity. God punishes and reveals.

God is all powerful. His acts ought never to be questioned. God is holy, righteous, and just. God judges humans, and his justice is retributive. But God is also loving; to those who repent and do God's will, God will be merciful.

The students using these texts were to understand themselves as among a chosen people with whom God had made a conditional covenant. If they did their part, God would reward them; if they did not, God would harshly punish them. God set firm requirements upon them and, to help them, gave them clear laws to obey. In return for obedience God promised them all good things, all that they needed and craved, and most importantly—peace. He also gave them a warning; if they failed to do his will they would suffer disaster and ultimately death and eternal punishment. God gave them a clear message about how to live to gain his approval. Indeed, God even punished them in order to move them to repentance and a return to doing his will, which is best understood in terms of an individualistic ethic.

The Scriptures used in the early nineteenth-century readers correspond to seventeenth- and eighteenth-century "evangelical" piety. There is a persistent hostility toward the self, a preoccupation with ways to annihilate any enduring sense of self-worth. Only by destroying the self can one conform to the sovereign will of God. People are encouraged to seek an experience of new birth, a transforming crisis that reshapes them in significant ways. In these school books, the Scriptures are taken to support an authoritarian world in which children are to "love and fear" both their parents and God. Submission and gratitude to a sovereign God are fundamental expressions of piety. Children are to be brought up in the ways of the Lord. They are to be taught to live pious lives founded upon significant religious experience. An authoritarian and repressive understanding of life prevails. Obedience is a dominant value; submission is praised. Punishment is a prevalent theme. Shame, guilt, and inner discipline are encouraged. Conscience is the inner voice of an external authority—the expectations and commands of God. Severity and gentleness, reward and punishment are alternating elements in God's creation. The will needs to be broken and the self suppressed. Students are to fear God and make themselves perfect by first denying and controlling their innermost feelings and thoughts. The aim of life is to escape sin and to achieve purity. Still it is an individualistic understanding of life, in which each person confronts God and determines his or her own fate directly and alone. A defense of the religious temperament of the American frontier, one familiar to the piety of the Protestant Sunday School movement, is found throughout these readers.

However, the common school movement could not survive in an ever-growing, pluralistic country without a change in the content of the nation's school books. Pluralism, a social order founded upon the principle of harmonious interaction for common ends among communities each of which possesses both identity and openness, was characteristic of the American dream. By the close of the colonial period, the nation was religiously diverse, and no agreement on a national religion was possible. If a new social order were to be created, a separation of state and church seemed necessary. As a compromise between those who desired an established religion and those who did not, a guarantee had to be provided for the freedom of religious identity in an open society.

Education was omitted from the constitution as a function of the national government. Church-supported schools, with clear religious identities and orientations, were expected to induct persons into life in the new nation. However, the increasing need for national unity, loyal citizens, and common values combined with a growing rationalism, skepticism, and empiricism to give the original principle of separation of church and state a new meaning. What occurred was understandable but not expected. Freedom in education *for* religious identity (so long as it did not promote separatism) became freedom *from* religious identity on behalf of civil harmony. Thus, the doctrine of separation of church and state had come full circle. Not only was the right to teach religion and interpret life and history from the perspective of a religious tradition prohibited from common schools, but public support of church-related schools was denied. A national commitment to the education of the public had become identified with public education. The state's right and duty to encourage education became the right and duty to educate. The result was a functional elimination of religion from its original place of central importance in the public schools.

Thus, the relationship between church and state has been at issue since the birth of the nation. In the early days schools were marginal and the issue of religion and education within a diverse society was less significant. As schools increased in the scope of their obligations and in the intensity of their influence, the problem became more serious. The state increasingly turned over to the nation's educational institutions the responsibility for providing a sense of unity through the development of a national *paideia*. The state significantly placed private identity in a subordinate position to group identity. Thus by mid-century the biblical theology that had dominated textbooks for almost fifty years and the biblical content so conspicuous in the nation's first readers began to diminish until by the end of the century it had almost been eliminated.

WORKS CONSULTED

Blake, J.
  1831   *A Geography for Children.* Boston: Richardson, Lord, and Holbrooke.

Commager, Henry Steele
  1968   *The Commonwealth of Learning.* New York: Harper and Row.

Goodrich, Samuel
  1827   *Outlines of Modern Geography.* Boston: S. C. Goodrich.

  1853   *A Comprehensive Geography.* New York: George Savage.

  1857   *Goodrich's School Reader.* Louisville: John Morton Co.

Lossing, B. J.
  1866   *A Primary History of the United States.* New York: Mason Bros.

McGuffey, William H.
  1836a   *Eclectic First Reader.* Cincinnati: Truman and Smith.

  1836b   *Eclectic Second Reader.* Cincinnati: Truman and Smith.

  1837a   *Eclectic Third Reader.* Cincinnati: Truman and Smith.

  1837b   *Eclectic Fourth Reader.* Cincinnati: Truman and Smith.

  1866   *McGuffey's Eclectic Fifth Reader.* Cincinnati: Sargent, Wilson and Hinkle.

The Sunday School Spelling Book.
  1822   Philadelphia: Episcopal Sunday School and Adult School Union.

Westerhoff, John H.
  1978   *McGuffey and His Readers.* Nashville: Abingdon.

Woodbridge, William
  1866   *Systems of Modern Geography.* Hartford: W. J. Hamersley.

III

The Public Schools Are Not Enough:
The Bible and Private Schools

Virginia L. Brereton

Rarely in American educational history has the Bible failed to provoke controversy. Some of the most elementary questions have revolved about the issue of what version should be used—the King James, the Douay, or biblical selections that do not involve any disputed doctrines? Even within a single religious tradition, the problem has often arisen: Which Bible should be used, the venerated one with which the group has become identified, the one individuals remember from childhood, with all its archaisms and possible inaccuracies, or one better designed for modern ears and modern understanding? Beyond this lies a more important set of questions dealing with whether study of the Bible is meant for the few or the many. This has been no idle inquiry for Americans, given their ideal of universal education, and it has particularly stirred up Protestants. Who is permitted—or encouraged—to interpret Scripture? Lay people or only the clerics? Possibly only biblical scholars? How important a part does knowledge of the original biblical languages play in true mastery of Scripture? How many people can really gain competence in Hebrew, Greek, and other biblical tongues? The question of age has come into play too: Can children and young people understand or appreciate Scripture themselves or must it be explained to them? What are the uses of Scripture? Theological, moral, aesthetic, or all three? Which is prior, Scripture or its uses? Is the Bible the servant of religious faith, or must belief be determined by it? Finally, a particularly vexing question in the late nineteenth and the twentieth centuries has concerned the "scientific" study of Scripture. With what presuppositions should the student approach the Bible? Is it the word of God, the work of human beings, or some combination of the two? No religious group has managed to evade this problem entirely.

These questions have almost always proven explosive. Given the variety in American religious experience, consensus has mostly eluded those who sought it. Certainly public school leaders have never been able to navigate successfully among the various questions and answers. Nor have the courts and legislatures. In the end, many have chosen to eliminate the object of contention—the Bible—altogether. /1/

Both the disputes over the Bible and its increasing banishment from public education have contributed to the creation of other, non-public schools. In the nineteenth century those who felt public schools taught the wrong translation of the Bible or misinterpreted the correct version formed their own schools; later, those who feared that their children would suffer moral and religious harm because no Bible at all was taught established schools of their own. Of course, the founding of new educational institutions seldom occurred only because of conflict over the Bible. Other cultural, social, ethnic, moral, racial, and philosophical factors came into play. Two basic categories of schooling grew out of discontent over public education: supplements and alternatives. Generally speaking, Jews and Protestants chose to supplement public education, while Catholics set up an alternative system of their own.

For as long as Protestants controlled public schooling—which they did for all of the nineteenth century and much of the twentieth—they were content to depend upon supplementary religious education in the form of Sunday schools. The major exceptions have been Lutherans and to a lesser extent Episcopalians. Parochial schools appeared with the first Lutheran immigration in America; however, these older Lutheran groups had trouble maintaining their schools in the face of competition from the public schools. After a high point in 1830, their system declined. Since then the only extensive Lutheran school system has been that supported by the Missouri Synod, in which the preservation of cultural distinctiveness and a strict confessionalism have been primary (Damm). Presbyterians were more typical of Protestants generally; during the early nineteenth century they set out to create a system of parochial schools, but their half-hearted attempts had largely ceased by the 1860s (Sherrill). Though they remained content to supplement primary and secondary education, Protestants of all traditions have reacted more strongly to the deficiencies of higher education. When they judged already-established colleges too unorthodox for the preparation of ministers, they founded theological seminaries (Andover Seminary, dating from 1808, was the first), and of course they were constantly creating new church colleges. In the late nineteenth century they set up training schools for the special preparation of lay Protestant workers, particularly missionaries. In the early twentieth century conservative Protestants made some of these training schools serve as alternatives to existing forms of higher education, which, they charged, had grown atheistic and disrespectful of the Bible.

Until very recently, the majority of American Jews have favored public education. Despite this loyalty to common schooling, however, they also felt the need to preserve distinctly Jewish teaching, and so during the nineteenth and twentieth centuries they established forms of education that were intended to supplement the public schools, offering instruction in the afternoons following regular public school sessions or on Sundays. /2/ As the twentieth century progressed, many Jews became keenly aware of the deficiencies of supplemental education. Some groups, especially the

Orthodox, reacted by establishing Jewish day schools at a rapid rate from the 1940s on. Many of these schools offered intensive programs in Hebrew language and traditional Hebrew texts.

Catholic Americans reacted adversely to public education almost from its inception; they complained of its Protestantism and later they rued its secularism. Accordingly, they established a system of parochial schools, which the faithful were required to attend. Occupied with the founding and maintenance of schools, the hierarchy addressed itself only half-heartedly to the question of supplemental forms of religious education for Catholic children who attended the public schools. Strictly speaking, the Catholic parochial system does not belong in a study of schools set up in reaction to public education to advance a different understanding of Scripture, for until recently the teaching of the Bible has played a relatively small part in the Catholic school religion curriculum. But it is impossible to ignore the largest alternative schooling system in the United States. In the past few decades, moreover, the church's educators have turned to Scripture teaching as a way to reform and enliven their religion classes.

Reactions to the Common Schools, 1820–1880

Early Jewish Schooling

American Jews by and large supported the common school during the nineteenth century. Understandably they complained of the custom of reading the New Testament in these schools, and they felt uncomfortable with the pervasive Christian emphasis. Yet they sent their children. Even an educational dissenter like Isaac Leeser, who established a parochial school in Philadelphia in the 1840s, basically approved the concept of the common school and would gladly have endorsed it had it been more religiously neutral (Todes: 33).

Jewish allegiance to public eduation is remarkable especially because Jewish religious education traditionally involved a sizable agenda. Jews, of course, valued their Bible, which Christians call the Old Testament, as the all-important record of their early history and as the foundation for their theology, ethics, and religious practices. Study of the Bible in Hebrew was always mandatory for anyone who claimed to be a true scholar of traditional Jewish learning. Jewish students usually started with a study of the first five books of the Bible—variously referred to as the Pentateuch, Humash, or Torah. If they continued their Jewish education, they went on to the reading of the Hebrew Prophets. But familiarity with the Hebrew Bible by itself did not make a learned Jew. Unlike American Protestants, many of whom distrust scriptural interpretation, Jews recognize a body of biblical, largely rabbinical, commentary which equals the Bible itself in value. Most traditional Hebrew literature, in fact, is at least indirectly exposition of the meaning and intent of the Bible. Among the most important commentaries are the midrashic texts, created over many centuries; the Talmud, primarily a record of legal discussions concerning the applications and meaning of biblical law; and Rashi's *Commentary to the Pentateuch,* composed in Europe in the Middle Ages. Despite the importance of these studies to many Jews, most sought to supplement the teaching of the public school only by weekly instruction in their own traditions. During the greater part of the nineteenth century the majority of Jewish children who received formal religious education attended congregational Sunday schools on the Protestant model. /3/ The Jewish ideal of studying ancient sacred texts was missing from these Sunday schools, partly because there was little time for such activity. Furthermore, most of these Sunday schools belonged to Reform Judaism, which rejected the rabbinic tradition represented in much of classical Jewish literature. The Bible was taught mainly as a series of stories to which moral lessons were often attached. Assorted psalms and occasional chapters from Scripture might be introduced as well; but there was little systematic Bible or Hebrew language study.

Besides these Sunday schools, Jews established a few parochial schools, exceptions to the general pattern. Though such a school was founded as early as 1731 by the congregation of Shearith Israel in New York City, most of the early day schools came into being in the 1840s and 50s. In part these schools made up for the initially sketchy pattern of public schooling, but their appearance also demonstrated that the ideal of Jewish learning still animated American Jews. Early Jewish parochial schools did not simply duplicate the public school, omitting the Christian influence; they taught Hebrew language and literature and inducted the child into Jewish culture and customs. Isaac Leeser's Philadelphia school offered the same English studies as the public school; but in addition it advanced the learning of Hebrew as a central goal of the curriculum. "That a Hebrew not to be a Hebrew in language when this is within reach is an absurd proposition which requires no argument to illustrate," declared Rabbi Leeser (Todes: 34). The school's teachers used Leeser's Hebrew textbook, which contained the Hebrew alphabet, "a portion of the Bible in Hebrew and its translations into English," and "prayers, blessings and Hebrew grammar" (Todes: 36). Another parochial school, the Hebrew National School established by the congregation of Shaary Zedek in New York in the early 1850s, offered

> Instruction in Hebrew Comprising, Reading and translating the prayers and the Bible into English—Grammar, writing, the reading of Torah with the musical accents—a regular and complete knowledge of all religious customs and observance as practised among the Israelites from time immemorial, as also all the higher Branches of Hebrew Literature whenever the pupils shall be found sufficiently advanced so as to receive the same with Benefit to themselves and the Institute in General. (Grinstein: 30)

By the late 1850s these few parochial schools had died out. Economic depression was a factor in the demise of some; a series of regulations requiring attendance at public elementary schools as a prerequisite for public high school entrance was another. But more significantly, Jews felt less need to send their children to parochial schools, for the public schools had begun to abandon textbooks offensive to Catholics, Jews, and other religious minorities and to abolish the reading of Scripture, particularly in places where Jews and Catholics had the strength of numbers. These measures did little to mollify official Catholicism; religious neutrality was hardly much of an improvement over Protestantism. But these steps did enhance the satisfaction of most Jews with the public schools.

The mid-nineteenth-century Jewish parochial schools were few and scattered; the Sunday school pattern persisted. The first substantial challenges to the prevailing Jewish Sunday school were those institutional forms imported by the almost three million Eastern European Jews who entered the United States between 1880 and the end of World War I. These schools will be treated in a later section of this chapter.

Catholic Dissatisfaction with the Common Schools

Beginning in the 1830s and 1840s many American Catholics strongly dissented from the common schools. In the overwhelmingly Protestant public schools they encountered hostility toward their religious beliefs and practices. Often they felt that their religious, cultural, and ethnic survival in predominantly Anglo-Saxon Protestant America depended on the establishment of parochial schools. A major symbol of Catholic dislike of the Protestant control of the public schools was the practice in those schools of reading the "Protestant" or King James Bible, usually without comment or interpretation. If Scripture was to be read at all, Catholics wished it to be their own Rheims-Douay version, accompanied by correct teaching of doctrine. In general, Catholics were not given to reading the Bible on their own, as were Protestants; rather, they derived much of their contact with Scripture from the liturgy and from the catechism, in which biblical quotations were used to illustrate or substantiate doctrinal statements. The feeling lingered that Bible reading on the part of ordinary Catholics had been discouraged by the Council of Trent, and that it was the church's teaching that was authoritative, not Scripture itself.

For their part, most Protestants could not understand why simple Bible reading did not strike Catholics as either edifying or doctrinally neutral. They sometimes identified the reading of the Bible with the very survival of the public school system and were alert to every Catholic criticism of Bible reading as an aspersion on Scripture itself. In this clash there seemed to be no compromise. Failing for the most part either to bar Bible reading or to secure the right to use their own version in the common schools, Catholics, led by their hierarchy, established a system of parochial schools as rapidly as the supply of money and personnel would allow.

Quite probably, Catholics would have insisted upon parochial schools even if the Bible—and the Protestant nature of public schooling—had not been an issue. They were accustomed to having their own schools in Europe, sometimes state-supported. At the very least the clergy were in the habit of maintaining control over the schools Catholic children attended, and there was no reason for them not to continue to do so in the United States. Indeed, when in the twentieth century many urban schools became less explicitly Protestant and the influence of Catholics in the public schools increased substantially, Catholic fervor for their schools did not diminish.

Catholic and Jewish Supplements and Alternatives to the Public Schools, 1880–1940

The Bible in Catholic Parochial Schools

Because the Catholic parochial system was so decentralized during these years, it is difficult to make sweeping general statements about the religious instruction in Catholic curricula, especially over so long a period of time. The particular practices of teaching orders, the preferences of various ethnic groups, the supplies of money and space, and the inclinations of the parish priests (who often taught religion classes) and of the bishops all shaped the religious instruction in any given school. However, it seems safe to say that Catholic school children very seldom studied the biblical text itself. Some student acquaintance with Holy Writ came through its use in the catechism and through the occasional memorization of selected and usually isolated scriptural quotations; but probably the main exposure to Scripture came through classes and texts in Bible history.

An early and popular Catholic *Bible History* was that of Richard Gilmour (1824–1891), bishop of Cleveland. Gilmour's text was first published in 1869 and ran through many later editions. Like most other Bible history texts, it served numerous purposes in addition to introducing students to biblical heroes and events in chronological order. It advanced church interests, celebrated Old Testament "figures" of the Pope, pointedly discussed "types" of the sacraments, picked out prototypes of church enemies, and highlighted Old Testament events that seemed to vindicate the prerogatives of priests and the subordinate place of lay people. On Jacob's struggle with the angel, for instance, the text commented, "This contest of the angel with Jacob is a lively figure of the Church. Pagan emperors, heresiarchs, and, above all, hell, have made constant warfare against her; but as Jacob was not overcome by the angel, neither has the Church been overcome, nor shall she be to the end of time" (29).

In Gilmour's text, Bible stories and characters became embodiments of moral teachings, a purpose they often served in Protestant and Jewish Sunday schools as well. Gilmour chose 2 Kings 2:23–24 to teach a lesson on behavior. It is interesting to compare the text of the Douay Bible with Gilmour's treatment:

23 And he [Eliseus] went up from thence to Bethel. And as he was going up by the way, little boys came up out of the city and mocked him, saying: Go up, thou bald head. Go up, thou bald head.

24 And looking back, he saw them and cursed them in the name of the Lord: and there came forth two bears out of the forest, and tore them two and forty boys. (Douay)

One day Eliseus was insulted by some rude boys, who mockingly called him "Bald head." The prophet threatened them in the name of the Lord: and at the same instant two bears came from the woods and tore forty of those wicked boys to pieces. (Gilmour: 92)

Gilmour left nothing to his pupils' imagination but rather pointedly added the adjectives "rude" and "wicked" where the biblical text was silent. The choice of such an obscure passage emended in this way indicates at least as great an interest in reforming mischievous schoolboys as in conveying the biblical narrative.

Stories also illustrated theological points. Jonas, for instance, taught about Christ: he "was cast into the sea that, by the loss of one, the crew might be saved. By the sacrifice of Christ the world was redeemed. Jonas was three days in the whale's belly; Christ was three days in the tomb" (95). Gilmour did not make much concession to the youth of his audience, incorporating words and phrases that even adults might have paused over, such as "cubits," "flesh-pots of Egypt," "chid," "calumniated," and "mammon." As these phrases illustrate, students imbibed a good deal of the biblical language, though they may not have been aware of doing so.

The subject of Bible history did not take first place in the Catholic school curriculum; it usually ranked below the study of Christian doctrine. For example, in 1911 almost four times as many hours went into the study of catechism as Bible history in grades 1 to 8 in the New York Archdiocesan schools (N.Y. Catholic School Board). But Bible study faced competition from more than catechism. Catholic religion teachers needed to cover the liturgy, the sacraments and other practices of the church, saints' lives, prayers, hymns, church history, the training of character—particularly the will and conscience—and the reading of Catholic literature such as *The Imitation of Christ* and "devotional books about the Blessed Sacrament, such as Father Russell's and Mother Loyola's" (N.Y. Catholic School Board: 28). In addition, much time went into the preparation of students for the sacraments, especially First Holy Communion and Confirmation.

In Catholic higher education study of the Bible was usually an adjunct of doctrine or theology or even ancient history. In the curricula of the major seminaries, which had been prescribed by the Third Plenary Council in Baltimore (1884), philosophy and theology courses ranked first, and "Biblical exegesis" came under the heading of "theological studies." Seminary students received instruction in biblical languages: Latin (for the Vulgate), Greek (for the reading of early church fathers also), and only one year of Hebrew. In seminary, the schema instructed, "The teacher of Sacred Scripture should begin by vindicating the authenticity and canonical authority of each of the books, demonstrating how hermeneutics and the rules of exegesis were applied, and then strive to open up this fruitful treasury to the minds of his students with a view to nourishing their piety, instructing the people and defending religion" (Cassidy: 283). Here again Scripture was serving chiefly as a servant to the church's dogma and practices.

Advancing Torah Studies:
The Heder, Talmud Torah, and Yeshivah

The flood of Eastern European Jews who immigrated into the United States between about 1880 and 1920 brought the kinds of schools they had known in Europe: the *heder,* the Talmud Torah, and the *yeshivah.* The first two usually supplemented public school education; the *yeshivah* substituted for it. However much these schools differed from each other, they all had a common purpose: to teach the classics of Jewish sacred literature.

The *heder* (plural: *hadarim*) was a one-room, usually one-teacher school for young children, taught by a man who derived his living from student fees. It was usually located in the immigrant ghetto. The instructor used Yiddish; indeed, he often knew no English. Students memorized the translations of the Bible and learned the Siddur, or Prayerbook, in a mechanical manner. Only if they received enough of this kind of exercise over a long period of time did they eventually, and somewhat accidentally, learn Hebrew. Generally the lessons started with the Pentateuch. In addition to the Bible, students learned prayers and customs important to their eventual participation in synagogue (Dushkin, 1918:66–68; Gartner, 1964, 1969:11). It is difficult to evaluate the effectiveness of these *hadarim.* Jewish educational reformers of the teens and twenties found conditions terrible (Ben-Horin: 56–60; Dushkin, 1918; Honor: 2), but being progressives and reformers they could hardly be expected to applaud traditionalist *heder* pedagogy. Some later Jewish commentators, disturbed in their own time by what they perceived as a lack of attention to Hebrew language and texts, looked back to the *heder* with a touch of nostalgia (Katzoff: 68; Soviv: 19). Probably the truth lies somewhere in between the two perceptions. For one thing, some *hadarim* were better than others. Though some *heder* teachers had difficulty maintaining discipline—a contemporary observer found a Harlem *heder* "full of boys fighting and hitting each other" (Ben-Horin: 59)—one must not forget that the community supported *heder* teaching methods, however boring they may sound to a later generation.

The Talmud Torah was larger than the typical *heder,* involving more teachers and students, and was generally more advanced in its curriculum. Like the *heder* it could usually be found in immigrant neighborhoods, but it was a communal not a proprietary effort. Designed as a five-year course, it met seven to ten hours a week, supplementing the instruction of the public school. Hebrew was often the language of instruction. The tuition of twenty to twenty-five dollars per year was augmented by community contributions. The Bible, particularly the first five books, stood at the center of the curriculum; the unabridged Hebrew text was used, as in the *heder*. Usually students also tackled the midrashic and rabbinic explanations of the Pentateuch, especially as transmitted by Rashi. Other subjects such as Hebrew, Jewish history, and customs and ceremonies were introduced as aspects of Bible study. Older students progressed to Talmud and other rabbinic commentaries (Dushkin, 1918:68–72, 304–326 and passim; Gartner, 1969:16–18).

The Talmud Torahs received better reviews from educational reformers than did the *hadarim*. The Bureau of Jewish Education, which was formed in New York City in 1910 and became a hotbed of educational progressivism, elected to shun the *hadarim* and concentrate its money and efforts upon the Talmud Torahs. The leaders of the bureau introduced new textbooks in place of European ones, organized more dependable sources of income, and promoted a new, more "natural" method of teaching Hebrew, *ivrit b'ivrit*, in which Hebrew was learned conversationally rather than phonetically or through text memorization or drill (Dushkin, 1918:100–128; Goren: 119–125). The influence of the bureau extended beyond New York City, as its efforts and achievements were imitated in other American cities. The Talmud Torah had problems that the bureau did not succeed in curing, however. One was the rapid turnover of students, which stemmed from the high rate of mobility in the ghetto and also from the fact that the Talmud Torah was, after all, only supplementary to the public school and therefore was sometimes regarded as dispensable. Boys often stayed no longer than three years. One sympathetic critic of the Talmud Torah questioned whether in America it was wise or possible to adhere to "East European standards" and "assume that every boy is capable of becoming a learned Jew" (Dushkin, 1918:312). This question, in one form or another, has continued to haunt Jewish educators.

The third type of educational institution imported by Eastern European immigrants was the traditional or talmudic *yeshivah* (plural: *yeshivot*). The *yeshivot* were all-day schools, not adjuncts to the public school, and were not nearly as numerous as the *hadarim* and Talmud Torahs. *Yeshivah* schooling was intensive, with students attending sometimes from 8:40 A.M. to 7:00 P.M. Students applied themselves to Humash and Rashi's commentary in the lower grades, Talmud and Shulhan Arukh (a sixteenth-century codification of Jewish law) in the higher grades, receiving their instruction in Yiddish. They also engaged in English studies but usually only in the late afternoon. Some schools taught only the legal minimum number of hours of public school subjects, and even when they offered more they strictly subordinated the non-Jewish part of the program (Dushkin, 1918:326–332; Kaminetsky: 105; Nardi: 24–25; Schiff, 1966:28–36). Not all educators or parents who desired intensive Jewish education were content with such a traditional format as that offered by the talmudic *yeshivah*. Beginning with the Yeshivah Etz Hayim, founded in Brooklyn in 1916, some *yeshivot* began to diverge from the strict focus on the Jewish past. They taught some subjects in Hebrew rather than Yiddish—usually a mark of modernity for that time. The students generally learned Hebrew through the *ivrit b'ivrit* method. If these newer *yeshivot* paid more attention to current ideas in pedagogy, however, the actual content of the curriculum closely resembled that of the more conservative *yeshivot*: Humash, Rashi, prophets, Talmud, and Jewish history (Shulman: 47–48). One difference was that the new *yeshivot* were more likely than their traditionalist counterparts to devote time to modern Hebrew literature. They were also apt to treat general English studies more seriously, although they still consigned them to a subordinate position.

In addition to the Eastern European imports, a native American form of Jewish education grew up at this time, the weekday afternoon school attached to a congregation, usually an Orthodox or Conservative one. (In contrast, Reform congregations continued to employ mostly Sunday schools to teach religious education.) These afternoon schools usually met for three or more sessions a week. Like most other Jewish schools, they set out to teach the Bible and other Hebrew literature, but critics claimed that most of their time was taken up in preparing boys for their Bar Mitzvah and their adult participation in the congregation. Thus, while students of the afternoon schools finished by knowing "Customs and Ceremonies," as the subject was called, they generally had gained little familiarity with Scriptures in either Hebrew or English. Further exacerbating the situation was the inability of most congregations to support fully the synagogue's educational program; teachers were poorly paid and poorly trained (Dushkin, 1959:185–188; Katzoff; Leibman).

Jewish Supplements and Alternatives
to Higher Education

In the case of higher education, three major institutions had their beginning in the late nineteenth century: Hebrew Union College in Cincinnati (1873); Jewish Theological Seminary in New York City (1886); and, also in New York, Rabbi Isaac Elchanan Theological Seminary (1897)— the foundation for what was to become Yeshiva University. The first two institutions, like Jewish schools on a lower level, started out mainly as supplemental institutions, offering almost entirely Jewish studies. Students attended secular high schools or colleges during the morning and early afternoon and spent the late afternoon and early evening hours at Hebrew Union or JTS engaged in biblical, talmudic, and other classical Jewish studies. Both schools were geared largely to the training of rabbis—Reform at Hebrew Union, Conservative at JTS. Beginning in 1903 JTS opened a Teachers Institute, which prepared young people to become teachers of Jewish education, giving them instruction in Bible, the Hebrew language, and other Hebrew studies. Even after Hebrew Union and JTS became full-time graduate institutions early in this century, the schools continued to confine themselves to the training of rabbis, religious teachers, and scholars. Students attended them after they had earned college degrees. The schools therefore served as complements, not substitutes, for public and secular higher education (Adler; Cohon; Liebman).

The history and purpose of Orthodox RIETS were different. Set up as a center for Torah study, particularly Talmud, it was specifically intended to counter secular forms of higher education. Students received modest stipends while they engaged in their studies, and in return they agreed not to pursue any secular forms of education simultaneously. So high a value was placed upon study of Torah that even ordination was considered somewhat incidental, and the directors frowned upon any practical training that applied directly to the students' future roles as rabbis. Nor did the directors sanction the teaching of other Jewish subjects, such as modern Hebrew literature, which fell outside the category of the classical Hebrew texts. The students on the other hand were eager to study secular subjects, practical rabbinics, and other Jewish subjects in addition to concentrating upon Torah. When they rebelled in 1906 and 1908, they caused a reorganization of the administration of RIETS and forced the gradual introduction of secular subjects into the curriculum. Bernard Revel, president from 1915 to 1940, vastly expanded the scope of the institution. Among other new programs, he created a talmudic academy (at the high school level), a college (Yeshiva College), a teachers institute, and a graduate school for Jewish studies. Despite the incorporation of secular subjects, the Bible, Talmud and other Hebrew studies continued to receive major emphasis. This combination of institutions made it possible for students to spend most of their educational career in the study of Torah.

At a time when the student populations of the public colleges of New York—City College in particular—were predominantly Jewish /4/, Yeshiva was viewed by its supporters as an alternative to a secular education, as a way of encouraging young people to seek and to value Jewish learning. What Revel said in 1925 to justify the founding of Yeshiva College applied to many of the other schools within the institution as well:

> The Yeshiva proposes to establish a College of Liberal Arts and Sciences . . . with the double purpose of educating both liberally and Jewishly a number of Jewish young men who have already been imbued with the spirit and sanctity of Judaism and its teachings, so that these men may not be lost to us. . . .
>
> In existing colleges, Jewish students are led to efface their Jewishness. . . . some of our idealistic and talented young men will find in a College of Liberal Arts and Sciences a congenial home, . . . a home where they will be able to realize their energies and mental endowments for the enrichment of general and Jewish culture. (Klaperman: 150)

American Judaism, then, had created a few institutions by the 1920s whose leaders self-consciously set out to provide intensive and not supplemental education in Jewish culture and classics. The imperatives—and the financial means—for such alternatives to public schools would increase as the twentieth century went on.

Protestants and Popular Interest in the Bible: The Bible School, 1880–1940

In the late nineteenth century American Protestantism experienced a biblical renascence, which strongly affected the shape of American education. The first generation of biblical scholars took upon themselves the task of popularizing their findings in the belief that they could give the public a "new" Bible, one that was fresh and living. William Rainey Harper, for instance, president of the newly founded University of Chicago, contributed to the prestigious International Critical Commentary in his capacity as biblical scholar; but he also popularized the study of Hebrew, edited a magazine of Bible study for the lay person, devised a correspondence course for Bible study, and experimented with Sunday school teaching methods.

Bible study was an important goal of the original Chautauqua founded by Methodist Bishop John H. Vincent in upstate New York in 1874 as well as of the spate of small imitative "chautauquas" around the country. New British and American translations of the Bible appeared: the English Revised Version (1881 and 1885) and the American Revised Version (1901). A renewal of interest in biblical prophecy took place in the post–Civil War decades, and premillennialism—the belief that Jesus Christ would soon return to earth to initiate personally a promised thousand years of peace and prosperity—enjoyed a resurgence. Dispensationalism, a system of premillennialism promulgated by an Englishman, John Darby, caught on in America after the Civil War, particularly after the publication of such books as W. E. Blackstone's *He Is Coming* (1878) and C. I. Scofield's *Rightly Dividing the Word of Truth* (1888). One of the best-selling American Bibles, the *Scofield Reference Bible*, published by Oxford University Press in 1909, spread the dispensationalist method of reading Scripture through its copious notes.

Beginning in 1868 premillennialists and others gathered for Bible and prophetic meetings, the most famous of which was the series of "Niagara Bible Conferences." There was a widespread hunger for "expository preaching," in which the expositor conducted a study or series of studies over time on some passage of Scripture. Periodicals catering to the desire for biblical knowledge sprang up. Many Americans longed to travel to the Holy Land in order to see the country described in Scripture.

The biblical renascence of the late nineteenth century also contributed to the appearance of a new form of schooling—the Bible or missionary training school, the first of which was founded in Chicago in 1881—the Baptist Missionary Training School for Women. In part these schools grew out of the missionary enthusiasm of the closing decades of the nineteenth century and the conviction that "the evangelization of the world in this generation" depended upon the recruitment and rapid training of a body of lay men and women. The training was brief (usually two years) and practical, with students trying out their skills in city missions, settlement houses, and other urban religious and philanthropic agencies. These training schools also arose out of the increasing conviction that Christian workers needed greater familiarity with their Bibles in order to go about their tasks more effectively. Thus, the study of the Bible in English assumed a prominent place in the curricula of the training schools. Since the teachers did not espouse any one theological viewpoint, neither did they employ any single approach to Bible study. At some schools an elementary form of higher criticism was taught; at others, some variety of premillennialism; at still others, some haphazard mixture of methods and theologies. Whatever the approach, however, the most important objective of such Bible study was for students to become thoroughly familiar with the entire Bible, to be able to employ it initially for their own spiritual nurture, and then to use their biblical knowledge to win others to a Christian life. /5/

The Protestant biblical renewal of the late nineteenth century flourished well into the twentieth century, but by the 1920s many of its sources were weakening. In the public school the reading of Scripture had been increasingly interdicted by law, court ruling, and the decision of school boards. In more and more colleges and universities the Bible was taught as a human document rather than a divine one. Increasingly, instructors applied the historical method, raising questions about the factual truth of much of the biblical record, defining its meaning in terms of the people who created it, and ignoring its hallowed status as the ultimate religious authority for each successive generation of Protestants. The tendency was for Scripture to become the exclusive concern of experts who were certified to pronounce on biblical matters by their extensive knowledge of ancient Near Eastern languages and their familiarity with archaeological discoveries. In the up-to-date Protestant theological seminaries that had come under the influence of the universities, higher critical methods were fast gaining credence. The last of the biblical scholar-popularizers such as William Rainey Harper had passed on. For the most part the heirs of such leaders rejected the task of enhancing the public's knowledge of the Bible. The Chautauquas grew less important, and their focus became less biblical. Many of the missionary training schools— particularly those that had been established for women—fell victim to the increasing concern with accreditation and with the precise categorization of institutions of higher education into colleges and graduate schools. Those that did not close down or conform to the new definitions were merged into theological seminaries and for all practical purposes ceased to exist.

But one set of missionary training schools did not disappear, those that espoused a conservative theological viewpoint and approach to Scripture. In fact, they multiplied rapidly during the twenties and thirties and became identified with the emerging religious phenomenon known after 1920 as "fundamentalism." /6/ This group of training schools became notorious or celebrated as "Bible schools," or "Bible institutes." As the most cursory glance at the Bible school will show, fundamentalism was one strain of American Protestantism in which preoccupation with the Bible did not diminish during the twentieth century. Bible schools became especially important when fundamentalists failed to win control over the regular denominational educational institutions during church political struggles that took place in the 1920s. This failure meant that the conservatives could not insure the soundness of the teachings in denominational colleges and seminaries. So distrustful did they become of the "modernism" of most of Christian higher education that they often preferred to send their children to state colleges and universities. At least these schools were neutral in matters of religion, they thought.

Fundamentalists could not immediately replace the colleges and seminaries that "the tides of apostasy" had swept away. These institutions were simply too expensive to duplicate immediately. However, the Bible schools required fewer resources to set up and sustain. Most of their teachers were part time and accepted modest remuneration. Generally the Bible schools were beyond the pale of accrediting agencies and state education departments, which, if they took any notice at all, regarded the schools as too much of an anomaly to bother with. Hence, it was possible to call just about anything a "Bible school" without being challenged. Moreover, they were capable of quickly producing practical-minded workers who could staff the many independent congregations, Bible conferences, and foreign missions organizations that fundamentalism was spawning rapidly during the twenties and thirties. /7/ Bible schools operated at almost any academic level, depending upon the needs and backgrounds of their constituencies. Some received students who had little more than a year or two of grammar school; others included high school graduates and even a sprinkling of students with a year or two of college. Most schools admitted a student body with a mixture of academic backgrounds and provided several different courses of study for them. It would probably be accurate to say that, on the average, most Bible schools maintained a high school level of study during the twenties and thirties.

One of the most important functions of the Bible school was to keep alive the intense American biblicism of the nineteenth century, a biblicism that included such elements as a reverence for the Authorized or King James version of the Bible, for its every word as the actual utterance of God; an intimacy with Scripture so constantly cultivated that the biblical rhythms became part of daily speech; the conviction that knowledge of the Bible makes a decisive and practical difference in the whole range of the individual's life, from the critical matter of the salvation of one's soul to smaller questions of how to conduct one's daily affairs. This Bible school biblicism manifested itself in many ways. The time spent on Bible study was immense. In addition to the hours of formal classes they attended, Bible school students heard constant injunctions such as, "Study the Bible everywhere" and "Bring the Bible with you always." They were taught that Bible study was tantamount to praying; if the Bible was the word of God, then study was like a dialogue with him. With this in mind, students sometimes read the Bible on their knees.

Biblicism also involved the conviction that the Bible had a myriad of practical uses, and one of the functions of the Bible school was to teach these uses. Above all, the Bible was the primary vehicle of salvation, for oneself and others. On the personal level, the Bible could mold noble character and train one's aesthetic sensibility. It could help resolve critical decisions; the practice was quite common of opening the Book at random and applying whatever verse appeared to the situation at hand. The right passage, recalled at the appropriate time, could stave off temptation. For every mood or occasion, there was an appropriate biblical commentary. This advice, delivered by a dean of Moody Bible Institute in 1915, captures the flavor of Bible school faith in the practical power of Scripture:

> In the morning read Psalm 19, and at even, Psalm 8. If you are going on a journey, Psalm 121 is appropriate. If it be Sunday, Psalm 122. If in perplexity, read Psalm 37. If you are grateful, choose Psalm 105, or 106, or 107. If your heart needs searching, Psalm 139 will accomplish it: . . . If it is comfort you need, you will find it in abundance in one or another of the following Psalms—34, 91 or 103. (Pope: 278)

But the primary business of Bible school students was evangelism; by preaching, teaching, and personal contact they were expected to win the souls of the unchurched and the un-Christian. In accomplishing this task the Bible was crucial. There was a biblical verse that would catch the heart of the most recalcitrant sinner, if only the Christian worker could locate it. Was the subject of the student's evangelism a fallen away Christian? Possibly Psalm 66—"Restore unto me the joy of thy salvation"—would move the sinner to return to the fold. Did the would-be Christian protest that he was unacceptable in the eyes of God? Try John 6:37—"Him who comes to me I will not cast out." The Letter to the Romans especially was celebrated for its abundance of effective responses to inquirers' questions and objections. /8/

In order to put Scripture to such practical uses, a Bible school student had to know the English text thoroughly; if he or she had memorized great chunks of it, so much the better. Such familiarity did not come easily. One needed a "method," a topic much discussed by Bible school educators. Probably no method was more popular than that of James M. Gray, teacher and dean at Moody Bible Institute from the 1890s until 1935. Gray called his system "Synthetic Bible Studies," which meant simply that the Bible was to be approached as a whole book, not in fragments as exegetes were accustomed to do. There were at least two reasons for Gray's emphasis upon study of the entire Bible. First, since all of it was God's word, no part of it was unimportant or irrelevant. In fact, one problem with present-day Christianity—according to fundamentalists—was that crucial passages from Old and New Testament prophecy had been ignored by Christians who studied only parts of Scripture, to the great detriment of their comprehension of God's plan for the world. Second, any dispensationalist understanding of God's scheme for human salvation—and many Bible schools, including Moody Bible Institute, taught dispensationalism—made a holistic reading of Scripture necessary. Dispensationalists believed that during different time periods, or dispensations, God employed a variety of methods to save human beings—each of which had failed because of human sinfulness. The Bible when perused in its entirety furnished a record of past dispensations and foretold the events of the present and future dispensations. Any Christian vitally concerned with God's methods and intentions for dealing with humanity could do no less than read the whole of God's word, and in sequence.

For Gray, reading the Bible as a whole involved reading it in books in the order of their appearance. Students were supposed to read a book, for instance Genesis, in one sitting, repeating the same reading on each successive day before the next class meeting if possible. They were encouraged to read rapidly, ignoring minor difficulties and puzzles, and fixing what Gray called the "main outline facts" of the book in their minds. Eventually, after several readings, the major themes of the book should become clear. As they progressed, students were also to explore and recognize the "organic" connection of each book to every other book. As one student of Gray's at the Bible Institute found, "It is wonderful what mere continuous and repeated reading reveals. With each reading a book shines out the clearer as if from a dissolving cloud-mist, until it stands a bold outline in memory; the relation of book to book grows plainer, and the Bible, as a unit, is ours in a new way" (Metcalf: 11). To grasp fully the impact of Gray's method on its practitioners, one must realize how frequently prior Protestant acquaintance with Scripture had been limited to single isolated verses—often used as proof texts—or had been subject to exhaustive but sometimes narrow-minded exegesis. The study of the Bible as a whole, allowing an appreciation of the sweep of its narrative, was a new idea to the late nineteenth century. (It was a viewpoint shared with the first higher critics, incidentally, though for different reasons and with different results.) Gray's method did not exhaust the list of possible approaches to Bible study, even at Moody Bible Institute. Students explored it topically (for instance, they could follow the theme of "faith" through both Testaments, using a concordance); they could study one or more of the great

Bible characters; or they could trace certain theological doctrines. Once students had a grasp of the whole Bible, they could narrow down their scope to the study of single books, or great chapters; they could even attempt the exegesis of important passages.

Bible school educators also sometimes employed the "Bible as literature" approach in teaching their students. This was not necessarily a conservative method; in fact, it was popular among some of the early higher critics, in addition to their other approaches. But, since literary study in the early part of the twentieth century was largely appreciative, the treatment of the Bible as literature was consistent with a reverent attitude toward Scripture. One of its virtues for Bible school educators lay in the fact that it skirted historical and relativistic questions about the biblical text. Furthermore, its use did not depend upon the knowledge of the original ancient languages. Still, Bible school students were warned never to forget that the Bible was of course much more than literature and that for true comprehension and appreciation they must rely upon the inspiration of the Holy Spirit, not only upon their own acuity as readers.

One reason for the concentration upon Bible study methods was the assumption of most Bible school educators that, armed with a system, most lay persons could study and interpret Scripture for themselves without the aid of biblical commentaries or even a teacher. Bible study could therefore be a lifelong pursuit. James M. Gray claimed that one "great advantage" of his synthetic method consisted of "getting the people to read the Bible for themselves" (10). He assured the student that "the Bible is wonderfully self-interpretative" (15) once the student had mastered the "facts" of the biblical narrative.

Bible school educators and fundamentalists in general believed that ordinary people, studying the Bible in a thorough and systematic manner, would come to similar conclusions about its meaning. /9/ The same could not be said of biblical scholars, who usually assumed that proper understanding of Scripture was impossible without the application of their expertise. Thus, Bible schools, not the universities, became primary centers for the popularization of Bible study during the twentieth century. Bible school educators taught appealing and easy-to-learn methods that any lay person could employ; Bible school leaders actively cultivated the widest possible audience for their instruction. They seldom limited their teaching efforts to regularly matriculated Bible school students; in addition they organized and led Bible conferences, addressed Bible study groups in churches, edited periodicals that spread knowledge of Scripture, offered correspondence courses on the Bible, preached the Bible constantly in Sunday services and on street corners, wrote manuals on how to study the Bible, and broadcast biblical instruction over the radio. Philadelphia School of the Bible, founded in 1914, typically set out to "teach the English Bible, and to promote its study by means of regular school work, correspondence courses, Bible Conferences,

Community Bible Classes, and the circulation of approved books, pamphlets, and tracts on Bible study and Bible doctrine; to publish a magazine devoted to Bible study" (Showers: 160). To a large extent, then, schools such as Philadelphia became Bible teachers to conservative Protestants who felt that the rest of the educational world had gone astray.

Disenchantment with Existing Education:
The New Day Schools, 1940–Present

The Dilemma in Jewish Education
and Some Answers

Whatever could be said in criticism of the various forms of Jewish education in the early twentieth century, one factor partially made up for its deficiencies. In their homes many Jewish children still learned from parents who were familiar with prayers and synagogue usages and read the Bible aloud both in Hebrew and in translation. A standard practice in the Eastern European home—presumably continued among many immigrant families— was the study and reading of the weekly Sidrah (the weekly selection of Scripture that was read in the synagogue) and the reciting of psalms (Gamoran: 16). Gradually, however, as Jewish families became partly assimilated and as further immigration was halted after World War I, many parents lost interest in the task of educating their youngsters in Jewish literature and traditions. (They were not alone; simultaneously Christian educators were complaining that Christian parents had ceased to worship, pray, and read Scripture with their children.) By the thirties and forties the chorus of complaints about the low estate of Jewish education, reinforced by periodic surveys, had become standard fare of publications such as *Jewish Education.*

Basically, the lament ran that the teaching of the Bible and other ancient Hebrew literature and the instruction in Hebrew, upon which Bible study depended, were woefully inadequate. The failures were ascribed to various causes, some of which overlap: the mechanical and boring methods of language instruction; poor teaching; competition from other subjects (for example, study of Israel and modern Hebrew culture); lack of parental interest; dispersal of the old concentrated Jewish immigrant communities; and sheer lack of instructional time due to the supplemental nature of most Jewish education. Jewish educational leader Alexander M. Dushkin wondered if the pragmatic, action-oriented American environment was somehow fundamentally inimical to the Jewish tradition of learning and study (1948:7). Since he was an educational progressive, it might not have occurred to him to ask if the philosophy of progressive education— especially in its more popularized versions—militated against the orientation to texts that traditional Jewish learning required. Perhaps progressivism in education rendered more undesirable the hard work of drill and memorization that was difficult to avoid if the student was to gain enough facility to read the Bible and other sacred texts with sufficient ease and understanding. Neither did Dushkin question whether the longstanding loyalty of most Jews to public education inevitably relegated Jewish education to a marginal place and minimal accomplishment.

The admitted failures of Jewish education on the elementary and secondary levels—either to attract students or to educate properly those it did draw—caused problems in Jewish higher education. By 1968 an observer noted that students who entered Hebrew Union College in Cincinnati rarely had acquired enough Hebrew to benefit fully from the Bible and other Hebrew literature courses the school offered. Students at Jewish Theological Seminary and Rabbi Isaac Elchanan Theological Seminary had received more thorough instruction in Hebrew but had often reached rabbinical school largely ignorant of the Bible and Bible-related literature. Since both of these schools (particularly RIETS) concentrated upon talmudic study, students never did become as familiar with the Bible itself as many of them had hoped. At RIETS Bible study was available primarily through the Bernard Revel Graduate School of Yeshiva, a circumstance leading to a split between rabbinical and secular studies. In the rabbinical school the Talmud was studied by traditional philological method, reverently and without exploration of the context in which the law was created; in the graduate school Bible was approached in the more "scientific," higher critical manner (Liebman).

And yet no matter what the apparent obstacles, the vast majority of Jewish educators, whether progressive or more traditional in orientation, continued to believe that the acquisition of the Hebrew language and lifelong study of the Bible was somehow basic to a Jew's concept of self, indeed to the survival of Jews as Jews. William Chomsky, long-time professor at Gratz College, Philadelphia, and author of Hebrew and biblical textbooks, put it strongly:

> Continuity of Torah study throughout life by every Jew, rich or poor, young or old, healthy or sick, is a basic tenet in Judaism. Indeed, the study of Torah outweighs all other precepts (see *Peah* 1:1 etc.). In the Greek tradition, as formulated by Aristotle, a liberal education was a privilege reserved only for freemen, that is, those exempt from the menial work of slaves. . . . In contrast, Jewish tradition stresses that "the only freeman is he who occupies himself with the study of Torah" (*Avot* 6:2); it is learning that renders man free. While the other religions emphasize belief and faith, Judaism repeatedly enjoins learning and study. "A heathen who engages in the study of Torah is put on a par with a High Priest" (*Sanhedrin* 59a) and "a learned bastard has precedence over an ignorant High Priest" (Hor. III, 8). (1969:13)

Despite the difficulties, then, Jewish educators were reluctant to give up the ideal of study of the Hebrew Bible in the interests of expediency and competing demands on students' time. The Bible read in translation was simply not the same: "Jewish teachers were always reluctant to formulate a

'catechism,' . . . Every commentator and every student of Torah found in
the Hebrew text new ideas and insights unnoticed by their predecessors.
This process cannot take place when translation is used" (Soviv: 18). Jewish
educators therefore faced a vastly more difficult task than, for instance,
Protestant Bible school educators, who, though they argued that all
Christians must study the Bible, regarded the English translation as
sufficient.

Thus, faced with the weaknesses of elementary and secondary education, Jewish educators spent considerable time and energy speculating upon
and experimenting with methods of improving the instruction in Torah and
in the Hebrew language, with which the study of Torah was so intimately
connected. Some observers complained that the technique of *ivrit b'ivrit*,
whatever its merits, was oriented too much toward conversational Hebrew
and too little directed toward a reading knowledge of the Bible and other
ancient texts. This argument was part of a more general conflict about the
goal of teaching Hebrew, whether it was for contemporary use or for the
purposes of traditional study. Such conflict became more acute with the
revival of Hebrew in Palestine and its adoption as the national language of
the new state of Israel. Some educators who urged increased attention to
students' reading ability tried to promote the learning of Hebrew vocabular-
ies that would be more functional for the study of Bible even if less useful
for the conduct of ordinary conversations. If students came to the study of
the Bible with better linguistic preparation, such educators claimed, they
would be less likely to regard Scripture as little more than a dull language
text (Chomsky, 1937, 1944, 1962, 1969:12; Kaplan).

Other critics thought the chief obstacle to the efficient learning of
Hebrew and study of the Bible was the proliferation of competing subject
matter; they felt a more effective and integrated curriculum could probably
be achieved by incorporating some subjects such as Jewish history and
"customs and ceremonies" into the Bible instruction. Many educators aimed
their fire at the common practice of teaching Scripture mostly as Bible
stories, especially as moral tales. The exclusive concentration upon the
narrative portions of the Bible, they argued, missed the spiritual kernel of
the Bible. As remedies, they advocated the use of unabridged versions of the
Bible or more carefully adapted and richer abridged versions (Chomsky,
1938:88–89; Soviv: 20). Some commentators thought the cure to Jewish
education's ills lay in the "differentiated curriculum," in the practice of
encouraging the best and most interested students to achieve as much as
possible in Hebrew and Torah study, leaving the others to study it in English
in a more limited fashion (Frost: 11–12; Gamoran: 17). Some observers,
echoing educators in other religious traditions, suggested that Jewish
teachers honestly confront the question of the "truth" of Bible stories and the
dilemmas presented by the actions of biblical heroes that seemed to be
unethical by current standards. Teaching students about the historical

context of these stories would help students appreciate the essential truth of the text (Chomsky, 1938:87; Gamoran; Greenberg; Scharfstein). Almost all critics suggested supplements to supplementary education: educational summer camps in which Hebrew would be spoken, organized trips to Israel, and cultivation of parental interest in Hebrew literature through more adult and higher Jewish education (Chomsky, 1971:24; Dushkin, 1959:190–91). Virtually everyone agreed that existing schools should increase their instructional time, that afternoon schools must extend their hours, and that Sunday schools should institute weekday afternoon classes (Leibman: 34). Some congregations, recognizing that youngsters were often sent to school only briefly to prepare them for Bar and Bat Mitzvahs, sought to combat this practice by establishing minimal attendance times for Bar and Bat Mitzvah candidates (Leibman: 35). Some believed that the ultimate solution would be an all-day school. Because of the prevailing Jewish attachment to the public schools, such institutions had appeared only in scattered fashion in the early twentieth century. However, beginning in the 1940s and continuing to the present, they advanced in numbers and enrollments to a degree that surprised observers who had earlier assumed that they would never play a significant part in Jewish education. /10/

Many factors help explain the new popularity of the day schools: growing disillusionment with public education, particularly in the cities; the entry before and during World War II of another group of Orthodox Eastern European immigrants who treasured ancient study and who desired to reproduce the centers for Jewish study destroyed by the Nazis; the example of Protestant and Catholic parochial schools, which were experiencing a boom at the same time; the disappearance during the thirties of most of the Talmud Torahs, which had represented the most thorough form of supplementary education available until then; and the sobering lesson of the holocaust that Jewish spiritual and physical survival was no longer a foregone conclusion, even in the relatively hospitable environment of the United States; and, on the more positive side, the increased sense of pride that accompanied the founding of a Jewish homeland. Most important for our purposes, however, was the universal realization that the prevailing forms of Jewish education in America were failing to keep alive the tradition of Jews as "people of the Book" (Dushkin, 1959:185–91; Leibman; Gamoran: 16; Pilch: 131).

Even many of those who expressed uneasiness about the potential of the Jewish day schools for eroding the traditional Jewish support of public education praised the day schools for tackling seriously the problem of literacy in Hebrew and the basic classical Hebrew writings. The traditional or talmudic *yeshivot*, similar to the ones described earlier, and the Hebraic *yeshivot*, also introduced before, were chiefly responsible for the concentration of larger numbers of students on the Pentateuch, prophets, and biblical commentaries in the lower grades and on Talmud in the upper grades. The methods of these schools varied from mechanical translation to a more self-conscious pedagogy that included such concepts as "relevance" and student interest. Most *yeshivot* (as opposed to the other Jewish day schools) were established by Orthodox groups. Ultra-Orthodox groups also turned to the *yeshivah*. The Lubavitcher Yeshiva, founded in Brooklyn in 1940 on the model of the original *yeshivah* in Lubavitch, Russia, which dated from 1897, offered classes in the Talmud and law codes, the Bible with Rashi and other commentary, Jewish history, and Hebrew language and literature. Not all groups advanced the study of Torah and Talmud equally. Progressive Jewish day schools, intended for students who probably would have attended private school anyway, tended to emphasize English studies, spending only five to eight hours per week on Jewish studies. Cultural Hebraic day schools stressed Zionism, spoken Hebrew, and recent Hebrew literature. Though traditional Hebrew studies received some attention, the main focus of the curriculum lay elsewhere (Dushkin, 1948; Nardi; Schiff, 1966, 1967).

The Christian Day Schools

Protestant parochial schools in modest numbers have existed for a long time in America, particularly among Lutherans and Episcopalians. In the past few decades such parochial schools have enjoyed a new popularity, just as have Jewish day schools, and the twentieth century has witnessed the advent of the "Christian day school." Three groups of Christian day schools that are of special interest because of their biblical focus are the Christian Reformed schools (now called Christian Schools International), the interdenominational and evangelical Association of Christian Schools International, and the American Association of Christian Schools. Christian day schools have been growing rapidly in the past few decades. /11/ Most are on the elementary level, but more and more seconday schools have been founded in recent years. Several general reasons account for the rise of these schools. One is the "secularism" and "naturalism" of the public schools, particularly the lack of Bible instruction or reading. Reportedly, the Supreme Court decisions that ruled against the constitutionality of school prayer (*Engel v. Vitale*, 1962) and of Bible reading at the beginning of the school day (*Schempp* and *Murray*, both 1963) caused an increase in Christian school enrollments (Hautt: 11). Divergent ideas of child-raising help explain the founding of some schools. Conservative Christians generally perceive the public schools as too permissive and too educationally progressive (though, to be sure, Christian schools have incorporated some concepts of progressive education). Desire to escape racial integration and its consequences has played a part in the expanding enrollment of some Christian day schools, although a leader of one of the national associations disclaimed this as a factor in the growth of these institutions (Hautt: 10–11).

The upsurge in the Christian day schools occurred in the fifties, sixties, and seventies rather than earlier probably because it took until about 1950 before conservative parents, churches, and other supporters had enough resources to make this expansion of education to the lower grades possible. The growth of conservative Christian day schools has greatly benefited from the national associations, which have publicized them, promoted the pooling of information through periodicals and conferences, and offered legal counsel and other forms of aid. The creation of the national associations in turn depended upon the development of greater cohesion among conservative evangelicals. The Christian day schools represent an extension downward of the Bible institute (and to a lesser extent of the conservative Christian college of the early twentieth century); in this sense they are a logical development in the conservative Christian system of education. Many of the same groups that founded Bible institutes also established Christian day schools. At least a couple of the current day schools probably started out as Bible schools at an indeterminate academic level. In addition, some day schools have actual ties to present-day Bible schools and conservative Christian colleges; through teacher placement services maintained by the ACSI, graduates of Bible schools and Christian colleges are funneled into the day schools. But the most important connection of all comes from the fact that many of the Christian day schools continue the traditional Bible-centered approach of the Bible institutes. Frank E. Gaebelein, the founder of one of the earliest day schools, seemed to echo the remarks of early Bible school leaders when he said, "The most disturbing lack of modern education with all its tremendous range of subject matter comes out in the Biblical illiteracy of its products. By and large they know nothing of the Bible. Their ignorance of the Word of God is matched only by the cocksureness with which they dismiss its claims upon their lives" (118).

Because most of the Christian day schools emphasize knowledge of the Bible, they start their pupils in this study as early as kindergarten. The Christian Reformed *Course of Study* offers some clues to teaching methods. Young children in the first few grades of these schools learn mostly through hearing their teachers recount Bible stories. The children also memorize a selection of simple Bible verses that apply to the stories they hear. The teachers use pictures, singing, and drawing assignments to increase interest and understanding. As the students advance through the higher elementary grades, they encounter the actual biblical text more and more, and they are introduced to Bible geography and use workbooks to help them fix the biblical "facts" in their memories. The older they become, the more independent study they are expected to do, with the aid of questions from the teachers, workbooks, and Bible atlases and dictionaries. The memoriza-tion of verses—and constant review of what has been memorized earlier—continues throughout.

The goals of such Bible study are similar to those of the Bible institutes. On the simplest level, study is meant to render the student as familiar as possible with Scripture. In the Christian Reformed *Course of Study*, for instance, the Bible is "covered" four times between kindergarten and eighth grade. Next, Bible study is designed to make the student realize that "God's Word is a unit. Many parts take on richer meaning and others become clear only in the light of the whole. . . . The Bible is a continuous, connected, growing, developing picture of God" (National Union of Christian Schools: 39, 92). To this end even the smallest children learn the Bible stories in the same sequence as they appear in the Scriptures. Another goal of Bible study is to accustom students always to apply themselves to the actual biblical text, with ever increasing independence of the teacher, so that as adults they will continue to engage in Bible study on their own. Children are also encouraged to recognize the practicality of Scripture for their lives. As the instructions for the *Course of Study* direct, *"The significance of the selection should be linked with an existing or possible need in the life of the individual.* For example, Psalm 23 reveals God as a loving Father who faithfully cares for His own. After this meaning has become clear, its potentiality for providing comfort in times of danger and trial is readily deduced" (44).

Not all of these objectives were met in all schools. Gaebelein in his report on independent schools indicated that much work needed to be done in developing more thoroughgoing methods of teaching the Bible and integrating Bible study with the rest of the curriculum (120–21). But there is little doubt that students who participated in the full course of Christian day school plus Bible school or conservative college had at the very least attained an intimacy with the biblical text and could quote much of it at will. This, in the minds of conservative parents, presented an enormous advance over what public education could offer.

The Catholic Biblical Movement

During the first half of the twentieth century individual Catholic educators occasionally called for more attention to the Bible in parochial school religion courses (e.g., Russell, 1924a, 1924b; anon., 1924). Usually their suggestions met with indifference or inertia. Hostility to and lack of information about the higher critical studies of the sacred text reinforced the old distrust of Bible study as a "Protestant" activity. Many Catholics tended to view the Bible as a sacred object rather than a living text. By and large Bible study in schools continued to amount to the memorization of Bible history events and dates; students' acquaintance with the actual text was limited to quotations. Religion teachers themselves generally lacked familiarity either with the text or with basic Catholic biblical scholarship. Gradually, however, as the twentieth century progressed, several countervailing factors combined to alter this picture. In the encyclical, *Divino Afflante Spiritu* (1943), Pope Pius XII encouraged Catholic scholars to engage in biblical studies, sanctioned vernacular translations, and enjoined bishops and priests to promote interest in the Bible among the faithful. New more readable versions of the Bible appeared: the Knox Bible in Great Britain during the 1940s and, in the

United States, the Confraternity Revision (New Testament, 1941) and the Confraternity Version (which appeared in parts, the whole Bible being published in 1970). In 1966 came the English translation of the French *Bible de Jérusalem*. Organizations for the promotion of Bible study on the scholarly and popular levels came into being: the Catholic Bible Association of America, founded in 1936, provided a forum for Catholic biblical scholars; the more lay-oriented Catholic Biblical Society chose as one of its specific goals the advancement of knowledge of the Bible in the Catholic schools.

The climax came in the early 1960s with the promulgations of Vatican II, particularly the constitutions on divine revelation and on sacred liturgy, which encouraged the reading and study of the "divine word," and its use in liturgy. The document on divine revelation urged, "Easy access [to Scripture] should be provided for all the Christian faithful," while the Constitution on Sacred Liturgy directed, "if the restoration, progress, and adaptation of the sacred liturgy are to be achieved, it is necessary to promote the warm and living love for Scripture. . . . " In 1962, not coincidentally, *The Bible Today*, a magazine meant for a Catholic lay audience, made its first appearance.

As a result of these and other exhortations and encouragements, periodicals devoted to Catholic educational matters abounded during the fifties and sixties with articles on how to teach the Bible in the classroom. Some sought to familiarize students with the actual text or simply to accustom them to using the Bible on an everyday basis. Others aimed at increasing teachers' acquaintance with Scripture and explored the new textbooks and teachers' manuals on Bible study that were becoming available in the Catholic book market. Writers groped with the problem of the relation of catechism and doctrine to Scripture. They asked if the Bible is illustrative of catechetical principles—or if the principles are actually derived from it. Others explored the place of Scripture in the religion class and its relationship to other more traditional Catholic religious subjects. Teachers exchanged ideas on how students could be encouraged to apply Scripture to their lives and to the problems of society. Some argued that teachers should emphasize the "message" (moral or theological) of Scripture; others, the story value; still others, the heroes and possible models that the Bible offers. Another point of discussion concerned the question of the "truth" of biblical accounts and the treatment of the complex matter of the historical setting of the biblical record. Others discussed how the approach should vary according to the ages of the students (Bertrand; Brown; Ceroke; DePasquale; Doherty; Hartman; Kevane; Moore; Teresita; Tos). Seminary instructors asked their own questions. What would be the new alignment between biblical studies and theology? One professor predicted that more exegetical courses, more "history of Israel" offerings, and more biblical theology would appear in the seminary curriculum and urged that prospective theologians receive more graduate instruction in the "biblical sciences" (Maly: 65). This change is still in process, and once again the Bible has become a potent influence in shaping an alternative to the public school.

Conclusion

Despite the immense popularity of public education, common schooling has never received universal support. One reason is that public education has been unable to satisfy even one religious group without incurring another group's charge of teaching in a sectarian manner. Thus, to many it has seemed best to omit religion—and the Bible—altogether from the purview of the public school. Those who wish to advance their views of the Bible and cannot conceive of any knowledge apart from biblical knowledge have had to resort to nonpublic forms of religious education. Each educational choice made by such groups has presented its own set of problems. Supplementary education has often been criticized for not being enough. Its critics question whether parents and students take it seriously and whether educators pour sufficient resources into it. This has been a particularly pressing concern for Jewish educators, since mastery of Hebrew—no easy accomplishment—has been so important in Old Testament study. Another problem with supplementary education has been that its attempts to teach a separate set of values—for instance a distinctly "biblical" viewpoint—have usually been overcome by the public school with its greater command over students' time and attention. As A. A. Hodge, a noted Princeton Seminary theologian, complained in 1887:

> The infinite evils resulting from the exclusion of religion from the schools cannot be corrected by the supplementary agencies of the Christian home, the Sabbath-school, and the church. This follows not only because the activities of the public school are universal and that of the other agencies partial, but chiefly because the Sabbath-school and the church cannot teach history and science, and therefore cannot rectify the anti-Christian history and science taught by the public schools. And, if they could, a Christian history and science on the one hand cannot coalesce with and counteract an atheistic history and science on the other. Poison and its antidote together never constitute nutritious food. (McSweeney: 788)

Alternatives to public education—full-time day schools—face problems because they run counter to the deep-seated American loyalty to public education and often feed the distrust of pluralism. Jews, Protestants, and Catholics alike have usually felt obliged to justify the establishment of parochial schools in the most vigorous terms. Supporters of alternative schools also face the problem of paying for both public and private schooling and must constantly worry about whether the constituency of the schools is large enough to sustain them. Furthermore, any group that diverges too far from the norm of public education—if indeed it is legally permitted to do so— must ask whether its students will be handicapped when they try to enter the mainstream of society. Will they be able to "mix" easily and acquire desirable occupations? Will the alternative school serve social and economic mobility? Bible school graduates, for instance, have not always been welcome in other reaches of higher education. Their speech, sometimes heavy with King James words and patterns, their aggressive use of the Scriptures to proselytize others, and their absolutistic understanding of Scripture as "the truth" offend many. Fortunately for them, evangelicals make up a large enough group in American society to supply employment for those who have received a conservative Protestant education. Even so, many Bible schools have found it desirable in recent decades to move closer to the practices of liberal arts colleges. Ironically, it may be equally risky for alternative schools *not* to depart substantially from the public school version of education. Why should parents undertake the expense if their children are not receiving a recognizably different sort of education? Catholics, Lutherans, and Protestant fundamentalists, as major founders of alternative schooling, have had to cope with these thorny issues.

Despite these obstacles, religious groups have persisted in creating new schools throughout the nineteenth and twentieth centuries because they have worried about issues of Bible study and scriptural interpretation. Their perseverance has testified to the continuing power of the Bible to influence, shape, and create American education.

NOTES

/1/   See Justice William Brennan's brief survey of instances in which the reading of the Bible has been prohibited from public schools from 1843 on by school superintendents, boards of education, state attorneys general, and courts (quoted in Duker: 195–98).

/2/   Samuel Benderly, director of the Bureau of Jewish Education, New York City, wrote to Judah Magnes, March 9, 1910: "As the great public school system is the rock bottom upon which this country is rearing its institutions, so we must evolve here a system of Jewish education that shall be complementary to and harmonious with the public school system" (Pilch: 55).

/3/   The rabbi usually served as "superintendent" of the Sunday school, and confirmation often replaced the Bar Mitzvah. One early Sunday school was even forced to use the King James Version, for lack of any other; this same school taught Scripture from a publication of the "Christian Sunday School Union," in which offensive passages were deleted (see Gartner, 1969:9, 54–60).

/4/   In 1906 it was reported that 90 percent of the City College graduates were Jews and that in 1908 three-quarters of the City College student body was Jewish (Klaperman: 83).

/5/   For an extended discussion of the missionary training school as well as of the biblical revival and the Bible school, see the forthcoming history of Protestant theological education in America (funded by the Lilly Endowment, Inc. and conducted under the auspices of Auburn Seminary).

/6/   The definition of fundamentalism has posed a knotty problem for historians of American religion, involving as it does complex religious, theological, experiential, sociological, cultural, political, and educational aspects. Fortunately the question of who the fundamentalists were has been addressed with greater seriousness in the past few years. For a review of the literature on fundamentalism, see Wenger, "Social Thought in American Fundamentalism," pp. 1–75. Recent and important contributions to a conception of fundamentalism have emerged from Sandeen (*Roots of Fundamentalism*) and reviews of his work by Marsden and Moore. George M. Marsden's book, *Fundamentalism and American Culture,* offers many new and fascinating insights into the nature of fundamentalism. I broach a definition in my doctorial dissertation on fundamentalist education (Teachers College, Columbia University, 1981).

/7/   For an idea of the scope of fundamentalist organization, see Joel Carpenter, "Fundamentalist Institutions."

/8/   For accounts of how the Bible was employed in the evangelism of others, see Metcalf (*Letters to Dorothy,* pp. 26–29) and Harkness (*Torrey,* pp. 124–26). The examples I use are from these books. Fundamentalist periodicals also abound with similar examples.

/9/   George's Marsden's book has an illuminating and extended discussion of this point (see chapter 13).

/10/   In 1945 there were 10,000 students in day schools in the United States; in 1962, 50,000; and in 1969, 80,000 (Gartner, 1969:28). Dushkin (1918:418) reported only 985 students in Jewish parochial schools in N.Y.C.

/11/   Exact statistics on total numbers of Christian day schools and total student enrollments are difficult to attain, since some schools report to no association at all, and some belong to more than one association. Available figures from individual associations indicate impressive growth since the 1950s.

WORKS CONSULTED

Adler, Cyrus, ed.
    1939   *The Jewish Theological Seminary of America.* Semi-Centennial Volume. New York: The Jewish Theological Seminary of America.

Anonymous ["A Benedictine Priest"]
    1924   "A High School Course in Religion." *Catholic Educational Review* 22 (September and October): 472–86.

Association for Christian Schools
    1962   *Schools Weighed in the Balance.* Houston, TX: St. Thomas Press.

Ben-Horin, Meir
    1969   "From the Turn of the Century to the Late Thirties." In *A History of Jewish Education in America,*

ed. Judah Pilch. New York: The National Curriculum Research Institute of the American Association for Jewish Education. Pp. 51–118.

Bertrand, M.

1967   "Introducing Scripture to the Elementary Child." *Catholic School Journal* 67 (November): 46–47.

Brown, Daniel

1968–1969   "Teaching the Old Testament to American Students." *Living Light* 5 (Winter): 65–74.

Carpenter, Joel A.

1980   "Fundamentalist Institutions and the Rise of Conservative Protestantism, 1929–1942." *Church History* 49 (March): 62–75.

Carper, James C.

1980   "In the Way He Should Go: An Overview of the Christian Day School Movement." *Review Journal of Philosophy and Social Science* 4: 118–31.

Cassidy, Francis P.

1948–1949   "Catholic Education in the Third Plenary Council of Baltimore." *The Catholic Historical Review* 34 (October and January): 257–305; 414–36.

Ceroke, Christian P.

1955   "The Bible Goes to Summer School." *The Catholic Biblical Quarterly* 17 (April): 154–57.

Chomsky, William

1934   "How Should the Bible Be Taught?" (Review of "Darche Limmud Hatanach," by Zvi Scharfstein) *Jewish Education* 6 (October-December): 172–74.

1937   "Vocabulary Studies as a Basis for a Hebrew Methodology." *Jewish Education* 9 (April): 58–60.

1938   "The Problem of Bible Teaching in Our Hebrew Curriculum." *Jewish Education* 10 (April-June): 85–90.

1944   "Aims and Methods in Teaching Hebrew." *Jewish Education* 15 (May): 148–54.

1962   "Another Look at the Aim of Teaching Hebrew in Our Schools." *Jewish Education* 33 (Fall): 45–51, 57.

1969   "This I Believe: The Credo of a Jewish Educator."
                Jewish Education 39 (January): 6–17.

1971   "American Jewish Life and Education in Retro-
                spect and Prospect." *Jewish Education* 40 (Spring):
                20–25.

Cohon, Samuel S.
1950   "The History of Hebrew Union College." *Publica-
                tions of the American Jewish Historical Society*
                39 (September): 17–55.

Damm, John Silber
1963   "The Growth and Decline of Lutheran Parochial
                Schools in the United States, 1638–1962." Unpub-
                lished Ed.D. dissertation, Teachers College,
                Columbia University.

DePasquale, Leonard
1964   "[don't hesitate to use] the Bible in the classroom."
                Catholic School Journal 64 (June): 39–41.

Doherty, John T.
1965   "The New Liturgy: Its Impact on the Elementary
                School, the Biblical Approach." *National Catholic
                Education Association Bulletin* 62 (August): 483–
                89.

Duker, Sam
1963   *The Public Schools and Religion: The Legal Con-
                text.* New York: Harper and Row.

Dushkin, Alexander M.
1918   *Jewish Education in New York City.* New York:
                The Bureau of Jewish Education.

1948   "The Role of the Day School in American Jewish
                Education." *Jewish Education* 20 (Fall): 5–15.

1959   (with Uriah Z. Engelman) *Jewish Education in
                the United States: Report of the Commission for
                the Study of Jewish Education in the United
                States.* New York: American Association for Jewish
                Education. Volume I.

1967   "Fifty Years of American Jewish Education: Retro-
                spect and Prospects." *Jewish Education* 37 (Win-
                ter): 44–57.

Frost, Shimon
1977   "The Position of Hebrew in the Supplementary School." *Jewish Education* 45 (Winter): 10–12, 38.

Gaebelein, Frank E.
1951   *Christian Education in a Democracy: The Report of the N.A.E. Committee.* New York: Oxford.

Gamoran, Emanuel
1930   "Problems in the Teaching of the Bible." *Jewish Education* 2 (January): 16–24.

Gartner, Lloyd P.
1964   "The Jews of New York's East Side, 1890–1893." *American Jewish Historical Quarterly* 53 (March): 264–84.

1969   *Jewish Education in the United States: A Documentary History.* New York: Teachers College Press.

Gilmour, Richard
1924   *Bible History.* New York, Cincinnati, Chicago: Benziger Bros. First published in 1869.

Gourary, S.
1948   "The Story of the United Lubavitcher Yeshivoth." *Jewish Education* 20 (Fall): 43–46.

Goren, Arthur A.
1970   *New York Jews and the Quest for Community: The Kehillah Experiment, 1908–1922.* New York: Columbia University Press.

Gray, James M.
1900   *Synthetic Bible Studies.* Cleveland: F. M. Barton.

Greenberg, Moshe
1959   "On Teaching the Bible in Religious Schools." *Jewish Education* 29 (Spring): 45–53.

Grinstein, Hyman B.
1941   "An Early Parochial School." *Jewish Education* 13 (April): 23–33.

Harkness, Robert
1929   *Reuben Archer Torrey: The Man, His Message.* Chicago: The Bible Colportage Association.

Hartman, Louis F.
1957   "The New Confraternity Translation and Religious
                       Education." *Religious Education* 52 (January–
                       February): 17–22.

Hautt, William David
1971   "The Effectiveness of Christian Schools in Achiev-
                       ing Religious Objectives." Unpublished Ed.D. dis-
                       sertation, Teachers College, Columbia University.

Honor, Leo L.
1952   "Jewish Elementary Education in the United States
                       (1901–1950)." *Publications of the American Jew-
                       ish Historical Society* 42 (September): 1–42.

Kaminetsky, Joseph
1955   "The Hebrew Day School Movement." *School and
                       Society* 82 (October1): 105–7.

Kaplan, Louis L.
1944   "A New Approach in the Teaching of Humosh."
                       Jewish Education 15 (January): 85–89.

Katzoff, Louis
1949   *Issues in Jewish Education: A Study of the Phi-
                       losophy of the Conservative Congregational
                       School.* New York: Bloch Publishing Co.

Kevane, Eugene
1955   "Sacred Scripture in the Catholic High School." *The
                       Catholic Biblical Quarterly* 17 (April): 136–53.

Klaperman, Gilbert
1969   *The Story of Yeshiva University: The First Jewish
                       University in America.* New York: Macmillan.

Leibman, Morris
1956–1957   "An Evaluation of the Afternoon Hebrew School."
                       Jewish Education 27 (Winter): 29–38.

Liebman, Charles S.
1968   "The Training of American Rabbis." *American
                       Jewish Year Book* 69: 3–112.

McSweeney, P. L.
1887   "Christian Public Schools." *Catholic World*
                       (March): 788–97.

Maly, Eugene S.
   1963   "Progress and Prospects in Scripture Studies in the Seminaries." *National Catholic Education Association Bulletin* 60 (August): 59–65.

Marsden, George M.
   1971   "Defining Fundamentalism." *Christian Scholar's Review* 1 (Winter): 141–51.

   1980   *Fundamentalism and American Culture: The Shaping of Twentieth Century Evangelicalism: 1870–1925.* New York: Oxford University Press.

Metcalf, Edith E.
   1893   *Letters to Dorothy.* Chicago and New York: Fleming H. Revell.

Moore, Joseph
   1976   "Is the Old Testament for Children?" *Living Light* 13 (Fall): 374–78.

Moore, LeRoy, Jr.
   1976   "Another Look at Fundamentalism: A Response to Ernest R. Sandeen." *Church History* 37 (June): 195–202.

Nardi, Noah
   1948   "The Growth of Jewish Day Schools in America." *Jewish Education* 20 (Fall): 23–32.

National Association of Christian Schools
   1964   *School Directory*

The National Union of Christian Schools
   1953   *Course of Study for Christian Schools.* Second Edition. Grand Rapids: William B. Eerdmans.

New York Catholic School Board
   1911   "Course of Study and Syllabus in Religion for the Elementary Schools of the Archdiocese of New York."

Pilch, Judah, ed.
   1969   *A History of Jewish Education in America.* New York: National Curriculum Research Institute of the American Association for Jewish Education.

Pope, H. W.
 1915   "Daily Bible Reading." *Christian Workers Magazine* (December): 278.

Russell, W. H.
 1924a   "The Aim and Content of the High School Religion Course." *Catholic Educational Review* 22 (March): 144–52.
 1924b   "The Method of the High School Religion Course." *Catholic Educational Review* 22 (April): 215–22.

Sandeen, Ernest R.
 1970   *The Roots of Fundamentalism: British and American Millenarianism, 1800–1930.* Chicago: University of Chicago Press.
 1971   "Defining Fundamentalism: A Reply to Professor Marsden." *Christian Scholar's Review* 1 (Spring): 227–32.

Sanders, James W.
 1977   *The Education of an Urban Minority: Catholics in Chicago, 1833–1965.* New York: Oxford University Press.

Scharfstein, Zvi
 1930   "Traditional versus Historical Approach in the Teaching of the Bible." *Jewish Education* 2 (January): 4–15.

Schiff, Alvin I.
 1966   *The Jewish Day School in America.* New York: Jewish Education Committee Press.
 1967   "An Appreciation of the Jewish Day School in America." *Jewish Education* 37 (Winter): 69–83.

Sherrill, Lewis Joseph
 1932   *Presbyterian Parochial Schools, 1846–1870.* New Haven: Yale University Press.

Showers, Renald
 1962   "A History of Philadelphia College of the Bible." Unpublished M.A. thesis, Dallas Theological Seminary and Graduate School of Theology.

Shulman, Moses I.
1948   "The Yeshivah Etz Hayim Hebrew Institute of Boro Park." *Jewish Education* 20 (Fall): 47–48.

Soviv, Aaron
1973   "The Function of Hebrew in the Afternoon Hebrew School." *Jewish Education* 43 (Fall): 17–22.

Spotts, Leon H.
1971   "Trends and Currents in Curriculum Development, 1930–1970." *Jewish Education* 40 (Spring): 36–45.

Teresita, M.
1965   "A Bible Vigil: Presenting Bibles to Students." *Catholic School Journal* 65 (Spring): 62–64.

Todes, David U.
1955   "The Life and Character of Isaac Leeser the Educator." *Jewish Education* 26 (Fall): 30–39, 56.

Tos, Aldo J.
1964   "Approaches to the Old Testament for High School Catechists and Students." *National Catholic Education Association Bulletin* 61 (August): 262–69.

Wenger, Robert Elwood
1973   "Social Thought in American Fundamentalism, 1918–1933." Unpublished Ph.D. dissertation, University of Nebraska, Lincoln.

IV

Stabilizing a Changing Culture: The Bible
and the Sunday School in the Late Nineteenth Century

William L. Sachs

The story of the Bible in the American Sunday school movement frequently is conceived as the growth of the Bible's influence on American life
or as the development of consensus about the social importance of Bible
study. Less noticed but more significant were two crucial developments in
the Bible's place in American Sunday schools. First, during the nineteenth
century, Sunday schools evolved a systematic approach to Bible study. Early
in the century Bible study involved memorization of disparate passages of
Scripture, but by the end of the century structured curricula focused attention on a planned pattern of lessons. Increased structure allowed for emphasis on portions of Scripture that curriculum designers deemed crucial to
Christian living and permitted attention to the psychological development of
students. The second development paralleled the emergence of structured
curricula. Over the course of the nineteenth century the context of Sunday
school education shifted from interdenominational agencies to denominations themselves. A rethinking of basic goals accompanied this shift. Early
American Sunday schools sought the moral betterment of their students as a
means of teaching effective citizenship and as an aspect of their personal
salvation. Later Sunday schools, set in the churches and armed with structured curricula, stressed above all the personal salvation of their students.
This chapter will sketch the development of these changes in the use of the
Bible by American Sunday schools.

Moral Restraint and the Rise of System

Sunday schools did not originate in the United States. They appeared
first in England late in the eighteenth century. Historians generally have
credited Robert Raikes with founding the first Sunday school at Gloucester in
1780. But Sunday schools presupposed several centuries of Protestant
organizations to educate children in religion. Raikes was one leader—albeit a
prominent one—of an explosion of schools to teach religion to poor English

children on Sundays after 1750. These pioneer efforts recognized the growth of an impoverished class but assumed that the poor were capable of being bettered by education. English Sunday schools stressed memorization of biblical stories and rudimentary instruction in reading and writing as means to spiritual and moral improvement. Undergirding this philosophy was a sense of moral urgency based on a conviction that the poor who remained untouched by knowledge of Scripture constituted a threat to society. English Sunday schools used a variety of biblical examples to convey instruction in proper behavior. In the long run this effort reflected the emergence of lay leaders who could apply religious beliefs to social problems. It also contributed significantly to the emergence of an English working-class culture by supplying a biblically based vocabulary and sense of life's flux (Laqueur).

American Sunday schools developed along similar lines late in the eighteenth century, though they were less dedicated to serving the working classes. Like their English counterparts American Sunday schools presupposed more than a century of efforts to educate children in Christian belief. It would be difficult to specify the first American Sunday school; however, several early examples stand out. In 1785 William Elliott, a Methodist layman, began to instruct children and a few slaves in the Bible at his Virginia home. Elliott subsequently moved his school to a nearby church. Other Sunday schools appeared at the same time. In 1786 Francis Asbury organized a school for instructing children at the home of Thomas Crenshaw in Hanover County, Virginia. Spontaneously organized Sunday schools quickly appeared in most of the former American colonies (Buckle: 273; Cope: 73). These schools operated autonomously and reflected a consensus only about the need for popular education in the Bible.

A move to Sunday school organization on a larger scale was the first significant development in the history of American Sunday schools. This shift occurred in two ways. First, interdenominational Sunday school societies emerged. Founded in 1793, the Philadelphia First-Day Society pioneered this trend. It was led by such philanthropists and noted clergy as Benjamin Rush, Matthew Carey, and William White. An interdenominational effort, the Philadelphia Society had a strong sense of philanthropic purpose. The society conceived of itself as a system of schools for the city's poor children where literacy would be taught and behavior improved. Though instruction in the society's schools was confined to the Bible, the schools also taught reading and writing based upon stories from Scripture (Pray: 206). The Philadelphia First-Day Society inspired a number of interdenominational Sunday schools in America's eastern cities. These schools were part of a massive benevolent effort. Inspired by a sense of national mission, many American Protestants organized voluntary agencies to promote Christian belief and virtuous citizenship. America's burgeoning cities were prime targets for this energy. Protestant agencies led by Lyman

Beecher, William E. Dodge, Arthur and Lewis Tappan, and other ministers and philanthropists tried to shape life in the cities through the communication of Christian benevolence. For this effort the Bible was the basic text. Convinced that the Bible was the primary repository of moral example, urban Protestants in the early nineteenth century began to distribute tracts and Bibles in enormous quantities. Sunday schools, designed to encourage faith and proper deportment among poor children in the cities, were part of this benevolent effort.

Surveying American Sunday schools of the early nineteenth century, Lewis Pray noted that the Sunday school "has for its basis the fundamental principle, that moral and religious instruction is an original and indispensable want of the child's nature; and that other and more efficient means than parental instruction and example, and the ordinary services of the Church, are requisite, in the progress of the ages . . . " (233). Interdenominational Sunday schools rallied around this perception. Sunday schools appeared in New York, Boston, and Portsmouth, New Hampshire, before sweeping the eastern seaboard. Soon state and local Sunday school societies were formed. Finally, by 1824 the American Sunday School Union appeared and began to push for uniformity in curriculum design and teaching methods. Interdenominational Sunday schools involved large numbers of lay people. Often wealthy, these people saw themselves as Christians summoned to spread the social influence of the Gospel. They were a united front capable of achieving divine ends beyond the powers of their individual denominations. Indeed they rejected sectarian goals to focus on revitalizing American life. Interdenominational Sunday school leaders assumed that the children whom they reached eventually would filter into the churches, if the schools did their job. It was their task to strengthen American society by instructing urban poor in moral principles of conduct.

A sense of the city as a moral threat strikingly influenced early Sunday school leadership. Sunday school promoters attempted to re-create the moral order of the village in their classes. The schools were surrogate families whose goals went beyond the attempt to convert children to the faith. Sunday schools presupposed the failure of traditional means of child nurture and assumed the responsibility of promoting "deferential and disciplined patterns of behavior based on an image of society as stable, orderly, and securely hierarchical." The biblically centered curricula used in urban Sunday schools stressed the social duties of husbands, wives, parents, children, masters, servants, magistrates, and subjects as depicted in Scripture. Loyalty, deference, obedience, responsibility, and courtesy dominated the biblically approved virtues (Boyer: 43).

Sunday school promoters assumed that knowledge of Scripture was essential for personal salvation and for social stability. Scripture was considered a fount of eternal truths that must be applied to modern social problems. A particular logic underlay this assumption. Sunday school organizers saw society as an amalgam of individuals, the sum of whose moral qualities determined society's nature. The moral improvement of society, according to them, must begin by uplifting the moral character of individuals. In an age of untamed cities and frontiers, the achievement of this improvement became paramount among Sunday school leaders. They also believed that training in proper living was their most important task. Feeling that society's destiny might largely be determined by their efforts, Sunday school leaders worked furiously to extend knowledge of the Bible in American society.

Though interdenominational societies took the lead in organizing Sunday schools and formulating more developed curricula, the churches were not far behind. After the earliest Methodist Sunday schools in the late eighteenth century, Congregational schools began to appear. In 1805 at Bath, New Hampshire, David Sutherland founded what was apparently the first Congregational Sunday school (Ewing: 2ff.). Soon other Congregational schools dotted New England. Denominational Sunday school societies followed. By 1840 the Unitarian, Lutheran, Episcopal, Baptist, and Methodist churches had their own Sunday school associations. The Methodist Church was the first denomination to organize intensively its own Sunday schools. By 1827 Methodists had founded a Sunday School Union. In its first annual report the Methodist Sunday School Union noted that Methodists enrolled an impressive 63,240 pupils in 1,024 schools. The same report revealed an emerging tension between the churches and interdenominational agencies over who rightly should control Sunday schools.

> Hence religious instruction is the grand and primary object of Sunday School instruction in our day, and among our children. On this account, however humiliating the fact, general union of all the parties becomes the more difficult. Whatever may be the intention, each teacher of religion will more or less inculcate his own peculiar views of Christianity, and thus insensibly create party feelings and interests. . . . The managers are of the opinion, that the most likely way for the several denominations to live and labor together in peace, is for each to conduct its own affairs. (*The Christian Advocate and Journal*, April 21, 1827:130; cited in Buckle: 583)

Both denominational and interdenominational schools shared a common approach to Sunday school education. Sunday schools lumped together children of all ages and stressed the beneficial effects of memorizing passages of Scripture. Although there was little pattern to memorization of the Bible, Sunday school designers conferred a magical quality on memorization. Sunday school teachers expected their charges to retain as much Scripture as possible. Triumphs of childhood capacity for memorization dot early Sunday school reports. One girl quickly learned ninety passages concerning human depravity and God's mercy. In Newburyport, Massachusetts, a ten-year-old girl memorized Matthew, several psalms, fifty-four assorted verses, twenty hymns, forty-four Scripture proofs, one tract, and a catechism in only a few months (Ewing). Between 1805 and 1820 Sunday school Bible study consisted simply of memorization of randomly selected passages of

Scripture. Often the passages chosen dealt with moral themes drawn from Jesus' ministry or the lives of patriarchs and prophets. Teachers assumed that the more Scripture one learned, the more one improved morally. As the limitations of this logic became apparent, Sunday school organizers began a more systematic approach to Bible study. At the same time Sunday schools became concerned with saving the souls as well as improving the conduct of their pupils.

Lewis Baldwin's *The Biblical Interrogatory*, published in 1816, was one of the first attempts to systematize Bible study in Sunday schools. Baldwin's work provided a series of questions to guide study through the Old and New Testaments. Truman Parmele and S. W. Seton followed with a series of questions on the New Testament and a limited plan of Scripture lessons, as did Albert Judson of the New York Sunday School Union (Rice: 75–108).

The New York Sunday School Union's "Selected and Limited Lessons," published in 1827, was one of the most comprehensive of the early curricula developed by an interdenominational agency. The Union declared that its system aimed "to exclude the unprofitable plan of committing large portions of Scripture to memory *without religious instruction*; and to introduce a method whereby the scholars shall receive particular instruction of *all* that they commit to memory, and the teachers themselves be more duly prepared for the Sunday School duties . . . " (New York Sunday School Union). The Union's curriculum stressed study at home and memorization of a selected passage. The New York plan focused on Christ's life as both a moral example and the means of personal salvation. For example Lesson XXXII, which highlighted Matt 19:13–26, was entitled "Christ blesseth little children. The rich man's questions what he should do to be saved." Study questions accompanying the lesson appeared in three categories of difficulty. Some of the simplest questions included: "Who were brought to Christ?" "Into what did Jesus say that such a rich man should hardly enter?" or "When the disciples had heard it, how were they affected?" The most difficult questions possessed a greater doctrinal flavor. "Are all children members of the kingdom of heaven?" "Has Christ always proved to be a good Master or Teacher?" and "What must you do if you would have everlasting life?" These questions reveal that the lessons moved beyond the goal of accumulating biblical information. Yet each lesson pointed above all to the moral benefits of knowing Scripture. The lessons were designed to begin with Christ's divinity and to follow Christ's ministry through the crucifixion. In this comprehensive sweep the New York Union hoped students would perceive a pattern of moral deportment by which they could improve their own conduct and achieve personal salvation.

As they moved to patterned programs of Bible study, Sunday schools became more conscious of the means to effect moral improvement. They also began to link salvation of the students' souls to improved conduct. Interdenominational Sunday schools took the lead in systematizing this trend.

With the birth of the American Sunday School Union in 1824, interdenominational Sunday schools reached the zenith of their organization in the first
half of the century. The Union attempted controlled growth and consensus
in teacher training, curriculum design, and philosophy of education. It published a variety of Bible study aids, including dictionaries, geographies,
commentaries, tracts, and inexpensive New Testaments. Among its most
prized publications was a series of Select Scripture Lessons, spanning forty-
nine selections on Christ's life. Unlike the New York Sunday School Union's
curriculum, this plan consisted merely of a list of suggested, randomly
selected New Testament passages without questions or commentary. The
American Sunday School Union's plan urged that schools be divided into
four classes: (1) children who read the Bible, (2) those who read indif-
ferently, (3) those unable to read but able to spell in two or more syllables,
(4) those restricted to some knowledge of the alphabet. The Union suggested
that this afforded a uniform means of instruction with attention to the
capabilities of pupils. Thus Sunday school promoters became increasingly
aware of the desirability of shaping their message to pupils' individual
circumstances (American Sunday School Union, 1826:110).

Even as Sunday school instruction became more systematic and more
attuned to personal salvation, interdenominational schools refused to relinquish their commitment to moral education. The 1831 report of the American Sunday School Union clearly expressed this philosophy of Bible study.
"A religious man must necessarily be a moral man, and a moral man cannot
be a bad citizen." "We are willing to avow that our grand object is, with
God's blessing, to make every child . . . a believer in the Bible, the whole
Bible, and . . . *nothing but the* Bible."

> On this subject, as on all other moral subjects, the Board esteem the Bible the
> only perfect standard. They here find sufficient sanction for the inculcation of divine
> truth by means of histories, which, though not known to have any foundation in fact,
> are fitted to illustrate and explain moral principle. The incidents in connexion with
> which the truth is exhibited, are wholly supposititious, but yet perfectly simple and
> natural, while the truth itself is plainly and prominently enforced.
>
> Nathan's inimitably beautiful and pungent reproof of David—the simple
> account of the creditor and his two debtors, by which Simon's unforgiving temper was
> rebuked, and the broken-hearted penitent comforted—the particular history by which
> the relation of a neighbour is illustrated in the case of the man on his way from Jerusa-
> lem to Jericho, where circumstances are minutely related—the great supper, by an
> allusion to which the fulness and freeness of the gospel salvation are represented,—and
> the story of the Prodigal Son, which declares, with unparalleled eloquence, the
> forgiveness and exceeding compassion of God,—all these, and others which might be
> cited, are pertinent examples of the style of writing to which we have just referred.
> (American Sunday School Union, 1831:22f.)

As long as the goal of teaching the Bible was to communicate illustrations of moral behavior, Sunday school organizers emphasized the purity of
the Bible's moral examples. The noted Princeton theologian Charles Hodge

spoke in this vein in 1833 when he delivered the American Sunday School Union's annual sermon. Hodge declared that the end of all Christian institutions was to bring the Bible to bear on the formation of human character and the regulation of human conduct. The truth of the Bible, said Hodge, lay in its containing a perfect rule of moral duty. Only through knowledge of the Bible could a person fully cultivate the moral aspect of the human constitution. As the primary agency for Bible education, the Sunday school had great responsibility for social welfare (Hodge: 5ff.). With this commitment in mind, the American Sunday School Union became more systematic in its approach to Sunday school organization. Teacher training increasingly preoccupied the Union. Early American Sunday schools had done little to define the teacher's role. At any given time teachers were to preserve order, ensure that students met the school's objectives, provide moral example, or explain bits of Bible history and doctrine. The American Sunday School Union's 1831 report advocated certain preparation for teaching.

> A man of ordinary education, with the Bible, a volume of Union questions, and a copy of our Bible Dictionary and Sacred Geography, could make a very useful Bible-class teacher, if he had the right spirit and would apply himself. If it is desirable, however, to enjoy still higher advantages, a few individuals can unite themselves into a society for the purpose of advancement in biblical knowledge; and under the tuition of some competent instructer [sic], soon become sufficiently familiar with it to enable them to be profitable teachers of others. (39)

As the teacher's role became more defined, manuals on Sunday school teaching appeared. A growing interest in child psychology characterized these manuals, as teachers attempted to ensure the success of their efforts by matching their lessons to the child's capacity for comprehension. In one popular manual, John Todd depicted children as susceptible to powerful examples. Because the child's mind is easily influenced, Todd continued, children must receive proper moral examples based upon biblical precepts. Another influential manual by W. F. Lloyd stressed that teachers in Sunday schools must have a knowledge of human nature in order to teach effectively. The teacher, Lloyd urged, must remember his own youth, apply these insights to teaching, and know the individual characteristics of his pupils. Only in this way could the teacher effectively infuse moral guidance into every activity. The teacher's role, Lloyd continued, is to "explain and enforce the precepts of divine truth. You will labour earnestly to enlighten the understandings, and form the tastes, and impress the consciences, of your scholars; you are to train them in the 'nurture and admonition of the Lord.'" Teachers must "endeavour to model [the students'] tastes, and form their judgments for useful instruction and pious reading."

> You will teach your scholars to consider the Sacred Scriptures as the standard by which everything is to be judged, and every doctrine examined, every opinion formed. You will often require them to prove Scripture doctrines and duties, and to compare one part of the sacred records with another, comparing 'things spiritual with spiritual.' (Lloyd: 47)

The primary goal of Sunday school instruction continued to be moral development. However, by the 1840s, changes in curriculum design and Sunday school organization spawned greater attention to the proper means of interpreting the Bible.

> The rules which many give for the study of the Bible seem to me too frequently to overlook one grand characteristic of the word of God;—*viz.*, that as it required supernatural aid to write it, so it does also to understand it. The Spirit which dictated it, is necessary to understand it; and the Bible cannot be understood, and its true spirit apprehended, except by the mind which is led and sanctified by the Spirit of God. You must have the aid of this Spirit, or you open the word of God in vain. The letter killeth: the spirit only maketh alive. . . . Some look upon the Bible as a garden of spices, in which you may walk, and at your leisure pluck the flowers, and gather the fruits of the Eden of God. But this does not accord with my experience. I have found it more like a mine, in which you must dig and labor,—the wealth of which is not to be obtained without labor; a mine, rich in gold and precious things, but it must be wrought day and night in order to produce them. (Todd: 187)

Todd added that the goal of Sunday school instruction was to recover children from sin. This goal could be achieved through imparting a comprehensive view of God's government revealed in Scripture. The teacher's task was to instill the proper spirit in children and to enhance this spirit by communicating detailed, accurate knowledge of the Bible. Thus Todd echoed the traditional goal of moral improvement and reflected the trend toward a systematized view of the Sunday school and its task, but his work also revealed a subtle change in process. As Sunday school leaders focused on instilling in children the spiritual quality they considered the essential prelude to moral behavior, the Sunday school's primary task began to shift away from moral education toward saving the souls of its pupils. As this change progressed, the Bible's place in American Sunday schools evolved from a collection of moral examples whose historical veracity was irrelevant to the record of God's dealings with humanity, a historical record whose literal truth was crucial.

Altered Context, Rethought Content

When Sunday school leaders began to rethink their approach to teaching the Bible, a conflict emerged over the context of Sunday school education. The denominations began to challenge interdenominational agencies for control of Sunday schools. Agencies such as the American Sunday School Union never had been free from internal tensions. Theological consensus across denominational lines was never achieved. By 1837 interdenominational agencies were experiencing a full-blown crisis (Foster: 222).

Denominational structures also asserted themselves. It is ironic that the same clergy and laity who promoted ecumenical cooperation frequently encouraged greater denominational organization. These leaders of benevolence tended to think of moral education and individual conversion as two sides of the same coin (Banner: 3, 5). Advocates of benevolence such as

Lyman Beecher and Charles Hodge felt that Sunday schools should convert as well as educate and should be supported by both churches and interchurch agencies. Their influence spurred more effective Sunday school organization but also set up tensions concerning the Sunday school's goals and contexts. Increasingly fewer Sunday school designers felt their schools *could* educate without converting or *should* educate without denominational sponsorship. Yet the ideal of the Sunday school as an interdenominational agency for moral training (and hence national improvement) retained powerful supporters. These tensions dominated the use of the Bible by American Sunday schools from the middle of the century.

The American Sunday School Union cautioned in its 1843 annual report that denominational Sunday schools threatened the great ends that they must serve. The nation required a general union of Christian people devoted to communicating the behavioral ideals contained in Scripture. Only such commitment could have significant social impact and serve the ends to which Sunday schools devoted themselves (20). Yet as the quest for conversion and the pursuit of denominational goals distracted Sunday schools, they began to lose the emphasis on social betterment that had obsessed early Sunday school proponents.

Episcopal clergyman Stephen Tyng provided an important mid-century perspective on the Sunday school's shifting nature. His stature as a Sunday school spokesman, partially a function of four decades of Sunday school leadership, made Tyng a significant bellwether. Tyng declared that conversion was the greatest goal of Sunday school instruction. This meant "the real spiritual turning of the heart to God, and its renewal for His service by the Holy Spirit." Tyng added:

> The instrument of conversion with children is the same as with adults—the Word of truth, the simple message of redeeming love. This message speaks in the simplest language in the sacred Word, and is perfectly intelligible to the youngest mind.... And if this message of actual pardon in the Saviour's blood, real salvation through His death for all who will receive it, is placed before the youthful minds as designed for them and belonging to them, with the evidence of sincerity and earnestness on the teacher's part, we may as reasonably look for a blessing to attend the truth in the experience of children as of adults. (37)

Though Tyng felt that instruction in the Bible encouraged moral improvement and bettered society, Sunday schools taught the Bible for another reason. "The simple principle of the Bible is to teach the Bible. I have no disposition to shrink from the responsibility of every part of it. There is not a history which does not exhibit some spiritual truth, able to make wise unto salvation, through faith in Jesus Christ. There is not a single narrative or fact which in the hands of a spiritually-minded teacher will not be brought out as a definite instrumentality for the instruction and, if God shall please, the conversion of the soul." Tyng felt that the Bible need only be presented simply and intelligibly. Unvarnished, it would attract children by its language and purpose. But Scripture had to be studied comprehensively. "Every portion of its history and its teaching should come up for study in its turn. Its various parts must be made to illustrate and confirm each other. Children must be familiarized with its use, and accustomed to refer to its various parts easily and freely." To this end Tyng was convinced that Sunday schools required a

> system of illustration, from every variety of source accessible to the teacher, and adapted to the minds of children. The whole system of divine teaching in the Scripture is of this description. An endless variety of story and biography and comparison is employed there to make every truth more clear and manifest in its personal application to those for whom they are all proclaimed. And the preacher or teacher most of all confined to the mere Bible without note or commentary for study, will habitually become in the very pattern of the Bible, the most disposed and ready to illustrate its truths by comparisons and facts bearing them out. (226ff.)

Tyng felt that Sunday schools should be organized by the churches. Sunday schools offered not simply moral training but also Christian nurture. To sustain Christian nurture was the churches' task, not the responsibility of broadly based agencies. As long as Sunday school instruction sought to teach knowledge of the Bible, there was danger neither of Sunday schools succumbing to sectarian goals nor of their losing their commitment to train American society in morality. As more Sunday school leaders agreed with Tyng that Sunday schools belonged to the churches, they became increasingly preoccupied with devising highly systematized curricula that related biblical knowledge to cultivation of their students' faith. Episcopal cleric F. D. Huntington said the Sunday school's goal was "to produce, to nourish, or to perfect, in the pupil, a personal and conscious relation to Christ: a relation of obedience, of trust, of sympathy, of affection, of loyalty . . . " (9). These qualities were biblical. Hence Sunday school instruction should highlight God's historic promises to humanity revealed in Scripture. For example, young converts needed to understand the biblical concept of covenant. Thus they could locate God's offer of salvation to them through the Holy Spirit in the context of God's covenantal relationships articulated in the Old and New Testaments. Because the Bible presented the drama of salvation as a pattern for the young Christian's life, Sunday schools properly belonged to churches, where the faith would be encouraged and sustained. "Separate the Sunday School from the Church and you break it from the parent stem . . . " (19). In the eyes of such advocates only sundering the Sunday school's dependence upon the Bible could have been a more fundamental error.

By mid-century, Sunday school representatives were espousing more systematic approaches to Bible study. They stressed that Scripture presented the pattern for salvation whose accurate replication was the condition of the Sunday school's success. The more closely students understood God's offer of grace, chastisement of the wicked, and dominion over history, the more likely they would be to read their own lives in this way, accept Christ's love, and grow in knowledge and love of the Lord. As Sunday school organizers defined child development more precisely in terms of Scripture, they slipped away from seeing their task as moral nurture and began to highlight conversion. Children must be primed for the intervention of saving grace before they can be instructed how to live the Christian life. At the same time Sunday schools became far more dependent upon denominational resources than upon interdenominational cooperation. As a result, Sunday school curricula began to reflect more doctrinal and apologetic concerns. As intellectual challenges to the Bible such as the theory of evolution arose, denominational Sunday school leaders felt compelled to defend what they saw as Scripture's essential tenets. In the quest of ammunition, they often resorted to sectarian dogmas. However, the interdenominational Sunday school ideal did not die. Nor would all Sunday school leaders relinquish the goal of moral training as the Sunday school's primary task.

Appropriately, historian Frank Lankard labelled the years between 1840 and 1872 as the "Babel" period in the development of American Sunday schools. This was a period of indecision and conflict over the Sunday school's proper goals, means, and context. Were Sunday schools supposed to nurture morally, or to convert, or both? Were they the churches' responsibility or must they be spearheaded by ecumenical groups? Moreover, how should the Bible be taught, and for what ends? On this last question answers abounded. The "Babel" period produced a flood of Sunday school curriculum options. For example, the Massachusetts Sabbath School Society, a Congregational agency, published an influential series of lessons and questions. By 1850 the society had expanded this series to include more than 192 different booklets. Other popular lesson plans at this time included *Journeyings of Abraham and His Descendants* (1856), *Line Upon Line*, and *Scripture Lessons For Sabbath School and Families* (Lankard: 179–90).

It is striking that these curricula reflected their designers' interest in overcoming the tensions of the era. Scripture was presented inclusively, joining the Old Testament to the New, emphasizing the Bible as both a textbook of morality and the pattern of salvation. Rote memorization of biblical passages remained the pedagogical ideal. "It was thought that mere memorization of the Book would work some magical change in the life [of the student] either presently or in the remoter future" (Lankard: 199]. Curriculum designers posed mechanical questions geared to reciting Scripture's contents. Yet the curricula of the "Babel" period stressed that Scripture was a historical narrative. Memorization must not be helter-skelter but should proceed according to the unfolding of God's word. Thus, Orange Judd's popular *Lessons for Every Sunday in the Year* connected each lesson with the preceding to form a chronological scheme while reiterating the necessity of memorization. Judd argued that his approach enhanced students' ability to retain what they memorized and encouraged them to understand the Bible as history that revealed God's universal offer of salvation.

The Limits of Consensus

The tensions that the American Sunday schools experienced during the "Babel" period, i.e., confusion about their proper means and ends, reflected a broader questioning of the nature of American life. After 1865, however, many Americans committed themselves to reuniting the nation by articulating a common sense of mission. There was a new focus upon group experience and upon the meaning of human interdependence. But many Americans found nationalism a burdensome priority. A new excitement for the individual emerged. American fulfillment depended upon the ability of individuals to effect good or evil. "By 1876, American thought took increasing solace in placing the citizen in a great drama stretching far into a romantic past and moving toward a glorious future" (Nagel: 204). Increasingly the individual became not simply a cog in the national wheel but a self-contained universe. Interest in human nature followed this perception and by the end of the nineteenth century the sciences of psychology and human development had ᵕcome the preoccupations of many Americans. The American Sunday school was influenced directly by this trend. In the short run, a few leaders attempted to restore the Sunday school's interdenominational heritage of moral tutelage. Ultimately their efforts were handicapped by conflicts over curriculum, which left control of Sunday schools more firmly in the hands of the churches. At the same time the impulse toward systematized curricula focused more surely on teacher training and awareness of child development. Encouraged by Americans' fascination with individual psychology, Sunday school curricula placed a premium on converting and nurturing children rather than on simply instructing them morally. The use of the Bible by American Sunday schools of the later nineteenth century was determined by these larger considerations.

Sunday schools experienced rebirth after the Civil War. Prominent lay people, working with ecumenically-minded clergy, established local schools joined by national networks. Revivalist Dwight L. Moody was a leader of this movement, as was Methodist clergyman J. H. Vincent. Powerful businessmen such as B. F. Jacobs, H. J. Heinz, and John Wanamaker participated. A commitment to awakening America morally animated these men. Fearful that America's urban slums were blemishes on the national character, these men promoted Sunday schools as vital means of teaching morality. Their efforts briefly reinspired interdenominational Sunday school cooperation. At the same time the successful businessman's influence encouraged a more systematized approach to Sunday school organization. From our perspective this resulted in elaborately designed curricula (Lynn and Wright: 56ff.).

With renewed interdenominational cooperation a new era in Sunday school curriculum design emerged. In 1865 J. H. Vincent began publication of the *Sunday School Teacher's Quarterly*. In 1866 Vincent added a course of lessons on Jesus' life in his magazine. Edward Eggleston continued Vincent's

Two Years With Jesus when he assumed editorship of the *Quarterly* in 1867. At the same time Vincent began to publish a series of lessons that he called the *Berean Series* while Eggleston designed his own *National Series.*

Vincent's *Two Years With Jesus* included twenty-four lessons, two Sundays per lesson. The heart of Vincent's system was a series of P's and D's. For each lesson there were Places, Persons, and Parallel Passages, as well as Dates, Doings, Doctrines, and Duties. Lessons were graded and accompanied by a text to be memorized. Thus Lesson XXXII, "Blind Bartimeus," included Mark 10:46–47; Luke 18:36–37 and 43. The same lessons taught the blessing of poverty and emphasized Christ's grace and power (Lankard: 208ff.). In this way Vincent continued to stress the moral benefits of memorization but suggested that moral behavior might depend upon cultivation of an inner state of grace that was keyed by conversion.

Eggleston's *National Series* was more comprehensive in scope. It consisted of one lesson per Sunday, arranged in tight chronological order. Simple moral themes highlighted the plan; for example, Lesson XIX, "The Rich Man and Lazarus," Luke 16:19–31, drew contrasts between the rich man's ultimate despair and Lazarus' rich reward in eternity. Eggleston stressed the historical setting of each passage, encouraging students to draw parallels and contrasts between past and present. In addition teachers received suggestions for how points could be illustrated. Morality, it appears, could not be taught in ignorance of sensitive pedagogy.

B. F. Jacobs carried the renewed interdenominational curriculum impetus to its zenith. He began to push for a national, uniform series of lessons. Improving the nation's morality was not the sole motivation for Jacobs's plan. He held that a uniform series would promote a more thorough and systematic approach to Scripture study by allowing the entire Bible to be covered. This approach would encourage parents to instruct their children at home. Comprehensiveness, Jacobs felt, ensured the greatest impact of Scripture's moral lessons. Jacobs appeared before the 1872 National Sunday School Convention in Indianapolis to promote his plan. The convention received Jacobs enthusiastically and organized a committee to formulate a comprehensive lesson system (Sampey: 86). The committee adopted Jacobs's principle that children at all age levels should study the same passage from Scripture. The committee added that each year's lessons should include selections from both the Old and New Testaments. Jacobs's chronological approach to Scripture received the committee's endorsement. The Bible must be taught as a comprehensive narrative of salvation featuring Christ's life and ministry. But the committee also suggested that salvation consisted of more than proper deportment. The rationale for teaching the Bible was to remake the students' souls.

The chief aim of the International Lessons was to convert children to faith in God through Christ based upon understanding the Bible as God's word. Detailed knowledge of Scripture was the key. The initial plan was a six-year cycle of lessons, from 1873 to 1879. For 1873, six months study of Genesis was halved by six months study of Matthew. In 1874, three months devoted to Mark preceded three months on Acts and six months study of Moses and Israel.

By the completion of the third cycle in 1893, 461 lessons from the Old Testament and 570 from the New Testament had been featured. More lessons came from Acts than from any other book, followed by Mark, Luke, Matthew, and John. Such emphasis reflected interest in the early years of the church as well as in the life of Jesus. Next in popularity were Genesis, Exodus, 1 Samuel, and 1 and 2 Kings. New Testament lessons stressed Jesus' life and teachings as well as the activities of early Christian communities. Old Testament highlights included God's design and creation of the world, the unfolding of salvation, and heroic figures of faith (Lankard: 240–41).

The International Lessons represented more than the triumph of a comprehensive approach to Bible study: they replaced memorization of passages with a didactic approach that stressed a theme related to the process of salvation for each lesson. For example, the *Lesson Commentary* for Lesson VIII of 1880, Matt 6:1–13, noted that every person looks for some reward and that what is done to earn human praise cannot merit praise from God. In time, lesson aids became more direct, emphasizing God's offer of eternal life to righteous people and threat of eternal punishment to the wicked. Moral admonition alone had been replaced by appeals for a changed heart as the necessary precondition for virtuous living (Lankard: 256–57). Sunday schools could no longer be content to prime their charges with Scripture and hope for the best. Only a precise, planned study of the Bible could lead students along salvation's path.

The International Lesson System was the greatest achievement of interdenominational Sunday school cooperation. The series represented a considerable didactic advance and solidified a long-standing trend toward systematized curricula. The Lesson System briefly retarded interdenominational fragmentation and reanimated the ideal of ecumenical consensus. Proponents of the Lesson System believed that they could isolate certain key tenets of Scripture to which all Christians could assent and from which peculiarly denominational concerns could be distinguished. Finally, the International Lesson System prompted a new burst of interest in Bible study highlighted by new study guides and commentaries. Unfortunately the Lesson System never achieved the unity its advocates desired. Critics of the initial cycle charged that the lessons lacked sufficient emphasis on social reform or, more frequently, complained that the lessons were not sufficiently flexible to include denominational doctrines. The latter criticism proved more telling. When the system's committee refused to arrange lessons according to the liturgical calendar in 1874, the Episcopal Church withdrew its support. Meanwhile German Reformed and Lutheran Sunday schools significantly rearranged the lessons to fit a liturgical calendar (Sampey; 120).

Even those denominations that continued to support the plan asserted their freedom to alter lessons to match their doctrinal priorities. Eventually every denomination screened the lessons with its own expositors.

Many critics also complained that the lessons ignored child psychology. Chronology, not doctrine or a plan of salvation, provided the lessons' unity. Use of the same lesson at all levels prompted bitter opposition. In 1894 the Lesson Committee responded with a separate course for younger children, and in 1901 an adult series crystallized (Lankard: 263ff.). By this time, however, numerous alternatives to the Lesson System existed, and most of them reflect the resurgence of denominational autonomy. Critics also complained about undue emphasis on certain portions of the Old Testament and charged that missions and temperance were not sufficiently promoted. Supporters of the International Lesson System insisted that it had achieved its primary goal. J. H. Vincent noted that the series has

> increased the influence of the Bible over the people. It has advertised the Bible; it has led to its wider use; has increased the popular knowledge of its contents; has exalted it as the only standard of faith and practice, and has promoted the love of the Book among the people. . . . Unity in the study of the Word has promoted the spirit of unity among the people of God. It reminds us that we all search the same Word, love the same truth, depend on the same Spirit, appeal to the same authority. (Vincent: 258)

Unfortunately for him, many of Vincent's contemporaries disagreed that unity of faith had such an obvious basis or was so desirable an end.

However, Sunday school leaders could agree that teachers required more elaborate training. This was the next step in the trend toward a systematic approach to Sunday school organization. Teacher training became highly organized in the late nineteenth century. Teacher training institutes and associations appeared and generated magazines, conferences, and manuals for aspiring Sunday school teachers. Intensified teacher training was the logical result of viewing the Bible as the vehicle for children's salvation. Schools expected that teachers would evolve sophisticated means to guide children through the Bible, not simply for moral instruction but to present the opportunity for personal acceptance of the Christian faith. At the same time a movement for graded curricula reached its peak. For example, biblical material adapted for use by kindergarten children was presented differently from that used by adolescents so that it could appeal to the interests and sensibilities of different age groups (Lankard: 282–83).

Committed to interdenominational Sunday school cooperation and to the trend toward systematized organization, J. H. Vincent presented an articulate example of the new concern for teacher preparation. One of the last great voices for interdenominational Sunday school leadership, Vincent insisted that teachers be both morally and spiritually qualified.

> This text-book—the Holy Bible—comes to us with a peculiar claim. The teacher, in opening it, professes to open an inspired book, by which God, the Creator of all, has

made known His character and His will to men. It is important, therefore, that the
teacher understand, at least to some extent, the evidences by which the divine
authority of the Bible is established, the men by whom its various parts were written,
the time and the place of writing, the questions of genuineness and translations, and
the actions of ecclesiastical councils concerning it. He should understand the laws of
interpretation by which we may approach the sacred pages in the right spirit, and by
the right methods arrive at the sentiments which the Divine author intends to reveal.
He should understand the contents of the book, first in general outline, and then in
detail—its history, chronology, geography, archaeological peculiarities, its doctrines
which relate to God, to man, to the God-man, and to life eternal. (92)

Biblical truth, Vincent continued, is not self-evident. It must be dug out as
from a mine. Teachers must pray for the Spirit to enlighten their minds and
must work hard, applying their personal experience to the lessons they
would convey. Teachers must isolate the point they would make, repeating
it often and drawing connections between lessons. These facts must be
related to God's present work of salvation. To do this teachers must
understand their pupils. Sensitivity to human nature should condition every
lesson. Growth or deterioration in each pupil's spirit could be detected and
appropriately handled by the teacher. Each step could be explained in terms
of the pattern of salvation revealed in Scripture (93–94, 173–74).

Concern for teacher training drew on a precise view of the Bible's
nature. For Vincent, as for all Sunday school leaders of the late nineteenth
century, the Bible revealed God's plan of redemption. God commanded
people to study his word because its every detail directed people to the offer
of salvation. Every bit of Scripture was important because of its divine origins and intentions. Step by step it led humanity to God.

There is order in it, for it was developed according to a divine order and under divine
direction. It is a history, extending through long ages of divine providence and revolution. The history had its beginnings—its seed-sowing, and then its germination, its
growth, its blossoming, and its fruit-bearing. Its confusion is only seeming confusion. . . . The Bible is not a classified cyclopaedia of things celestial and divine. It has
no alphabetic arrangement by which, as in a dictionary, one may turn at a moment to
the sum total of divine revelation on a given topic. Its history reaches through the
whole book. It is a book of geography from Eden to Ephesus. Its prophecy and poetry
are found almost everywhere. (249–50)

For Vincent, the key to understanding Scripture lay in grasping its
inner coherence and in rightly applying this coherence to one's life. "There
is a hidden system in Scripture. The student seeks and finds it. There is a
mechanical system which may be constructed after the larger and less
apparent divine system, and by which the student may the more easily
master the Word—'rightly dividing it.' This mechanical system the teacher
should employ for his own guidance, and for the guidance especially of his
pupils" (249–50). Vincent did not feel that a system could be imposed upon
Scripture. The ideal system would allow Scripture to speak for itself, thereby
freeing the Holy Spirit for the work of salvation. A proper system would

secure the most thorough study of Scripture possible. Vincent broke down a suggested system of Bible study into seven points:

1. Salient facts of the Bible, e.g., history, biography.
2. Leading Christian doctrines.
3. Recognition of Bible names, usages.
4. Devotional literature of the ages.
5. Principal characters and events of Church history.
6. The evangelical basis of all missionary and reformatory efforts.
7. Denominations must be careful not to contradict or avoid various parts of the Word. (249–50)

Vincent had more success in articulating a systematic approach to Sunday school organization than he had in promoting interdenominational Sunday school cooperation. By the end of the nineteenth century interdenominational cooperation had been reduced from actually sponsoring schools and regional societies to promoting consensus in curriculum through the International Lesson System and through ecumenical institutes and workshops. In general Sunday schools were run by the churches. Vincent acknowledged that Sunday schools should be arms of the churches, sustained by them and furthering their extension into the world. But bringing children into the church was only one aspect of the process of leading children to salvation. "The aim of the school should be the Biblical, spiritual, practical education of its members in order to [obtain] useful lives and a blessed eternity" (25).

Vincent not only attempted to retain the interdenominational aspect of Sunday schools, but he also rearticulated the Sunday school's commitment to providing moral guidance. Sunday schools must "lay foundations of Christian character by the conveyance of Bible knowledge, teaching the susceptible, filling their memories with the facts and words of revelation, alluring them by the delights of association, of song, and of wise tuition—that the coming Spirit in youth or in later years may find truth ready for the kindling fires of grace" (13). But moral guidance could not be provided in isolation from the effort to lead students to salvation. The students' outward demeanor was a function of their inward states. Students could be led to the offer of salvation, methodically, systematically. To do this the Sunday school needed only to teach the Bible. "The truth it teaches is Bible truth—the facts and ethics and doctrines and promises of God as contained in that great treasury of holy learning" (49).

Nineteenth-century Sunday school leaders never wavered in their belief that teaching the Bible was their primary responsibility. During the century, commitment to teaching the Bible became increasingly sophisticated as systematized methods came into use. By the end of the century it was not enough to have students digest large chunks of biblical material nor to spice their portions with historical and geographical facts. Students had to be led programmatically through a plan of study geared to conveying a series of lessons appropriate to their ages. This methodical approach took root as the context of Sunday school education shifted away from voluntary associations toward the denominations. More often Bible study related to denominational priorities.

Similarly, the Sunday school lost much of its early role as a weapon against social disorder. With the growth of systematic curricula and with the Sunday school's shift in context, Sunday schools no longer taught the Bible as an ahistorical collection of moral lessons. Every detail of biblical narrative mattered, for each point—however minute—was integral to the offer of salvation. During the nineteenth century, therefore, the Sunday school's task evolved from moral indoctrination to priming students for salvation. Despite the tensions endemic in this change, the Sunday school of the nineteenth century disseminated knowledge of the Bible throughout American society. For this reason the Sunday school achieved its primary goal.

WORKS CONSULTED

American Sunday School Union
  1826,
  1831,
  1843   *Annual Report*. Philadelphia: American Sunday School Union.

Boyer, Paul
  1978   *Urban Masses and Moral Order in America, 1820–1920*. Cambridge, MA: Harvard University Press.

Boylan, Anne M.
  1979   "Sunday Schools and Changing Evangelical Views of Children in the 1820s." *Church History* 48 (September 1979).

Buckle, Emory Stevens, ed.
  1964   *History of American Methodism*, I. New York and Nashville: Abingdon Press.

Cope, Henry Frederick
  1911   *The Evolution of the Sunday School*. Boston: Pilgrim Press.

Ewing, William
  1918   *The Sunday School Century*. Boston: Pilgrim Press.

Hodge, Charles
  1860   "The Place of the Bible in a System of Education."
                         In *Anniversary Sermons Delivered at the Request
                         of the American Sunday-School Union*. Philadel-
                         phia: American Sunday-School Union.

Huntington, F. D.
  1860   *The Relation of the Sunday School to the Church*.
                         Boston: Henry Hoyt.

Knoff, Gerald E.
  1979   *The World Sunday School Movement*. New York:
                         Seabury Press.

Lankard, Frank Glenn
  1927   A *History of the American Sunday School Curric-
                         ulum*. New York and Cincinnati: Abingdon Press.

Laqueur, Thomas Walter
  1976   *Religion and Respectability: Sunday Schools and
                         Working Class Culture, 1780–1850*. New Haven
                         and London: Yale University Press.

Lloyd, W. F.
  n.d.   *The Teacher's Manual; Or, Hints to a Teacher on
                         Being Appointed to the Charge of a Sunday
                         School Class*. Philadelphia: American Sunday
                         School Union.

Lynn, Robert W. and Wright, Elliott
  1971   *The Big Little School*. New York: Harper and
                         Row.

Nagel, Paul C.
  1971   *This Sacred Trust: American Nationality 1798–
                         1898*. New York: Oxford University Press.

New York Sunday School Union Society
  1827   *Eleventh Annual Report*. New York: Gray &
                         Bunce.

Pray, Lewis G.
  1847   *The History of Sunday Schools, and of Religious
                         Education*. Boston: Wm. Crosby and H. P.
                         Nichols.

Rice, Edwin Wilbur
    1917   *The Sunday-School Movement, 1780–1917, and the American Sunday-School Union, 1817–1917.* Philadelphia: American Sunday-School Union.

Sampey, John R.
    1911   *The International Lesson System: The History of Its Origin and Development.* New York: Fleming H. Revell Company.

Todd, John
    1837   *The Sabbath School Teacher.* Northampton: J. H. Butler.

Tyng, Stephen H.
    1866   *Forty Years' Experience In Sunday-Schools.* 5th ed. New York: Sheldon & Co.

Vincent, John H.
    1887   *The Modern Sunday School.* New York: Eaton and Mains.

V

Intellectual Ferment and Instruction in the Scriptures: The Bible in Higher Education

Thomas H. Olbricht

In the last quarter of the nineteenth century a number of ideational changes swept educated circles in America. These new perspectives were mediated to the larger reading populace through books, periodicals, and newspapers. This cultural change involved new views of truth that tended to reflect either Hegelian idealism or an empiricism nurtured by rapidly developing scientific breakthroughs. Hegelianism and empiricism, though in some respects at odds, intersected in the conviction that reality, human life, and the physical universe can be understood ultimately only from a historical perspective. The widespread American acceptance of the Judeo-Christian Scriptures as the basic source of insight into reality was slowly eroding. As a result the Scriptures lost their singular epistemological privilege, though their significance was still affirmed. Consequently, the manner in which the Scriptures were conceived and taught in American colleges, universities and seminaries was revised.

At the midpoint of the nineteenth century the Scriptures were seen as applying in various ways to contemporary life and religion, depending on confessional commitments. In some traditions the Scriptures were chiefly the source of piety and devotion. In others they served as the grist out of which doctrinal formulas were generated. In still others they provided foundations for traditionalism, ecumenicity, or methods in evangelism, polity, or liturgy. Regardless of the basis for applicability, all the major confessions were agreed that in some manner the Scriptures spoke directly to major human religious needs and fundamental relationships. The compositional or historical contexts of various biblical materials were not altogether ignored, but they were not considered vital for determining relevance. No deep historical chasm separated Scripture from the current age. Scholarly study of the Bible focused on philological (an intensive and minute scrutiny of the grammar and vocabulary of the original languages of the Scriptures) and theological concerns. By the end of the century, however, the consensus within American evangelical religion disintegrated precisely at this nexus. So William Henry Green of Princeton wrote:

> Now however, by a natural reaction perhaps, the period of theological controversy among us seems to be yielding to one of doctrinal indifferentism. Questions affecting the Trinity, the atonement, human ability, the parity of the ministry, the mode of baptism, which have agitated the Christian community by strifes between different denominations, or different factions in the same denomination, no longer engage public attention to anything like the same extent. People are growing impatient of doctrinal and ecclesiastical dissensions, and the tendency of the times is rather toward a Broad Church liberalism, and sinking the differences between hitherto discordant bodies in a more catholic fellowship, if not organic union. (Green, 1883:24–25)

The result was a major shift in the manner in which the Scriptures were taught. This essay will trace this shift as it emerges in the writings of six prominent biblical scholars, showing the influence of late nineteenth-century cultural perspectives on biblical pedagogy. These scholars, who taught at the major American seminaries, approached the Scriptures from various directions; yet each reflected the shifting scene. The changes may be seen by taking up these scholars according to their dates of birth. We shall examine the approach to the Scriptures proposed by William H. Green (1825–1900) Princeton, Old Testament; Joseph Henry Thayer (1828–1901) Andover, Harvard, New Testament; Crawford H. Toy (1836–1919) Harvard, Old Testament; Charles A. Briggs (1841–1913) Union Theological Seminary, Old Testament; Benjamin W. Bacon (1860–1932) Yale, New Testament; and Shailer Mathews (1863–1941) Chicago, New Testament.

William H. Green of Princeton

The Princeton approach to theology and Scriptures was ground out in the crucibles of mainstream nineteenth-century American evangelical Christianity. The contributing components were the revivalistic fervor of the Second Great Awakening, an antideistic apologetic, and the theological foundations of the Westminster Confession and Calvinistic scholasticism, particularly that of the Swiss theologian Francis Turretine (Loetscher: 20–22). For these reasons Scripture was read either as a document heralding salvation and blueprinting the contours of conversion or else as a solid foundation for mainstream creedal views. Charles Hodge, an early commentator of the school, spent most of his time reflecting on contemporary controversies related to central Westminster tenets (Olbricht, 1979b:128–29). He paid scant attention to the meanings of the biblical writings in their original settings, a topic that was to occupy so much effort of scholars fifty years later.

In the first three quarters of the nineteenth century the Princeton scholars were open to the new philological skills acquired and disseminated from Germany. Charles Hodge, as well as later Princeton biblical scholars, spent time in Germany to work specifically in the biblical languages and textual studies (Olbricht, 1979b:120–25). The Princetonians saw these tools as the means through which to discern the correct meaning of each word. They were confident that the mastery of linguistic studies would support rather than erode their confessional stance. They grew increasingly aware that German positions on literary composition and authorship were changing the complexion of biblical studies. But such interests had not yet become widespread in America and the Princeton scholars had no intention of introducing them as the central focus (Green, 1883:23–24). They were content to read the Scriptures for their salvific and theological relevancy to contemporary church life. Such a reading was concerned with immediacy; little interest surfaced for backgrounds or a historical perspective that separated the text from the current scene by centuries of development.

Though the Princeton biblical scholars defended the epistemological significance of the Scriptures, plenary inspiration, and the Westminster position—with certain modifications of their own—they became increasingly sensitive to the historical settings out of which biblical statements were made and the historical nature of biblical documents. Even for them biblical studies departed from a focus upon devotion, conversion, and consensus Calvinistic theology. They too now read the Scriptures from a historical and literary perspective. Green made a clarion call for this new scholarship: "We must have an English and American scholarship that is fitted to grapple with these questions as they arise. We need, in the ranks of the pastorate, men who can conduct Biblical researches and who can prosecute learned critical inquiries . . . " (1883:32). They differed only with the conclusions reached by German higher criticism. By the end of the nineteenth century most German biblical scholars agreed not only that the Scriptures must be scrutinized with history at the forefront but also that scepticism in regard to historical accuracy, alleged authorship, and the unity of biblical books is healthy if not mandatory. The Princeton scholars, in contrast, argued that accuracy, authenticity, and integrity were all supported by history itself.

This position is stated clearly in the writings of William Henry Green, sometimes labeled an arch-conservative. Green, who received his B.D. at Princeton in 1846, stayed on as an instructor in Hebrew from 1846 to 1849. After a two-year ministry in Philadelphia, he returned to Princeton in 1851 to begin a teaching career that continued until his death in 1900. His official title was Professor of Oriental and Old Testament Literature. The last decade of his life was one of his most prolific in respect to materials that appeared in print. The titles of his books show that in the nineties, whatever had been his prior focus, the questions that occupied his attention were those having to do with the character and history of the Scripture. In 1895 Green published *The Higher Criticism of the Pentateuch* as well as *The Unity of the Book of Genesis*; in 1899 *General Introduction to the Old Testament* in two books—*The Canon* and *The Text*. These books focus on the manner in which the biblical text came about rather than on context. The approach is historical. Green had no quarrel with the thesis that reality emerges historically even in the Scriptures. What he challenged was the particular account of that history originating in German higher criticism. As a result, university and seminary biblical instruction no longer emphasized the theological controversies revolving around certain proof texts. Instead, they centered on the historical and literary manner in which the Scriptures came about.

In *Higher Criticism* Green spoke favorably of the discipline but decried its perversion: "It seeks to ascertain by all available means the authors by whom, the time at which, the circumstances under which, and the design with which they were produced. Such investigations, rightly conducted, must prove a most important aid to the understanding and just appreciation of the writings in question" (v). Green discussed first of all the overall structure of the Old Testament. The basic approach was much like that of contemporary canonical criticism as represented by Brevard S. Childs (*Introduction to the Old Testament as Scripture*, 1979), but the process was considerably less complicated. In the rest of the book Green argued for Mosaic authorship, the unity of the Pentateuch, and the genuineness of the laws. While he approached these topics from a historical perspective, he relied almost completely on evidence from within the Old Testament itself. He offered no external history in the manner of William F. Albright a few decades later. His basic approach was to sum up viewpoints of the more radical critics and then mitigate their positions by denying Old Testament support. Similar methods were pursued in *The Unity of the Book of Genesis* except that Green took up consecutive sections of Genesis, refuting what he considered spurious critical conclusions.

In *The Canon* Green's historical predilections are the most obvious. He stated in the preface that the topic is treated "not theologically but historically" (vii). The reason is that he seeks to meet the critics on their own ground.

> The various arguments urged by critics in defense of their position that the canon was not completed nor the collection made until several centuries after the time traditionally fixed and currently believed are considered; and reasons are given to show that it might have been and probably was collected by Ezra and Nehemiah in their time. (p. viii)

Green began with a short history of how earlier scholars had dealt with questions of date and authorship and then examined what the Old Testament itself says about these issues. After identifying critical views, he examined statements on the canon in Josephus and other intertestamental literature. Following this historical analysis, Green discussed the so-called great synagogue, the views of the rabbis, the statements of Christ and the apostles, and the canon of the Christian church. Green was quite content to rest his case for the canon, which argued early collection, on historical grounds.

While the Princeton school for the most part supported traditional views in regard to authorship, date, and literary composition of the books of the Bible and even sometimes took more conservative positions than the tradition, yet even they changed their approach to biblical pedagogy because of the new cultural winds blowing in, especially from Germany. Rather than studying the Scriptures so as to comment on Westminster theological positions, they scrutinized the Bible in regard to its historical development and literary features, especially in order to respond to the views of the radical higher critics. Biblical study now centered on the origins and development of the Bible rather than its content.

Joseph Henry Thayer of Andover and Harvard

Biblical studies at Andover Theological Seminary (1808) and Harvard Divinity School (1816) commenced when Congregationalism was in the throes of delineating Arminianism from Calvinism and Trinitarianism from Unitarianism. For that reason, in the early years from 1810 until at least 1830 both wings of the Puritan church anticipated that the new biblical criticism and philology developing in Germany would provide ammunition for the battles being waged (Brown: 10–74). However, by the middle of the century interest in biblical studies among the Unitarians had declined, and it remained for the Trinitarians of Andover to lay the foundations in America for twentieth-century academic biblical studies. By 1850 a majority of the biblical scholars in America had been educated at Andover. When the now prestigious Society of Biblical Literature was founded in 1880, seven of the thirty-two charter members had received at least some of their training at Andover. If one were to add those who had studied with a scholar from Andover the number totals more than one-half. By the 1890s Andover's influence began to wane, but a remnant of past glory remained in the work of Joseph Henry Thayer who both was trained at Andover and taught there until he felt he could no longer subscribe to the Andover creedal position. He then changed his professorship to Harvard.

Thayer complemented his studies at Harvard and Andover with further work in Germany, specializing in biblical languages. He published both a *Grammar of the New Testament* (1873) and a *Greek-English Lexicon* (1887). Thayer was heir to a tradition that believed an accurate understanding of the Christian faith lay in precise knowledge of the original languages of the Scriptures. But Thayer himself came to view the Scriptures from a different perspective. His new approach to the study of the Scriptures was set forth cogently in a lecture before the American Institute of Sacred Literature in Boston in June 1889. The sponsors of this series tended to reflect devotional, conversion approaches to the Scriptures. The lecture was printed in 1891 under the title *The Change of Attitude towards the Bible.* Toward the end of the lecture Thayer addressed the question of the correct view of the nature of the Bible. He declared:

> It might be given in a single word . . . I refer to the word "historic". . . .
> The "historical" view and method aims to use all the knowledge of this sort which is still attainable. It looks at the Biblical books in their original relations; strives

to ascertain and take into account the particulars relative to time, place, person, which
called them forth, and shaped them. It is styled the "historic" view according, not in
the sense that it regards the Bible as primarily consisting of history, or designed to
teach history, but as a book to be studied and understood and used in the light of history. (56–59)

In Thayer's view the only proper way to understand the Scripture is to situ-
ate it as clearly as possible in its historic context. When this is done, one
discovers, according to Thayer, that the Scripture loses its absolute authority
as affirmed in Calvinism and popular American religion. Nevertheless,
Thayer maintained that through Scripture Christians are nurtured in the
ways of God.

Thayer was aware that the historical approach to Scripture created a
gap between the then and the now. He believed historical insight disclosed
that certain parts of the Scripture have no relevance for the contemporary
person. But he valued this as a contribution because historical investigation
makes explicit that Christianity cannot rest upon the antiquarian features of
the Scriptures. The new historical approach, therefore, enables modern
humanity to affirm Christianity despite certain antiquated features of the
Bible. Green, in contrast, sought to establish the current relevancy of
passages declared outmoded by the critics.

Thayer affirmed that the changed attitude toward the Bible was not at
the same time a change of commitment to the Christian faith. He argued, in
fact, that because of the confusion in the minds of many engendered by
cultural change it was only the revised attitude toward the Bible that made
the Christian faith viable. The change had to do with a revised view of the
role and significance of the Scriptures. In the past, according to Thayer, the
reformed or Calvinist tradition—especially in America—"laid a disproportionate emphasis on the full and final character of the Scriptural teaching
relative to the whole range of speculation and conduct, life and destiny"
(10). These views formerly were relatively harmless, but now "by reason of
improved methods of philological study, of progress in science and discov-
ery, of accumulating results in archaeological and historic research, the
theory has come to occasion restlessness and perplexity, at times not a little
distress, in thoughtful souls" (10, 11). For Thayer, Christianity was not so
much a religion of a book as a living loyalty to Christ. He believed that
assigning the Scriptures a secondary role would in fact enhance commitment
to Christ as a person. "The blessing and promise of the new view of Scripture lies in the circumstance that it remands externalities, whether books or
systems, to their proper secondary place, and brings to the front the central
and all-conquering truth of Christianity, viz., personal loyalty to a personal
Master,—the crucified, risen, reigning Christ" (69).

Thayer's purpose in his speech was to assure his listeners that a revised
attitude toward the role and significance of the Scriptures was occurring and
in fact should be encouraged. He offered seven reasons for relegating the

Scriptures to a subsidiary role. First, the Scriptures were not at the center of the life of the early church, and in fact other documents, for example the *Epistle of Barnabas*, were favorites in the early centuries. Second, several decades passed before the present New Testament canon received acclaim. The New Testament authors did not claim scriptural authority for their own writings, and in fact some of their writings were not preserved. For them Scripture meant the Old Testament, which they used for the most part in the inferior Greek translation known as the Septuagint. The New Testament also incorporated a number of "local and temporary forms" (26) and numerous variations in the Gospel accounts of the story of Jesus. Third, the view that all parts of the New Testament are coequal and infallible authority is set aside by the centrality of Jesus and the fact that the Gospels focus on him. Fourth, the Scriptures do not claim to be the word of God but rather to contain the Word. Fifth, Thayer argued that the Bible cannot be consistently applied even by the most clever interpreter. Sixth, since scholars have through constant contact with the Bible discovered that they cannot assign it a paramount position, they are at odds with the typical Christian. Seventh, to assign the Bible a first position is to repress the spiritual life of the church. "The present and abiding indwelling of the Holy Ghost seems to be forgotten" (54). It is only since the Reformation that the Scripture has been assigned such an exalted position. In view of the controversies over Scripture that were then current, Thayer concluded that it seemed the better part of wisdom to return to earlier views and assign the Scriptures a secondary role.

In Thayer's vision the new historical approach to Scripture should be appropriated in full though not to the extent of radical destructive criticism. From this new perspective the Bible would be studied for what it was and would still retain its role as an aid to commitment and piety. Such study would not appear threatening as long as it recognized that the Christian faith is founded on Jesus Christ and the work of God through his Holy Spirit. Thayer thereby sought to provide a rationale for living with the erosion of the epistemological privilege of the Bible.

Crawford Howell Toy of Harvard

The earliest American academic interest in German biblical criticism occurred at Harvard, where it was encouraged by the new literary magazine *Monthly Anthology and Review* and the visit of Joseph Stevens Buckminister to Germany in 1806–1807. Buckminister returned with three thousand volumes centering on biblical criticism. In 1811 he was appointed first Dexter Lecturer on Biblical Criticism. However, before assuming his post, he died in 1812 following an epilepsy seizure (Brown: 26). Convinced of the value of biblical criticism for their attacks on traditional dogma, the Harvard leaders determined to train biblical scholars by sending them to Germany. To this end they encouraged such men as George Bancroft, Edward

Everett, and others to pursue studies in biblical criticism at Göttingen, but none engaged in an academic career upon returning. It remained therefore for home-trained talent such as Andrews Norton and John Gorham Palfrey to take up the challenge. By the 1840s, confronted by other tasks, interest in biblical criticism at Harvard had waned.

Since Harvard found no biblical scholars among its own products after the Civil War, it drew from the pool of those trained elsewhere whose views had become amenable with Unitarianism. In the area of New Testament it was Ezra Abbot, trained at Bowdoin, who functioned as a librarian before his appointment. As the century drew to a close, more and more excitement was generated over biblical criticism, particularly higher criticism, both at a popular and an academic level. Harvard did not escape the effects of these trends. By traditions generated from Puritan and Unitarian predilections, Harvard preferred biblical studies over dogmatic theology. Against this background and in view of increasing expectations for biblical studies, it comes as no surprise that when Crawford H. Toy, who had been trained at the University of Berlin, was forced out of his position at Southern Baptist Theological Seminary in Louisville, Harvard appointed him Hancock Professor of Hebrew and Oriental Languages. (Harvard President Charles W. Eliot was also at this time promoting a revitalization of the Divinity School [Williams: 147–70].)

Crawford Howell Toy was born at Norfork, Virginia, in 1836. He was educated at the University of Virginia, the Southern Baptist Theological Seminary, and the University of Berlin. During his two years in Berlin he studied Semitic languages and German biblical criticism (Brown: 202). He taught English at Albemarle Female Institute in Charlottesville, Greek at Richmond College, applied mathematics at the University of Alabama, and Greek at Virginia and Furman Universities. In 1869 he was made Professor of Old Testament Interpretation at Southern Baptist Theological Seminary, then located in Greenville, South Carolina, but later at Louisville. After ten years there, he felt the pressures to resign because of the views on inspiration that were newly insisted upon. After a year in Norfolk and New York, where he was literary editor for *The Independent*, he was appointed Professor at Harvard. He became emeritus in 1909.

Though ostensibly the issue at stake in Toy's separation from Louisville was the doctrine of inspiration, one could argue that the underlying issue was the method for teaching the Scriptures. In the view of those who affirmed verbal and plenary inspiration, the Bible finally and irrevocably had God as its source. Therefore, since God is beyond time and history, Scripture should be studied as a timeless piece of divine literature. To scrutinize the Bible rigorously as historical—especially in the light of historical contingencies and perhaps miscues—is to deny divine authorship. An effort was made on the conservative side to offer a doctrine of inspiration that would protect the Scriptures from the problems resulting from increased information about biblical languages, the nature of the composition of the Bible, and the world from which the Bible came. Toy clearly accepted the historical approach to the Scriptures with its attendant openness to the fallibility of human authorship. His later works emphasized the historical approach. In fact, in 1901 he organized a Boston area club on the history of religions. One of his most important works reflected on the manner in which religious and ethical ideas in early Christianity developed from Judaism (*Judaism and Christianity*, 1890). Charles Briggs called this work "the best statement of biblical ethics and sociology that has yet been produced" and offered a typical complaint in the footnote: "It is discreditable to German and British writers that they so generally ignore a volume which is on the whole the best that has ever been written on the subject" (1899:587–88). Toy obviously was more interested in a study of the Scriptures that ascertained developmental aspects of religion, literary forms and documents, institutions and canon, than in a study that increased personal piety and commitment or that struggled with historical doctrinal stances. These commitments are obvious in *The History of the Religion of Israel* (13th edition, 1900), a work that had wide circulation among Unitarian Sunday schools, for which it was explicitly written. "It is hoped that the Primer in this shape will not be beyond the grasp of children of twelve years and upwards" (iii). In this book Toy concluded that in such a historical study, one came upon certain fundamental religious ideas pertaining to God, sin, redemption, the future life, and a pure spiritual or inner religion (150). Apparently he felt no need to argue the merits of historical study, since by this time in the circles for which he wrote the value of the historical approach had become axiomatic and commonplace.

It might be important here to notice how Toy's approach to the history of the religion of Israel differed from typical contemporary American biblical studies. First, a historical approach to the biblical period was not common among American biblical scholars prior to the last part of the nineteenth century. Before that time the biblical centuries were indeed taught as history—especially from the beginning of the seminary movement in the early part of the century (Olbricht: 1980)—but traditional Christian interpretations were presupposed, and the history was often presented from the perspective of God's loving work and of encouragement to be God's person because of past great leaders. In Toy's presentation these interests were almost completely dropped out. Toy emphasized the human agencies "that God has employed to preserve this religion which has been so powerful a factor in the history of the human race" (148).

Second, Toy considered it imperative that even the teacher in the church school be familiar with the scholarly literature. "To aid him in this task a short list of books of reference is appended to each lesson. Only such books are mentioned as it is believed will be useful to Sunday-school instructors" (iii). Despite what Toy called a short list, he recommended about 140 volumes that covered the gamut from the most radical to the most conservative and from

the most scholarly—such as the works of Wellhausen, Duhm, and Kuenan—
to the most popular, including Hitchcock's *Analysis of the Bible* (1870) and
The Speaker's Commentary (1871-75). What is more surprising, Toy
recommended several works in French and German. No doubt an occasional
church school teacher among the Unitarians read French or German or
both. One would expect, however, that even among the Unitarians this
would be an exception rather than the rule. From his bibliography it is
obvious that Toy anticipated that even in the church school the approach
would be that of historical biblical criticism.

The attack on Toy's work from the right centered on the manner in
which he constructed (to conservatives reconstructed) the history of Israel.
Toy argued that Israel's history followed the same laws of origin and growth
as that of all ancient or national religions (148), but he admitted that certain
national differences obtain. According to him, the early stages of Israel's
religion are hidden in the mists of antiquity. When the records begin, the
Israelites are polytheists much like their neighbors the Canaanites. For Toy
the best-documented period began with the time of Samuel. From Samuel
until the exile a major conflict between polytheism and monotheism ensued.
During this time Israel came to believe that Yahweh alone was God, whereas earlier they regarded the gods of the other nations as real beings, even
though they themselves worshiped only Yahweh. It was to the prophets that
Toy attributed this change of commitment. "The prophets insisted that Yahweh alone, to the exclusion of all other gods, was to be worshipped by Israel;
and at last they preached that there was no other god but Yahweh, and that
he should be worshipped not only by Israel, but by all nations" (2). The
period after the exile was different, however, in that great effort was put
forth to order human life in accordance with the will of God. The result was
the formalizing of fixed rules. Toy's reconstruction was much like that of
Wellhausen in its main outlines. While Toy accepted the historicity of Moses
and his contribution to Israel, he rejected the account whereby the whole of
the Pentateuch was authored by Moses. "The law grew up gradually, and
hundreds of years after Moses, when pious prophets and priests gathered
together the religious usages of their times, they thought that it must all
have been revealed in the beginning by the God of Israel, and so they came
to believe that their great deliverer from Egyptian bondage had received it
all at once. But we shall see that the succeeding history does not bear this
out" (20). The specifically Christian nature of Toy's interpretation can be
seen in his view that these laws became "burdensome and injurious" (149).
The problem was that the laws established the obligation of one to be holy
but failed to show the way. "It was at this point that Jesus of Nazareth came
forward, and taught that holiness was reached, not by rules, but by the
inward disposition of love to God" (149).

By the time the thirteenth edition of Toy's history was published even
the more conservative seminaries were teaching the historical development

of the Old and New Testament religions among their biblical courses. The conservatives by now agreed with the need to obtain historical insight, but they argued that history should be read as it appears on the surface of the Scriptures and as, in their view, it had been conceived from the beginning. Certain modifications might be needed here, and adjustments there, but the age-old reading of the text should be supported. From the conservative perspective reconstruction such as that of Toy conceived the Scripture as a human production and subject to human laws of misplaced emphases and errors. They objected to such radical historicizing on the ground that Scripture was given by divine inspiration and was not therefore a product of fallible humans.

The work of Toy clearly shows the ramifications of the cultural shift. Scripture lost its status as a privileged literary collection. It is to be studied as an instance of the universal phenomenon of religion. The highest aspects of biblical religion occur in the final stages and are to be located inward. The influence of Hegelian idealism on Toy is obvious.

Charles A. Briggs of Union

Charles A. Briggs was identified with Union Theological Seminary in New York both as a student and as a teacher. The beginnings of biblical studies at Union are rooted in the work of Edward Robinson, earlier a student and colleague of Moses Stuart at Andover. Robinson studied in Germany from 1826 to 1830, principally at Halle, and was the first American biblical scholar to achieve an international reputation. Robinson published both Greek and Hebrew lexicons but achieved international acclaim for his publications on the geography of Palestine. In the 1830s Robinson saw American biblical scholarship as derivative; he pointed out that both the biblical manuscripts and the specialists were to be found in Europe. Robinson believed Americans had been more active, particularly in philology, than British scholars, but he despaired of any major contribution by seminary professors. Rather, he laid the challenge to clergy to advance the discipline in America (155–56). Robinson was correct in his analysis of the American scene. Biblical studies were to remain essentially at that point until the next generation of scholars, many of whom studied in Germany after receiving their early education under Robinson and others. Robinson himself was traditional on a number of matters, for example, the unity of the book of Isaiah and the Mosaic authorship of the Pentateuch.

Solid foundations were laid by Robinson at Union in biblical philology and geography. Such foundations were destined to inspire further scholarly rigor and they culminated in Charles A. Briggs. Briggs, born in New York, studied at the University of Virginia from 1857 to 1860. Crawford H. Toy was there at the same time teaching in a female institute, but whether Toy and Briggs met at that time is not clear. In 1861 Briggs spent a few months in the Civil War, then attended Union Theological Seminary from 1861 to 1863. Robinson was professor during those years, but he was ill and died in 1863. Robinson probably encouraged Briggs to go to Germany, and he first took up his studies in Berlin under E. W. Hengstenberg, who was admired by Robinson. According to Briggs's own testimony he was eager to be convinced by Hengstenberg's position but ended up otherwise.

> In 1866 it was the author's privilege to study with Hengstenberg in the University of Berlin. His studies were at first chiefly on the traditional side. He can say that he worked over the chief authorities on that side, and they had all the advantages of his predilections in their favor. But Hengstenberg himself convinced him in his own lecture-room that he was defending a lost cause. (1893:62)

Briggs gave credit to Robinson in discussing philology but implied that higher criticism was new in America with his generation. Apparently he viewed higher criticism as a set of conclusions rather than as the raising of specific questions concerning the literary characteristics of biblical books, their authorship, sources, and historical backgrounds. The basic questions of the higher critics had been asked by American biblical experts from at least the days of John Cotton in the 1630s, but in this regard Briggs posited a discontinuity in Union's biblical scholarship. "It is only within recent years that any general interest in the matters of Higher Criticism has been shown in Great Britain and America. This interest has been due chiefly to the labors of a few pioneers, who have suffered in the interest of Biblical science" (1899:285). Concerning beginnings among the Presbyterians Briggs stated, "The discussion of the Higher Criticism in the United States began for the Presbyterian body, in the plea for freedom of criticism in my inaugural address as Professor of Hebrew in the Union Theological Seminary, N.Y., in 1876" (1899:286–87). By the time Briggs made these claims he had narrowed the definition of higher criticism. In his 1876 lecture he did not employ the term higher criticism but "Sacred Isagogics" (1876:14). These had to do with determining "the historical origin and authorship, the original readers, the design and character of the composition, and its relation to other writings of its group." Briggs said essentially the same in *Biblical Study* (1885). However, this work asserts that the questions must be raised with no presupposed answers and that matters of integrity, authenticity, and credibility are imperative (1885:86–87). In 1899 higher criticism meant for Briggs those literary questions the answers to which need not be traditional and presumably in many cases would not be. "The Higher Criticism devotes its attention to the literary features of the Bible." "Having secured the best text of the writings, criticism devotes itself to the higher task of considering them as to integrity, authenticity, literary form, and reliability" (1899:92).

Briggs, perhaps more than any other biblical scholar of his generation, set out to change the manner in which the Bible was studied. He did so by arguing in the name of the Protestant principle that affirms "the divine authority of the Holy Scripture over against tradition" (1899:246). On this basis, he contended, the reformers eliminated the apocryphal books, returned to the original Greek and Hebrew texts rather than the Septuagint and Vulgate, and rejected the Massoretic points as merely traditional. Furthermore, they rejected the allegorical method of interpretation for the plain grammatical sense. Briggs also identified a second critical revival under Cappellus and Walton, in which the interpretations of the rabbis were rejected. In Briggs's view biblical scholars were now in the third revival, which commenced at the close of the eighteenth century, in which higher criticism rejected the traditions concerning the literary features of the Scriptures. "The first critical revival had been mainly devoted to the Canon of Scripture, its authority and interpretation. The second critical revival had studied the original texts and versions. The third critical revival gave attention to the Sacred Scriptures as literature" (1899:246–47).

Briggs spoke out in the name of literary analysis rather than history. He admitted the value of the historical approach but argued that the inductive study of literary features should take precedence over the historical.

> But a history of Biblical literature might be constructed which would distinguish between facts and theories, and though it might be imperfect and not altogether satisfactory, it might prepare the way for something better, and it would certainly present the material in a most attractive form. But the dominant method in all biblical studies should be the inductive and not the historical. (1885:77).

He did not repeat this observation in the 1899 work.

Throughout his writings Briggs emphasized that conclusions must be formed on the basis of available evidence rather than dogmatic commitments. While history is always crucial for placing a work, raw data and generalizations depend on the document itself. Briggs was well schooled in the German predilection for basic distinctions in disciplines and the assigning of appropriate tasks to each. Briggs set out his basic delineations in his 1876 inaugural address, and they are repeated in *Biblical Study* (1885) and *The Study of Holy Scripture* (1889). The umbrella term for biblical studies was exegetical theology. The subareas are biblical canonics, textual criticism, higher criticism, biblical exegesis, biblical hermeneutics, biblical history, historical criticism, biblical archaeology, biblical theology, biblical religion, faith, and ethics (1899:12–41). In the rest of the book Briggs set forth conclusions on these topics as he understood them. For the most part he reflected advanced German views, mediated by his less radical stance, which attempted amelioration to American sensitivities but of course not always successfully. There is no question that Briggs changed the manner in which the Scriptures were read at Union and over the next several decades in most of the Presbyterian churches. His efforts were dedicated to taking up the biblical documents without any presuppositions about their origins. In that manner they joined the ranks of all other literary manuscripts.

Benjamin W. Bacon of Yale

It was Josiah Willard Gibbs who introduced scientific biblical philology to Yale. He was appointed instructor in Sacred Languages in 1824, became professor in 1826, and continued until his death in 1861. Gibbs lived with Moses Stuart from 1815 to 1818, during which time he pursued studies and became impressed with Stuart's work in lexicography. He himself published a Hebrew lexicon based upon Gesenius in 1824 and again in 1833 (Brown: 172). The generation of professors before Bacon was abreast of German efforts in philology and exegesis. George E. Day translated various German works including Oehler's *Old Testament Theology* but objected to reconstructed views on inspiration and authorship such as those of W. Robertson Smith, the Scottish professor who was dismissed from his chair at Aberdeen in 1881 (Bainton: 175). Timothy Dwight edited a translation of the twenty-volume Meyer German New Testament commentary, which according to its title was critical-exegetical but in Bacon's way of thinking was little advanced over the traditional (Harrisville: 10).

William Rainey Harper was the first professor at Yale in biblical studies to embrace the essential features of German critical studies, but it remained for Benjamin W. Bacon to implement these ideas after Harper left in 1891 to become president of the University of Chicago. R. A. Harrisville affirms that "Bacon deserves the title 'founder' in the area of biblical criticism, because it was he who inaugurated and gave direction to what contemporary scholarship takes for granted as belonging to the curriculum of biblical studies" (1976:iv). This statement ignores the contributions of the other scholars scrutinized in this essay, but it must be admitted that Bacon more than any of the others proceeded without amelioration to standard American sensitivities. He could do so in part because of those who preceded him, who laid the foundations and suffered the brunt of the ire against the advanced positions.

Benjamin Wisner Bacon, born in Connecticut of illustrious clerical heritage, spent two of his pre-college years in Germany and three in Geneva, Switzerland. He graduated from Yale in 1881 and from Yale Divinity School in 1884. He then served pastorates in Old Lyme, Connecticut, and Oswego, New York, until 1896, when he became professor of New Testament at Yale Divinity School. Before his Yale appointment Bacon had plunged into critical studies of the Pentateuch and had published several articles and books on the subject with William Rainey Harper as his mentor (Harrisville: 2). After his appointment at Yale he devoted most of his time to New Testament studies, the area of his unique contribution.

Harrisville has set out Bacon's presuppositions as revolving about the historical. Bacon insisted on a "rational and scientific conception of the process and history from which the religious and spiritual consciousness of Christendom had issued" (Bacon, 1890:302). He saw even matters of the

Spirit and miracle lawful according to principles not yet fully explicable. God is at work in history according to evolutionary laws both biologically and spiritually. It is spiritual evolution that for Bacon is the focus of the biblical scholar (Harrisville: 9–11). He understood the Gospels as having evolved in the early church. He called his approach "aetiological," by which he meant that the Gospels consisted of a series of anecdotes strung together with the purpose of explaining or defending the practices of the early church. The result was that the words of Jesus could not be considered absolute ground for doctrine or morals. The words attributed to Jesus in the Gospels may or may not have emanated from his lips. The reading of the Gospels was therefore dramatically, if not traumatically, different in that no longer could the Gospels be read as though Jesus spoke directly from the pages of the New Testament.

In one of his earlier works Bacon described higher criticism in a manner that made the historical dimension obvious.

> It inquires how the text thus established came to assume that form. Was the writer an editor or compiler merely, as the writers of Kings and Chronicles declare themselves to be? Then what were his sources, and what was their authority? Was he an author, as in the case of the fourth gospel? Then who was he? When and where did he live? Under what circumstances and for what purpose did he write? What were his materials, and if his personal opinions enter into the writing, what is the ground and degree of the respect to which his opinions are entitled? (1891:1, 2)

While the categories of these questions had been raised from time immemorial, the implied answers show the shift. For the most part it was assumed that biblical books had been produced by authors rather than editors; that the source was from heaven by divine inspiration rather than human; the authors were precisely those received in tradition; and that authors wrote down what came from God rather than expressing their own opinions.

Bacon divided his work on the Hexateuch into source analysis and historical criticism (1894:vi). Clearly, both have a historical dimension since explorations of sources involves dating origins and establishing provenance. His approach to the New Testament was similar. About the formation of the New Testament he wrote: "The literature of the New Testament must be understood historically if understood at all. It must be understood as the product, we might almost say the precipitate, of the greatest period in the history of religion" (1912:247). In the case of the Old Testament this meant specifically that one must examine the Hexateuch to determine how it was composed. Bacon argued that the major Old Testament scholars had agreed that the Hexateuch was a weaving together of four basic sources and went so far as to declare "the existence of a real and extraordinarily minute agreement of all schools of documentary analysis" (1894:iv). These sources Bacon called the traditional Jahwist, Elohist, Deuteronomist and Priestly writer (6), J having originated in Judah and E in Ephraim (21). The Jahwist source he dated in the ninth century B.C., the Elohist in the eighth, the Deuternonomist in the seventh, and the Priestly in the fifth. While the Hexateuch contained these basic strands the canonical form came about through the repeated redactions of the text (1894:lvii). Bacon considered his unique contribution the unraveling and sorting out of these redactions, as is obvious in *Triple Tradition of the Exodus*. Bacon proceeded in this work not by first reconstructing the history of Israel and then locating telltale signs of that history in the documents but by the reverse procedure of locating sources in the books and then raising the question about their provenance.

Bacon's approach to the New Testament was much the same. In *An Introduction to the New Testament* (1900) chronological sequence provided the overall structure for the work. After discussing questions pertaining to history, Bacon commenced with the letters of Paul under the affirmation that these were the earliest New Testament books. He likewise took up each epistle according to date beginning with Galatians, which he assumed to be the earliest. He then discussed the pastorals and Hebrews, the rest of the general epistles, the synoptics, and the Johannine writings. In discussing the synoptics Bacon reflected the consensus that Mark was the earliest of the Gospels, followed by a Q source, which Matthew and then Luke utilized. This is commonly labeled the Two-Source Hypothesis, that is, the thesis that Mark and Q provided the basic stuff out of which all the Gospels were constructed. In addition he conceived each Gospel as resulting from a much more complex development. His position on Matthew—a Gospel concerning which he made landmark contributions—assumed a three-stage development: (1) an Aramaic *Logia* or collection of sayings without frameworks, (i.e., Q); (2) a Greek edition with an outline of the public ministry and passion; and (3) a final recasting of the discourse material into five great masses and also taking up additional material from Mark (1900:202). In some cases Bacon was more traditional than the Germans, but in terms of origins he offered more involved explanations: "in the anonymous historical books my personal study has led to the conviction that our present gospels and Acts are the outcome of a longer and more complex process of growth than most critics admit" (1900:vi).

Bacon was a thoroughgoing historian. Not only did he reconstruct the chronology of the sources of the various biblical books, but he also struggled with the overall history of the biblical period and argued that any particular section of the Scriptures must be understood in the light of its historical location. Furthermore, external historical witness must not be ignored on matters of authorship and provenance. He considered the second-century tradition to be as important as the New Testament itself for determining origin and authorship (1900:277). Because of these traditions he sometimes came out differently from the German consensus, for example, on the authorship of Revelation (1900:278).

Bacon was sensitive to the fact that the approach to the Scripture with which he worked changed the manner in which Scripture was commonly read and taught. It was the difference, in his terms, between a devotional and a scientific reading. He assumed that the scientific provided a necessary backdrop for the devotional. "In conclusion let me urge the general reader to remember that while the devotional and scientific treatment of the Bible are widely different, they are neither incompatible nor independent" (1904:x). The traditional position held that since God himself has provided the substance if not the words of the Bible, all sources point to him and historical insight is generally irrelevant when one seeks to ascertain the will of God for his people today. While Bacon proposed that the historical was a stage on the way to the devotional and theological, he did little to contribute to the last stages.

Shailer Mathews of Chicago

Biblical studies at the University of Chicago commenced in the era of higher criticism and with a commitment to it. The University opened its doors in 1892 with William Rainey Harper as President. Harper himself had accepted the historical-scientific approach to Scripture and looked about for professors with the same view. He himself chaired the Old Testament department and brought Ernest D. Burton from Newton Theological Seminary as New Testament chairman. In 1894 Burton persuaded Shailer Mathews to accept a position as Associate Professor of New Testament History. Under the influence of Harper and his professors Chicago developed a focus that influenced biblical studies. C. Harvey Arnold characterized these early years as "The Era of the Socio-Historical Method" (1966:27). Gerald Birney Smith characterized the commitment of the University, then related it to the study of Christianity. "The only common presuppositions of the various portions are the acceptance of the historical method and the belief that the interpretation of Christianity must be in accord with the rightful tests of scientific truthfulness and actual vitality in the modern world" (1916:vii). The key word was scientific. Mathews, in speaking of those in biblical studies stated, "It was inevitable that we should share in the enthusiasm for scientific research which has always marked the University of Chicago" (1936:58). In the early years the specific focus was grammar and lexicography, but considerable effort was expended on the history and sociology of the biblical faith. The newer critical views on the literary features of the text were widely accepted, but theological positions remained for the most part traditional (Funk: 17; Olbricht: 1979a:96).

Shailer Mathews (1863–1941) was born in Portland, Maine, and was educated at Colby College and Newton Theological Institution. Mathews was not committed to the ministry but was attracted to the seminary since he felt the attention to detail and accuracy required by the biblical languages were valuable. He was appointed an assistant professor of rhetoric at Colby, then professor of history, political science, and sociology. In 1890 he spent a year at

the University of Berlin studying history and political economy. He returned
to Colby and taught these subjects until he moved to Chicago in 1894. In 1905
Mathews transferred from New Testament to systematic theology and from
1908 to 1933 was Dean of the Divinity School.

In view of the inclinations of the age and Mathews's training in history
and sociology, it only was natural that he would approach the New Testament from a historical, sociological point of view. He anticipated pioneer
vistas in these regions and felt that such study would not only contribute to
scholarship but also to social change. Mathews spoke of this vision in his
autobiography.

> . . . I knew I was not adapted to conventional New Testament instructing. I had never
> worked in the field proposed and knew nothing about it. In that I had plenty of com-
> pany for the historical method had not yet been applied in any serious way to the
> study of the New Testament. I doubt if Dr. Burton himself foresaw the revolutionary
> effort of such a method. . . . But Professor Burton overcame our hesitation. I caught
> his enthusiasm for a university in the making. My inherited interest in religion took
> form in an ambition to have a part in extending its frontiers. A new age was in the
> making and religion was needed in social change. I had at least some mastery of his-
> torical method which could be applied to the New Testament field. (1936:50, 51)

With Ernest Burton he published handbook materials for class studies that
represented these historical approaches, *The Life of Christ* (1900) and *Constructive Studies in the Life of Christ* (1900). His own works likewise
reflected these interests along with a penchant for sociology. *A History of
the New Testament Times in Palestine 175 B.C. to 70 A.D.* (1899) and *The
Social Teaching of Jesus, An Essay in Christian Sociology* (1897). Mathews
offered courses at the Divinity School on both the social teachings of Jesus
and the social teachings of the apostles (Olbricht, 1979a:87).

For Mathews, not only was the historical approach necessary in order to
attain the desired application of Scripture to life but also the Scriptures
approached from the standpoint of sociology supplied the foundations for
newer societal structures. It was Mathews's considered judgment that the age
in which he lived was a new one, the era of modern humanity. This new
age differed considerably from the age of the Scriptures.

> The world we live in is obviously very different from that of the apostles, and
> the presuppositions of our thinking are vastly different from theirs. Indeed, it would be
> difficult to overestimate the contrasts between the age of the New Testament and our
> own as far as the fundamental attitudes of the social mind are concerned. (1910:35)

With this vast chasm between antiquity and the present, the question must
be addressed as to the role of biblical studies. Mathews's observations show
the obvious shift from the tone that was being set in the American university
by theological and biblical studies to the task of determining what its new
role was to be once it had been demoted from hegemony. In Mathews's
analysis, most persons react to the disparity between then and now in two

characteristic ways. First are those who, deeply disturbed by the chasm, divorce their religious life from their best intellectual efforts and relegate religion to a matter of sentiment, unquestioned acceptance, and a literalistic interpretation of the gospel (1910:66–70). At the other extreme, according to Mathews, are those who hold aloof from the gospel "on the ground that it is utterly inconsistent with the current science and philosophy" (70, 71). They make religion into an inherently human phenomenon, a phase of sexual and social development. Their interest in the Scriptures, if any, is purely antiquarian. Though Mathews did not so indicate, it was the latter point of view that was beginning to obtain in the major American universities.

Mathews proposed a third alternative for the student of history.

> He knows that there is a third alternative, that of true conservatism; viz. such an historical evaluation of the gospel as it stands in the New Testament as will disclose both its historical and its timeless realities and will make possible a formulation of its content in modern terms and in accordance with constructive principles which are the equivalents of the controlling expositions of Jesus and his message to be found in the New Testament. (1910:71)

In other words, a historical approach to Scripture will enable the sorting out of the eternal verities found therein from what is temporary and fleeting. The expertise of the historian is important in biblical studies, therefore, because reality itself unfolds historically, and it is the historian who will snatch biblical faith from the flames of modernity, which threaten to consume it.

The platform for this program grew out of that sort of biblical studies that had attained consensus among the higher critics. The shift in the approach to the Bible for Mathews was more than simply retooling and modernizing. It was the means by which biblical studies could keep its toe in the door of the academy and other intellectual circles. Mathews identified five stages in this undertaking: (1) The documents of the primitive Christian faith must be scrutinized by the methods of historical-literary criticism. (2) The world view of the New Testament era must be ascertained and the elements of that view in the New Testament identified. (3) A distinction must be made between this first-century world view and the basic spiritual life of the gospel. (4) A determination must be made of those aspects of the world view itself that are constructive principles of the gospel. (5) Those concepts in the gospel that are permanent and eternally valid must be identified (1910:72).

Quite clearly, the correct reading of the text in Mathews's program is not the result of commitment, faith, correct piety or doctrine. It depends rather upon having acquired philological, historical, and sociological tools in order to weigh and sift and set aside a residue that can provide the foundations for human values. The reading of the Scripture before the shift, however, depended variously upon the former attributes. For Mathews a historical approach to Scripture was not important simply because history was in vogue but because through these means a visible platform for modern humanity was still available in these ancient documents. A person with more traditional commitments might argue that when one begins to separate the wheat and chaff in Scripture one is treading on dangerous grounds because the enterprise is purely human, subjective, and arbitrary. In contrast, the one who begins with the commitment that the whole Scripture is the eternal word of God has a certain, objective, divine basis from which to proceed. Mathews would admit that without a viable modus operandi, picking and choosing from Scripture would be subjective and arbitrary. But it is precisely for this reason that the historical-literary approach to the Scriptures emerges from a number of quarters. It is crucial first of all ontologically, because reality itself is characterized by historical emergence. It is crucial theologically, because the biblical faith itself embraces the significance of the historical. And it is imperative hermeneutically, because only through historical investigation can the question be settled of what in Scripture is viable for the modern world.

Conclusions

As the nineteenth century wore into the twentieth, the Scriptures were read variously for conversion, personal piety, denominational defense, or dogmatic construction. However, at the academic cutting edge the Bible was read with a new set of presuppositions, those of history. That the past is our surest guide to the future was academia's persistent conviction, which eventually permeated all of society. In the age in which history reigned supreme, the historical examination of Scripture created great excitement and inspired great rigor and detailed labors. The supremacy of history, however, did not persist. That era was succeeded by an age desperate for meaning. The result was a new crisis in biblical studies known as the biblical theology movement. In the 1930s and 1940s scholars honed the tools for reading the Scriptures so as to combat the overshadowing specter of meaninglessness. They sought methods for discovering a meaningful theology in the Scriptures. In the present time, another crisis has arisen that some have called a hermeneutical crisis. Such a label is accurate but perhaps belies the fact that all crises in biblical studies are hermeneutical.

The cultural crisis of this age is the feeling of powerlessness. In an age seeking power, whether individual or corporate, as the searchlight revolves across the Scripture, the interest centers upon whether any power sources emerge. This is the dawning of the age of Star Wars, the era of the Force. Already the surging charismatic movement is exploring every mist-enshrouded region of Scripture to locate sources of untouched power. Those who propose psychoanalytic models of hermeneutics have likewise offered a reading that locates sources of personal power. Even the counter-hermeneutic, the effort to explode the myths of the super hero, gives recognition to the hunger for power in the present era. Given the allusion to power in Scripture it seems no less viable to hold it up to the demands of a new age than it did to seek out its historical dimensions in a former time. The Scripture always has been and no doubt will continue to be searched under the floodlight of the cultural demands of an era.

WORKS CONSULTED

Arnold, C. Harvey

    1966   *Near the Edge of Battle*. Chicago: University of Chicago Press.

Bacon, Benjamin W.

    1891   *Genesis of Genesis*. Hartford: Student Publishing Company.

    1894   *Triple Tradition of the Exodus*. Hartford: Student Publishing Company.

    1900   *An Introduction to the New Testament*. New York: Macmillan.

    1910   *The Fourth Gospel in Research and Debate*. New York: Moffat, Yard and Co.

    1912   *The Making of the New Testament*. New York: Henry Holt.

    1914   *Christianity Old and New*. New Haven: Yale University Press.

    1925   *The Gospel of Mark*. New Haven: Yale Universiy Press.

Bainton, Roland H.

    1957   *Yale and the Ministry*. New York: Harper & Brothers.

Briggs, Charles A.

    1885   *Biblical Study*. New York: Charles Scribner's Sons.

    1889   *Whither?* New York: Charles Scribner's Sons.

    1893   *The Higher Criticism of the Hexateuch*. New York: Charles Scribner's Sons.

    1899   *The Study of the Holy Scripture*. New York: Charles Scribner's Sons.

Brown, Jerry W.

    1969   *The Rise of Biblical Criticism in America, 1800–1970*. Middletown, CT: Wesleyan University Press.

Childs, Brevard S.
    1979   *Introduction to the Old Testament as Scripture.*
                   Philadelphia: Fortress Press.

Funk, Robert W.
    1976   "The Watershed of the American Biblical Tradition:
                   The Chicago School, First Phase, 1892–1920." *Journal
                   of Biblical Literature* 95/1:4–22.

Giltner, John H.
    1956   "Moses Stuart: 1780–1852." Unpublished Ph.D. disser-
                   tation, Yale University.

Green, William Henry
    1883   *Moses and the Prophets.* New York: Robert Carter and
                   Brothers.
    1895   *The Unity of the Book of Genesis.* New York: Charles
                   Scribner's Sons.
    1896   *The Higher Criticism of the Pentateuch.* New York:
                   Charles Scribner's Sons.
    1899   *General Introduction to the Old Testament.* New
                   York: Charles Scribner's Sons.

Harrisville, Roy A.
    1976   *Benjamin Wisner Bacon.* Missoula: Scholars Press.

Loetscher, Lefferts A.
    1954   *The Broadening Church.* Philadelphia: University of
                   Pennsylvania Press.

Mathews, Shailer
    1897   *The Social Teaching of Jesus.* New York: Macmillan.
    1910   *The Gospel and the Modern Man.* New York:
                   Macmillan.
    1936   *New Faith for Old.* New York: Macmillan.

Olbricht, Thomas H.
    1979a   "New Testament Studies at The University of Chicago:
                   The First Decade, 1892–1902." *Restoration Quarterly*
                   22/1,2:84–98.
    1979b   "Charles Hodge as an American New Testament
                   Interpreter." *Journal of Presbyterian History*
                   57/2:117–33.
    1980   "Understanding the Church of the Second Century:
                   American Research and Teaching, 1890–1940." In

Tradition and History, ed. W. Eugene March. San Antonio, TX: Trinity University Press.

Smith, Gerald Birney, ed.
1916   *A Guide to the Study of the Christian Religion.* Chicago: University of Chicago Press.

Robinson, Edward
1834   "Philology and Lexicography of the New Testament." *The Biblical Repository* 4:154–82.

Thayer, Joseph Henry
1891   *The Change of Attitude Towards the Bible.* Boston: Houghton, Mifflin and Company.

Toy, Crawford H.
1900   *The History of The Religion of Israel: An Old Testament Primer.* Boston: Beacon Press.

Williams, George Huntston, ed.
1954   *The Harvard Divinity School.* Boston: Beacon Press.

VI

New Attitudes and New Curricula: The Changing Role of the Bible in Protestant Education, 1880–1920

Charles R. Kniker

The period from 1880 to 1920 was one of traumatic change for American society in general and the Protestant community in particular. This chapter will examine two changes—the shifting attitudes of Protestants toward the Bible as a result of critical scholarship and the responses of private and public educators to these shifts. In 1880 few challenged the Bible as the inerrant word of God. By 1920 there were a number of Protestants who preferred to speak of the Bible as the world's best literature. At the beginning of this period, the Bible was held to be society's sourcebook of moral precepts. At the end, its undisputed value in solving moral problems was questioned. At the same time, the warm partnership that the Protestant establishment enjoyed with the public schools dissolved into an uneasy alliance.

Three distinct attitudes toward the Bible can be discerned in this period, and each elicits its own pedagogical response. Those who saw it as "the words of God" sought ways to instill these words in the minds of students. Those who saw it as a "guide for life" were forced to grapple with great social changes in science, in school population, and in female emancipation. Those who saw it as "the world's great literature" sought to develop appropriate linguistic and literary techniques for understanding it. These three topics will form the major sections of this chapter. The content of each of these sections is derived in good part from national and local educational reports and curriculum studies, court decisions on the use of the Bible in public schools, Sunday school literature, and publications from the Chautauqua Literary and Scientific Circle, usually referred to as the Circle or C.L.S.C. /1/

The Bible Viewed As God's Word

For Americans living in Reconstruction days, the key to interpreting life was the Bible. The McGuffey *Eclectic Readers* presented the Bible as the unchallengeable word of God, which could and should be applied to almost every aspect of daily life (Handy: 382; Commager: vii; see Chapter II above). Therefore, it deserved to be studied daily.

Hearing about Darwin's theory of evolution and reading the findings of higher critics, many Protestants believed that the authority of the Bible would be destroyed, especially if God's authorship was denied. A number of authors and preachers rose to the occasion to argue that biblical truths had not been disturbed. In a widely distributed book, *The Tongue of Fire*, English preacher William Arthur stated that the greatest question for humanity was "Hath God spoken?" He responded affirmatively proclaiming that the Bible was the vehicle of God's speech, a book that contained more than the "guesses of thinkers" and "the juggling of priests" (73, 74). Luther Tracy Townsend, a prominent Methodist theologian who had studied in Europe, agreed: "We repeat, science, philosophy, archaeology, and all the correlated sciences have added not one new fundamental truth to our theological knowledge, and have changed nothing" (Schlesinger: 5; Townsend: 192). Other religious educators disagreed. Charles Hodge of Princeton Theological Seminary in *What is Darwinism?* pointed to the perils of the English scientist's theories for biblically grounded faith. John Fiske's *Outline of Cosmic Philosophy* tried to absorb some of Darwin's concepts, and Fiske penned a sentence, "Evolution is God's way of doing things," which became widely used in religious circles.

Darwin's theories were just one frontier of new learning that challenged the supremacy of the Bible. The most direct challenge to a biblically centered piety came from the higher criticism movement, which originated in German universities in the early 1800s and found its way to the United States in the 1870s and 1880s. Higher criticism was the critical literary and historical investigation of biblical records; it assumed that the Scripture's messages might be illuminated by placing them in historical perspective (Hudson; Flood, 1889; De Vries). Another factor that stretched the boundaries of knowledge was the missionary movement. Tales of other religious practices and exposure to such sacred writings as the Qur'an tended to undermine the uniqueness of the Judeo-Christian message. James Freeman Clarke's sympathetic treatment of world religions, *Ten Great Religions*, went through twenty-one reprints between 1871 and 1886. Specifically, then, what happened from 1880 to 1920 regarding the perception that the Bible was the word of God? And what were the responses by religious and educational professionals?

Defending Divine Authorship

Many clergy and Sunday school teachers during this time believed that God had directly supervised if not in fact actually written the Scriptures. The literature of the period regularly makes two related arguments: that the Bible is of divine authorship and that it contains only the truth and no error. Townsend, like others, contended that the so-called modern findings of science and medicine had been predicted by the Bible. "If there are scientific errors in the teachings of the Bible," the Boston Seminary professor reasoned, "it follows that the book is not in a special sense God's book, and, therefore, its claims upon us are not supreme." To those who might argue that the Bible's language was outdated for the modern world Townsend counseled that God's truth is scientifically accurate even though it does not employ the language of science (8, 9). To prove that the Bible contained sufficient truth for all ages, Townsend resorted to proof texts. He asserted that Prov 4:23, "Out of the heart are the issues of life," was a forecast of what the physician Harvey had proved in 1616—the heart pumps blood through the circulatory system (37–39).

America's awakening to the challenge that the Bible might not contain all truth was evident in the 1880s, as revealed in numerous church publications. But such publications still proclaimed that the Bible held the ultimate truth. John Vincent advised Sunday school teachers to develop the "spirit of cordial assent to all that it teaches, whether the truth be clear or obscure to the understanding, palatable or unpalatable to the moral taste." He concluded that "eventually the divine interpretation will make it clear to the persistent, even dull student" (1882:11, 12). In another publication in 1910, Vincent argued similarly: "Read as a scoffer, read as a Pharisee, and it will be useless to you" (1910:122, 123).

For many Protestants, then, the Bible was to remain the word of God. The Bible cradled the faith of Protestants and Catholics who believed that God acted in history. To deny God's authorship of the Bible was to deny the existence of God, the creative power revealed in the universe, and ultimately the concept of salvation.

Claiming an Infallible Text

A corollary to the divine authorship of the Bible is the infallibility of the text. A God of truth would not permit errors in the Old and New Testaments. Developments in the field of biblical translation in England and the United States between 1881 and 1885 introduced the public to textual problems in the Bible (Sims). In the 1880s it was common for defenders of the Bible to point out the accuracy of the Bible. Jesse L. Hurlbut, later the writer of the best seller *The Story of the Bible*, stated in 1883 that the Bible contained references to two thousand places and it had made no errors in location, as archeologists had verified (176). By the 1890s, however, it was not possible to ignore the evidence from the higher critics. Typical of many responses was that of R. F. Weidner of Augustana Theological Seminary in Rock Island, Illinois. He asserted that the Bible was still authoritative and error-free. He held to Mosaic authorship of the first five books of the Old Testament but did allow that "a few of the disagreements evidently arise from errors in the transcription of the original texts" (312, 315).

Weidner's two-part article was written on the eve of some of the most newsworthy events of the higher criticism controversy—the proceedings and trials of Charles A. Briggs and Henry P. Smith in 1891 and 1892 and the proclamation of Pope Leo XIII in his encyclical, *Providentissimus Deus* in 1893, which held to a rigid view of biblical inspiration and infallibility. The following year a "providential" call was issued to eighty thousand clergy inviting them to join in a campaign to defend the "evangelical Christian faith against the assaults of its infidel adversaries." The result was the formation of the American Bible League and a journal, *The Bible Student and Teacher*, which included a "Council of War" section. In 1895 at Niagara Falls, a similar conference drew up some "fundamental" points for evangelical Christians, headed by the inerrancy of the Scriptures (Cole: 46, 47; Nichols: 273). From 1910 to 1915 a more formal publication called *The Fundamentals* would continue the debate on the infallible text.

Redefining Revelation

A subtle change began to occur as these debates continued. Some religious educators and public school teachers and administrators began to claim that the Bible contains the word of God. Washington Gladden, leader of the social gospel movement, in his popular book *Who Wrote the Bible?* (1891), took such a stand. In 1913, Samuel C. Schmucker adopted a similar position:

> If we are to understand, in conformity with the thought of the age, any particular books in the Bible, there are three steps through which we must pass. We must first ask ourselves the kind of people to whom the book was originally written. We must know their habits of life and of thought. . . . We must next decide what is the inherent truth taught to the people of that time by the book under consideration. Much that is written must be simply the setting in which alone that truth could teach them. This extraneous detail gives vigor and color to the message but is not the message itself. The last step and the hardest one to take, the one that some minds see as almost irreverent, is to decide the form that message must take today to convey to our minds the same truth which the original message conveyed to the people of its time. . . . (281)

Educational Responses

The debate about the Bible's authorship and inerrancy caused much agony and confusion among religious educators, public school teachers, and legal experts. Obviously, the future could not be the same as the past. Three educational changes emerged from this theological crisis.

Less study of the Bible in public schools. In the nineteenth century the Bible was still a textbook used extensively in both the public schools and religious schools of the nation. The first law requiring that the Bible be read in public schools was passed in Massachusetts in 1826. By mid-century it is estimated that half the schools in Connecticut used the Bible as a reading textbook, despite some resistance from religious quarters. In the early years of the twentieth century, states were still requiring that the Bible be read (Boles, 1965). The importance of the Bible in Sunday schools and other religious enterprises is documented more fully in other chapters. That it was important during the late nineteenth century is certainly seen in the adoption in 1872 of a uniform lesson plan by many Protestant denominations. The lessons not only were printed by denominational publishing houses but also were reprinted weekly by newspapers across the country (Lynn and Wright: 65). In a similar manner, when the American Standard Version of the Bible was released, newspapers carried large excerpts of the new version. As the debate flourished during these years, public schools felt constrained to remove from the curriculum the Bible and books containing biblical passages.

New study methods in denominational curricula. The Bible continued as the major resource in most Protestant and Catholic curricula (Pease). The Old Testament and Talmud were used extensively in Jewish schools (Gartner: 138, 139). But during these years major changes occurred in approaches to Bible study.

John Vincent developed a twenty-step model for individual Bible study in 1877. The future Methodist bishop assumed that one of the chief purposes of Bible study is devotional. He advised owning two Bibles, the second one being "suitable for carrying in your pocket to the shop or on the railroad train" (1877: 13). In addition to committing something to memory each day from the Bible, he suggested that the best method of study was to break down the Bible into component parts for study: study the words of Scripture using a concordance; study phrases, paragraphs, chapters, and whole books.

The most common method used in teacher training classes was to provide a set of questions on a variety of topics, from doctrinal issues to personal and social problems, along with answers consisting of biblical verses. The curriculum guidelines prepared for church schools revealed much the same approach with a heavy stress on memorization of verses (Russell). New forms of biblical instruction emerged with the new century. In 1901 the Rev. Robert G. Boville of New York City, noting the inactivity of children during the summer, began the daily vacation Bible school movement. Ministers in Colorado and North Dakota instituted plans for Bible study for credit in high school and college in 1910. In these states, courses concerning biblical history and literature were developed (Lotz: 32, 33). Some school districts, like Gary, Indiana, began programs which released students at various times during the week for instruction at other agencies in the community, including the places of worship. In Lotz's survey of the objectives of these various programs, he, as a progressive educator, was dismayed to find that many were Bible-centered rather than child-centered. "Some had in mind the practical use of the Bible, such as learning to locate the different books of the Bible; some had in mind the memorization of certain passages from the Bible; some had in mind a general mastery of the contents of the Bible; and some had in mind the cultivation of the spirit characteristic of the

Bible" (72). He estimated that from 75 to 90 percent of the teachers were literalists or fundamentalists. His survey found that many weekday church schools stressed memorization of Bible verses, for such diverse reasons as helping to learn table graces and hymns (101).

Lotz, like his colleagues in the newly formed Religious Education Association (1903), believed that more attention should be given to the historical background of the Scriptures and that religious education should begin with the needs and interests of the young students. In adult education, the American Institute of Sacred Literature, a correspondence program begun by William Rainey Harper, organized materials around issues and problems confronting modern men and women. In these materials, use of memorization decreased while more concern was devoted to the situation of the learner.

Bible reading in the public schools. The first significant court case on Bible reading in the public schools occurred in Cincinnati in 1870. Between 1880 and 1920, a number of similar cases occurred in Wisconsin, Illinois, Nebraska, and Louisiana (Boles: 33 n. 68; Steiner, 1924.) There is virtually no disagreement in the opinions of the judges and lawyers in these cases that the Bible is a significant literary work. Even those who opposed the Bible in the public schools expressed some reluctance not to use it. The point of argument centered on the question: Is the Bible a sectarian book? If it is, then it should be banned from public schools because of the divisiveness it will cause. And most of the court decisions concluded that because the Bible is viewed as the word of God, it is a sectarian book. (This battle about the Bible as a sectarian book was very much a part of the *Abingdon* v. *Schempp* case in 1963.) /2/

Contrary to the belief that there was widespread agreement on Bible reading in the public schools during these years, sources such as Daniel Unger's dissertation on the situation in Pennsylvania reveal that the period was filled with legal hassles both in the state's courts and in the legislature. In 1895 in *Stevenson* v. *Hanyon*, Bible reading was supported, a position reaffirmed in 1898 in *Curran* v. *White*. Despite, or perhaps because of, opposition to Bible reading, supporters were able to have the legislature pass an amendment to the School Code in 1913 requiring the use of the Bible (Unger).

The Bible Viewed as a Guide for Living

Theologians and educators who spoke of the Bible's divine origin often added that it was important to study because it served as a personal and social compass of salvation and a guide to civilization. Some believed it was in fact the only necessary source of moral teaching. Luther Townsend, the young Methodist theologian, wrote that the Bible "arms conscience with a divine power, awakes religious sensibilities, refines the moral sentiments, evolves devout affections, displays well-directed philanthropies, promotes denominations to do exactly right at all times and in all things; . . . leads to industry, inspires courage, patriotism, and intelligence; [and the Bible] will aid in establishing the prosperity and perpetuity of the American Republic." Recalling what he had learned in his European studies about higher criticism, he wrote in conclusion: "Far, far above the fogs and mists with which immoral men and women, English free-thinkers, German free-livers, and American free-lovers, have sought to fill the sky, Bible morality stands unrebuked and unchallenged" (85, 86, 188).

Written at the beginning of the period under investigation here, Townsend's defense of the Bible as the all-consuming authority for life contrasts sharply with a later judgment (1916) by Union Seminary President, A. C. McGiffert:

> Biblical criticism has had theological effects of the very greatest significance. It is not that simply our view of the Bible has changed as a result of it, but our whole view of religious authority has changed. As we have learned not to think of the Bible as a final and infallible authority, as the ultimate court of appeal in all matters of human concern, we have come to see that there is no such authority and that we need none. (326, 327)

The Only Rule for Faith and Practice

For many persons in this period, the Bible was more than a book to guide daily conduct; it was the *only* rule of faith and conduct, as the Chautauqua material indicates. In 1883 Jesse Hurlbut commented: "By this we mean that the Bible contains God's law, and was given to us as the standard of life. It contains 'the only rule, and the sufficient rule, for our faith and practice.' No doctrine is to be accepted unless it is in accordance with the teachings of the Bible, and no law is binding which conflicts with the higher law of the Scriptures" (176). In C.L.S.C. literature, the last lengthy attempt to argue that the Bible was the only rule of faith and life was found in Weidner's article: "The greatest minds that ever lived have accepted and do accept the Bible as their only guide and hope of life. The Bible alone solves the great problem of salvation; it alone meets the deepest yearnings of our human being; it alone furnished the power by God's grace of perfecting holiness . . . " (445, 446).

In the wake of the Edgerton, Wisconsin, court decision banning Bible reading, numerous denominational bodies passed resolutions at their national meetings condemning the presumed omission of the Bible in public schools. The Presbyterian General Assembly at Syracuse, May 26, 1890, stated: "As the Bible is the source of the highest moral teaching, we regard its exclusion from our public schools as a menace to national welfare." Fundamentalists and Catholics were also disturbed by the apparent turning away from this book, which they considered the ultimate authority on morality. A byproduct of the higher criticism movement was the questioning of the authority of the Bible, as McGiffert's comment indicated. In the early 1890s, such books as Washington Gladden's *Who Wrote the Bible?* and Orello Cone's *Gospel-Criticism and Historical Christianity* admitted that the Bible was difficult to understand and to use in daily life. By sharing their reservations about the efficacy of a complex book, they helped to push open the door of doubt about the Bible's merit as the only tool of salvation.

The Guide for Civilization

In 1872 the General Conference of the Methodist Episcopal Church concluded that the Bible was "the charter of our liberties and the inspiration of our civilization." This thread runs throughout religious and educational documents and personal correspondence for the duration of the period under study. A common sentiment was voiced in a letter written by a C.L.S.C. member as the country erupted in a financial depression in 1893. "The Bible is absolutely essential to mercantile, political, social, and literary life. . . . Had the spirit of Christianity prevailed in Congress, in the office, and in the mill, our Ship of State would not be tossing in perilous waters" (Durrell).

Zalmon Richards, quoted in the U. S. Commissioner of Education's Report of 1888, was not surprised to find "the seeds of anarchy, socialism, communism, infidelity, insubordination, and licentiousness" in the youth of the country when the school curriculum was stripped of everything moral and religious (1888: 623). Courts in Kansas and Minnesota in the early 1920s echoed similar sentiments. "What is more natural than turning to that Book for moral precepts which for ages has been regarded by the majority of the peoples of the civilized nations as the fountain of moral teachings" (Minnesota, 214 N.W. at 18; cited by Boles: 75, 76).

Educational Responses

Educators who wished to retain the Bible as a book of moral instruction had to respond to three crises.

The emergence of a scientific spirit. The findings of emerging fields of science and higher criticism challenged the Bible as the most effective moral guide for the "modern" world. For some the best way to resolve the conflicting claims of science and religion was to declare that they were mutually exclusive arenas. The Bible was a rule of conduct and guide to faith and not a scientific textbook. As John Vincent once remarked, "The object of the Bible is the revelation of religious facts and of duty, and not to give us solutions to the mysteries of science or religion." He reinforced his position by quoting a sixteenth-century cardinal and Vatican librarian, Baronius, who had written, "the purpose of holy Scripture is to teach us how to go to heaven, and not how the heavens go" (1879: 53). Public educators, such as Austin Bierbower of Chicago, argued that the quarrels the Bible raised were outweighing the questionable benefits gained from spending a small portion of the school day reading moral passages. Interestingly, he favored dropping the reading of the Bible, unless there was opposition to it (U.S. Commissioner of Education, 1891:627). This stand was reinforced by U.S. Commissioner of Education William T. Harris in 1903, who argued that the approaches to the truth by science (used in the public schools) and religion were different: "The principle of religious instruction is authority; that of secular instruction is demonstration and verification. It is obvious that these two principles should not be brought into the same school, but separated as widely as possible" (1841–43).

A changing school population. The influx of immigrant children and the increased number of female students staying for more years of schooling sent school population soaring. In 1880 there were 9 million students in elementary and secondary schools. By 1920 the number was 21.5 million. Most impressive was the growth of the public high school. In 1875 there were fewer than 25,000 secondary students; by 1900, there were 500,000 (U.S. Bureau of the Census: 207–210, 214). As immigration brought many new students from diverse religious and cultural backgrounds to the public schools, teachers and administrators could make fewer assumptions about what parents wanted taught. Many of the court cases involving a church-state issue in schools were based on a religious group disputing the way their members' faith was being jeopardized in the schools. For example, the Edgarton, Wisconsin, case of 1890 involved Roman Catholic parents who argued that the use of the King James version of the Bible was incorrect and incomplete and that teachers needed to be better trained in how to interpret the text considering the diverse student population. The five Protestant judges agreed with their point. In 1915 the highest court in Louisiana found that both Jews and Catholics were discriminated against when the King James version was used. In 1922 the Central Conference of American Rabbis produced a book, *Why the Bible Should Not Be Read in Public Schools,* another example of the feeling that the schools should not favor one religious tradition over others.

Parochial schools were one response to the perceived difficulty of moral instruction in the public schools. Bishop John J. Keane, who also was rector of the Catholic University, wrote in the *Independent* that logic dictated that the public school had to be Christian if Americans wanted a Christian society. Keane argued that if the public school system could not be Christian, then an alternative school system had to be established. He chided those who hoped somehow that a general morality could be adequately presented in public schools (U.S. Commissioner of Education, 1891:625, 626). A number of school officials, quoted in the same article, disagreed.

The new role of women in society. As the suffrage movement gained momentum during this period and more and more spokespersons for women's rights came forward, attention was given also to the use of the Bible to "put women in their place." By the late 1860s and early 1870s,

Elizabeth Cady Stanton was giving private talks to women in which she pointed out that the biblical picture of maternity as a curse is the result of Bible translation by men and for men (*Des Moines Register*, July 19, 1871). By 1895 Stanton and Mrs. Robert Ingersoll had become the principal authors of *The Woman's Bible* (Old Testament, 1895, New Testament, 1898). Their English translation utilized the results of higher criticism, but their text tended to be polemical (Rossi). Other women, such as Julia E. Smith of Connecticut, made translations that tried to adhere to the Greek and Hebrew idioms (Sims: 149–51).

In summary, educators of the period, whether in public schools or churches, continued to hold to the belief that "wherever the Scriptures are read, and only there, do we see a higher order of civilization" (Vincent, 1891:31). Most educators in the public domain also continued to hold to a position advanced by California school officials that "the one *great* want in the public schools is a closer attention on the part of teachers and other authorities to moral instruction—to character building. To turn out good, honest, clean-living men and women should be the principal end and aim of the public schools" (U.S. Commissioner of Education, 1887:25). But changes did occur. C.L.S.C. members who completed their course of study after 1892 had a noticeably different religious curriculum from those who had graduated earlier. The frequent reference to the Bible as the "Word of God" was replaced by "the Book that describes the activities of God." This new way of speaking about the Bible must now be examined more closely.

The Bible Viewed as Great Literature

Those who viewed the Bible as providing a unique and superior moral system found their position more difficult to defend as the years passed. Major social movements conspired to weaken public support for such a view, and the evolution of higher criticism and comparative textual analysis raised questions about the infallibility of the Bible. Comparative studies of other ancient cultures and even the fairly positive new discipline of archaeology raised questions about the uniqueness of the Jewish heritage. In addition the rise of modern comparative studies of religion, fueled in part by the missionary movement, contributed to a sense that Christianity was one religion alongside others.

From Unique to Superior

In 1868 Bradford Peirce wrote a widely sold book, *The Word of God Opened: Its Inspiration, Canon, and Interpretation Considered and Illustrated*, setting out the absolute claims of divinely revealed truth. The movement of this era can be seen in a contrasting opinion expressed by M. S. Terry in 1881. Writing for the C.L.S.C., this Garrett Seminary professor mused, "Where is the race of people who have not some tradition of a creation, or a happy garden, of temptation and failure, and of a mighty flood of waters" (9). But if not unique, certainly the Bible was superior. There emerged a constant refrain in religious writing of the period emphasizing the literary superiority of the Bible. Thus, while Lyman Abbot, Congregational clergyman and editor of *Outlook*, had reservations about studying religion in public schools, he strongly favored studying the Bible for its literary merits.

> I do advocate the use of the Bible in the public schools as a means of acquainting our pupils with the laws, the literature, and the life of the ancient Hebrews, because the genius of the Hebrew people pervading their laws and their life and their literature was a spiritual genius. The United States is more intimately connected with the Hebrew people than with any other ancient people. Our literature abounds with references to the literature of the ancient Hebrews; they are probably more frequent than the references to the literature either of Greeks or Romans. No man can read the great English or American poets or authors understandingly unless he knows something of his English Bible. Historically we are more closely connected with the Hebrew people than with the Greeks. Our free institutions are all rooted in the institutions of the Hebrew people, have grown out of them. . . . A man is not a truly educated man who knows nothing of the sources and foundations of our national life, and they are found in the Bible. (221)

Public school officials expressed similar sentiments. A. P. Marble, Superintendent of Schools in Worcester, Massachusetts, stated his preference for daily Bible reading on the grounds that "first, this book is the basis of the morality of this country; and secondly, because it has so influenced our civilization, and it so permeates our literature, that ignorance of it is more noticeable and less excusable than no acquaintance with Shakespeare" (U.S. Commissioner of Education, 1891:628).

Educational Responses

The Bible as literature. Not everyone could support the position that the study of the Bible for its literary and historic values was appropriate. Journalists, in addition to some members of religious communities, saw it as a thinly disguised strategy for returning religious indoctrination to the schools (Boles: 277–80). One of the most outspoken critics of the study of the Bible in public schools was E. Haldeman-Julius, publisher of the "Little Blue Books," a series of inexpensive paperbacks that were widely sold in the first decades of the twentieth century. One of his commissioned books, *The Bible: Should It Be in the School Room?* by Franklin Stiener, offered fifteen reasons for the exclusion of Bible study from public schools (38–61). A number of his reasons consist of attacks upon the literary merits of the Bible. He argued that the book was dull, outdated, and that Abe Lincoln was greater than Abraham, Ben Franklin a wiser and clearer man morally than Solomon, and Edison did more good than Ezekiel. It should not be taught, he added, because its stories show oriental tyranny and "kingcraft" in addition to the "subjugation and slavery of women." Steiner concluded that to teach that the Bible was a special book above all others was wrong, and he preferred to accept the poet Lowell's observation that "Slowly the Bible of the race is writ, and not on paper leave or leaves of stone; each age, each kindred, adds a verse to it. . . . "

What the courts of Nebraska (1902) and Illinois (1910) seemed to confirm was that it was very difficult not to accept the Bible as a sectarian book. But efforts to change state constitutions to include regular Bible readings in the public school curriculum failed, as for example in Illinois between 1920 and 1922.

Proper translations and study guides. The interest in the Bible that was spurred by higher criticism, archaeological discoveries, and the publication of the British revisions of the New Testament (1881) and Old Testament (1885) and the American Standard Bible (1901) promoted many other individual and group projects either to translate the Bible or to provide additional study guides. Some of the translations were by scholars (Moffatt's 1901 New Testament), and some were published for specialized audiences (the *Young People's Bible*, 1901). From 1900 to 1920, over twenty-five English translations appeared (Kubo and Specht: 208-13). Other works, such as Moulton's *Modern Bible Reader* (1907) were called translations but were actually study guides or attempts to modernize the language. There was no lack of books about the Bible. Matthew Arnold's *God and the Bible* (1903), which argued for comparative studies of the miracle stories, was a popular book. The International Lesson series, however, was slow to change. In the early 1890s their lessons did not show evidence of the distinctive literary forms—folktales, oral traditions, myths— which higher critics found in Genesis (Lankard).

The Bible Viewed from the Perspective of Critical Scholarship

A fundamental dilemma gripped those who wanted to make the Bible relevant in the age of "robber barons" and the Gibson girl. To embrace everything the biblical scholars uncovered was to invite the criticism that the Bible was no different from any other book, which would destroy the central authority that the Bible had for most religious heritages. As the findings from various scholars raised questions about the originality or authenticity of biblical passages, Protestants especially were galvanized into groups that either supported or denied the evidence. The major groups, which often cut across denominational lines, were the fundamentalists, the conservative orthodox, the evangelical liberals, and the scientific modernists. /3/ The letters from C.L.S.C. readers suggest that most were in the evangelical liberal camp or the conservative orthodox group.

The Support of Archaeology

Most Protestants, bewildered by the findings of the higher critics, found comfort in the work of the archaeologists. For the most part, the discoveries of the nineteenth century seemed to confirm biblical statements. Travel conditions in the 1860s made the Holy Land more accessible than before, which encouraged trips by many American ministers, including John Vincent. Growing interest in archaeology led to the formation of the Society of Biblical Archaeology in 1870. Journals like *The Chautauquan* devoted space to stories about the explorations and findings of archaeologists such as James Breasted and their discoveries, including the unearthing of Hammurabi's monolith in Persia (1909). In 1880 an active participant in the Society of Biblical Archaeology, J. E. Kittredge, addressed the summer Chautauqua assembly. He traced the brief history of modern archaeology and spoke about the significance of the digs for biblical stories. Because the "monuments of the past" corroborated the scriptural records, Kittredge encouraged the audience to embrace the budding science. Whenever he concluded each of his major points, he thundered, "The Word of the Lord endureth forever," to which his listeners responded with great applause (Kittredge).

Another reason religious groups were inclined to be receptive to the work of archaeologists was the conviction that a better understanding of the Bible could be gained by learning more about the historical context of the biblical writers. Archaeology helped to recreate life situations of the past. As one of the first books of the Circle declared: "In order to appreciate the meaning, the force, and the beauty of the sacred writings, it is necessary to be familiar with the geography of biblical countries, and of the former and present appearance of Scripture places" (Peirce: 101).

The Absorption of Higher Criticism

By 1880 higher criticism in Europe had already celebrated its diamond anniversay (Grant; Neill). Although the synoptic problem—or the literary similarity of the first three gospels—was little known in America until Theodore Parker, a Unitarian preacher from Boston, translated a major work in 1843. By the end of the Civil War Ernst Renan's *Life of Jesus* and K. H. Graf's monumental research on the "four document" theory of the Pentateuch had appeared in English translations. Religion writers tended to react to the higher critics in two ways. Many of the early books used by the C.L.S.C. (which were often taken from commercial publishing companies or denominational presses) ridiculed or attacked the continental professors. Townsend felt they had brought much confusion into the theological world. John Hurst, a Methodist bishop who had himself studied in Europe, commented: "Many of our younger theological writers have studied in German universities, and in some instances have brought over with them some views which would have been in better place if left in the Fatherland. As they advance, however, they indicate a disposition to lay aside some of the superfluities called 'Higher Criticism,' and to adapt themselves to the sphere of ascertained Scriptural truth" (126). Until the 1890s many American theologians resisted the findings and held to Mosaic authorship of the Pentateuch.

William Rainey Harper, the Baptist leader who became the first president of the University of Chicago and founder of the Religious Education Association, was one of these. Another was James M. Freeman, who accepted both the literal view that the Ten Commandments were written on two stone tablets and the critical view that other parts of the Pentateuch were written by a number of authors (25–26, 32).

The second major way in which religion writers reacted to biblical scholarship was one of guarded acceptance, which eventually developed into a strategy of absorption. In 1889 Theodore Flood, the editor of *The Chautauquan* and a conservative, pleaded for a fair trial for higher criticism, after explaining its methods.

> By higher criticism, we mean literary investigation or research. But what is literary investigation? Its aim is to discover by examining the words and style of a book, and by comparison of the words and style, to ascertain who wrote a given book and the date of his work and his motive in writing it and other matters of interest in interpreting the book. Applied to the Bible, the Higher Criticism (or literary criticism) proceeds just as it would in examining any profane author of antiquity. . . .
>
> It is plain enough that the truth cannot be harmed by any new knowledge. Those who believe that the Bible is the truth of God have no fear of literary criticism. Let us have all there is. . . . We must give literary criticism a free hand. (212, 213)

The major event in Chautauqua history that signaled the effort to embrace and eventually absorb higher criticism occurred in the summer of 1892. William Rainey Harper delivered a series of addresses on "The Rational and the Rationalistic Higher Criticism." His major lecture attacked both biblical literalism and rationalistic criticism. The result of the former was "a degradation of the God it was desired to honor, a dictating to Him how to act and what to do." And what had rationalistic higher criticism made of the Bible? "A few harmless stories; a few well-meant, but mistaken warnings; a few dead songs; many unfulfilled predications; a large amount of fairly good literature" (7). Yet he admired research that was done in the proper spirit of trying to illuminate biblical truths.

Interest in comparative religions and the development of form criticism were emphasized in the final years of the nineteenth century. Adolf Harnack's lectures on the organization of the early church were published in 1899 under the title *The Essence of Christianity*. Two other widely sold books of the new century, Albert Schweitzer's *Quest for the Historical Jesus* and James Frazer's *The Golden Bough*, a classic in comparative religion, may have made older Chautauquans, like fundamentalists, uneasy. For younger religious leaders in America, including Shailer Mathews, Dean of the Divinity School at the University of Chicago, such investigations were welcome (Bray; Mathews, 1906). Mathews wrote the last major article on higher criticism in *The Chautauquan*. He accepted the tenets of the movement and spoke positively of the theological schools in Europe, mentioning with enthusiasm the leading scholars—Harnack, Ritschl, and

Herman. He was intrigued by the approach of *Religionsgeschichte*, which he saw as "a genuine theology from a study of religious evolution in general and of Christianity in particular." This approach, Mathews explained, did not begin from a basis that assumed that the Scriptures were inerrant (Mathews, 1913). Katharine Lee Bates, in a book on American literature in 1907, summarized the feelings of a number of the evangelical liberals when she said: "higher criticism has lost its terrors . . . " (227).

Educational Responses

New interest in biblical geography. One of the most fascinating reactions of religious groups to archaeology and, to a lesser extent, to higher criticism was the interest displayed in geographical studies. Sunday school papers and religious publications were filled with advertisements for Holy Land atlases, travel guides to the world of the Old and New Testaments, and concordances for biblical terms. Jesse Hurlbut's *Story of the Bible* (1904) sold more than three million copies. Sunday school conventions were noted for memorization contests of place names and personal names from the Bible.

The epitome of this interest in biblical geography was John Vincent's Palestine Class (L. Vincent: 91). Vincent sparked interest in the Bible by building a scale model of Palestine in the yard of the church; the Dead Sea, major cities, and highways were included. Vincent developed sets of questions that were used to determine degrees of knowledge about the Holy Land. Songs were created that set biblical places in rhymes to facilitate memorization. Vincent spread this technique for learning throughout the Midwest when he moved from New Jersey to Illinois. Beginning in 1874, many features of biblical geography were introduced to the thousands of Sunday school teachers who attended Chautauqua conferences. A huge relief map of Palestine was constructed, and models of the Jerusalem tabernacle and an Egyptian pyramid were built at the New York lakeside retreat center. A volunteer dressed as a Muslim demonstrated the prayers of that faith.

Why this seemingly disproportionate amount of interest in biblical geography? It might be argued that it was a fad or that keeping up with archaeological discoveries was a mind-expanding avocation. Could it also have been a vehicle for by-passing discussions about denominational doctrines? Might such interest in geography also have been a convenient way to avoid consideration of the really serious questions of biblical authorship?

Attempts to avoid controversy. Textbooks of the period show little interest in higher criticism per se. Public schools in particular were inclined to view the Bible as a source of morality. In order to avoid controversy, such questions as the authorship of the Pentateuch were not discussed. Biblical content was gradually eliminated from other textbooks, especially in the sciences. Wittmer's study of geology textbooks shows that authors became less inclined to give a theistic viewpoint or to claim that geology agreed with Christian doctrine. The same was true of books in astronomy, chemistry, and biology.

In curriculum material used in Sunday schools, parochial schools, or Torah schools, there was some mention of higher criticism, but it was not extensive and was more likely to come at the seminary level. In his inaugural address Kaufmann Kohler, President of Hebrew Union College, noted: "Yes, a store-house of spiritual power the theological school must be, and it is foolish and wrong to evade the discussion of vexatious problems of the day. You fail to train men of power for the ministry, if you ignore or simply condemn the Higher Biblical Criticism and Comparative Religion and Law as detrimental to the faith or to reverence for the Bible" (Gartner: 115). There was little discussion in parochial schools (Kane). Within denominations, those who were inclined to accept higher criticism were those who were more liberal. These individuals were likely to support the Religious Education Association and to accept theories of developmental stages of human growth, which were used to determine content for different levels of curriculum materials (Pease; Maring; Johnson).

Summary

In 1880 the biblical foundation of the Protestant life seemed secure and victorious. In 1920 some, such as Shailer Mathews, were equally sure that the rejection of the infallibility of the Bible and the use of the scientific method would likewise mark a triumphant day for the Christian faith. The period reveals that three lines of defense were presented by evangelical liberal and conservative orthodox leaders. The first held that the Bible was the revealed word of God, authoritative without question, divinely inspired, and infallible. Despite the warnings of apologists such as R. F. Weidner, many C.L.S.C. readers compromised this stance to hold that the Bible *contained* the word of God. The second defense was that the Bible contained rules for life, indeed, for some the Bible was the only rule of life. Higher criticism and comparative religion made evident to others that finding simple rules for life in the Bible was not so easy as they had been led to believe. These two lines of defense occupied a significantly less important place in religious education literature after 1895. The third position regarding the role of the Bible grew in importance after that date. In it, the Bible was presented as a repository of unique literature. For a while the field of archaeology seemed to support such a claim to uniqueness, but archaeology relied on comparative data. The findings of scholars in the area of comparative religion forced the Circle members to admit that the Bible messages were not unique. Higher criticism brought evidence that the Israelites were not so unique a community as had been believed before. Increasingly, the references to the Bible's literature described it as the best literature.

The changes in attitude toward the Bible were accompanied by changes of attitude toward biblical scholarship. At first, despite the country's commitment to public and higher education, doubts were expressed that academic investigations outside the realm of archaeology would aid biblical faith. Those who feared that such scholastic labors would disrupt faith ridiculed and leveled charges of infidelity against some of the pioneering work in the field of higher criticism. There is some indication that educators welcomed archaeology because it seemed to support biblical piety and also because it was an area free of denominational squabbles. Some religionists and most public educators ignored the findings of the higher critics, but the dominant response came to be that of absorption. Those who followed this approach argued that the findings of the higher critics did not contradict essential Christian truths but only extended what had been known previously. The public argument seems to have ended, and the literature reveals little evidence of confrontation after 1895.

In the public schools the period marked a time of disputes. The courts upheld the contention of Roman Catholics, Jews, atheists, and liberal church members that the Bible was a sectarian book. Educators increasingly agreed to limit Bible reading because it was controversial but tried to cling to it for moral instruction purposes. The general attitude toward the Bible is best represented by Lyman Abbott's plea for an educated piety. Groups like the C.L.S.C. had put so much trust into the sphere of education that their allegiance to the higher critics and its subscription to their methods was virtually inevitable. By 1914 the C.L.S.C. placed more faith in the scholarly analysis of religious questions than it did in the individual's untutored reading of the Bible. For the Protestant constituency of the nation, the Bible was no longer the central guide to God's revealed plan for salvation. The key to the new educational piety that marked the Protestant style of life was "scientific reasoning."

NOTES

/1/   The Circle was a part of the wider Chautauqua movement. It became America's first successful book club claiming members from Jewish, Catholic, and Protestant traditions. It was established to meet the needs of those individuals who desired a "college outlook" on life and religion. Its founder was John Vincent, a Methodist minister who had gained a national reputation for his successful training of Sunday School teachers (Vincent: 1886).

/2/   Before the Supreme Court's ruling in 1963, a total of thirty-seven states permitted Bible reading in their public schools. No state constitution prohibits Bible reading as such; twelve states and the District of Columbia have required that the Bible be read (Boles: 48).

/3/   For a more thorough discussion of these categories, see Hudson (*Religion in America:* 269–81) and Handy ("Fundamentalism and Modernism," *Religion in Life* 24: 388ff.). Briefly, fundamentalists believed the Bible was the inerrant word of God; the conservative orthodox maintained the Bible was the ultimate truth but acknowledged minor textual flaws; the evangelical liberals granted multiple authorship of the Bible and held to it as the best "rulebook"; the scientific modernists tended to see it as a good book that contained numerous textual errors.

WORKS CONSULTED

Abbott, Lyman
1901   "Editor's Comment." *Outlook* 68 (May 25): 221.

Arthur, William
1880   *The Tongue of Fire, or the True Power of Christianity.* New York: Harper and Brothers. First printed in 1856.

Bates, Katharine Lee
1907   *American Literature.* Chautauqua: The Chautauqua Press.

The Bible in the Public Schools
1870   New York: Da Capo Press. 1967 reprint.

Blodgett, H.
1898   "Sunday Schools." *U. S. Commissioner of Education Report 1896–97,* I: 293–423. Washington, DC: United States Government Printing Office.

Boles, Donald E.
1965   *The Bible, Religion, and the Public Schools.* Ames: Iowa State University Press.

Bray, F. Chapin
1900   "Topics of the Hour." *The Chautauquan* 30/4 (January): 356, 357.

Cole, Stewart
1931   *History of Fundamentalism.* New York: R. R. Smith.

Commager, Henry S., ed.
1962   "Foreword." In *McGuffey's Fifth Eclectic Reader.* 1879 ed. New York: New American Library.

De Vries, S. J.
1962   "History of Biblical Criticism." *The Interpreter's Dictionary of the Bible.* New York: Abingdon Press. 1:413–18.

Durrell, J. M.
1893   Letter to Kate F. Kimball, Executive Secretary of the Chautauqua Literary and Scientific Circle. Found at Smith Library, Chautauqua.

Flood, Theodore
1889   "What is the Higher Criticism?" *The Chautauquan* 10/2 (November): 212, 213.
1893   "Editorial Outlook." *The Chautauquan* 32/5 (August): 628, 629.

Freeman, James M.
1880   *The Book of Books.* New York: Phillips and Hunt.

Gartner, Lloyd P., ed.
1969   *Jewish Education in the United States.* New York: Teachers College Press.

Grant, Robert
1948   *The Bible in the Church.* New York: Macmillan.

Handy, Robert
1955   "Fundamentalism and Modernism in Perspective." *Religion in Life* 24/3 (Summer): 381–94.

Harper, William R.
1892   "The Rational and Rationalistic Higher Criticism." *Chautauqua Assembly Herald,* August 4.

Harris, William T.
1903   *Independent* 55 (August 6): 1841–43.

Hudson, Winthrop
1965   *Religion in America.* New York: Charles Scribner's Sons.

Hurlbut, Jesse L.
1883   "The Bible from God through Man." *The Chautauquan* 4/3 (December): 176.

Hurst, John
    1890   *Short History of the Church in the United States,*
                            A.D. *1492–1890.* New York: Chautauqua Press.

Johnson, Frank, ed.
    1907   *Bible Teaching by Modern Methods.* London: Andrew Melrose.

Kane, John Joseph
    1955   *Catholic-Protestant Conflicts in America.* Chicago, Regnery.

Kittredge, J. E.
    1881   "Bible History in the Light of Modern Research." *The Chautauquan* 2/3 (December): 150–56. Lecture given August 14, 1880.

Kubo, Sakae, and Specht, Walter
    1975   *So Many Versions?* Grand Rapids, MI: Zondervan. Pp. 208–13.

Lankard, Frank
    1927   *The History of the American Sunday School Curriculum.* New York: Abingdon Press.

Lotz, Philip H.
    1925   *Current Week-Day Religious Education.* New York: Abingdon Press.

Lynn, Robert W., and Wright, Elliot
    1971   *The Big Little School.* New York: Harper and Row.

Maring, N. H.
    1958   "Baptists and Changing Views of the Bible, 1865–1918." *Foundations* 1 (July): 52–78.

Mathews, Shailer
    1906   *Biblical World* 27 (January): 59–62.
    1913   "Contemporary Theological Movements in Europe." *The Chautauquan* 70/3 (May): 309–10.

McGiffert, A. C.
    1916   "The Progress of Theological Thought During the Past Fifty Years." *American Journal of Theology* 19 (July): 326, 327.

Neill, Stephen
1964   *The Interpretation of the New Testament, 1861–
                  1961.* London: Oxford University Press.

Nichols, James
1956   *History of Christianity.* New York: Roland Press.

Pease, George W.
1904   *An Outline of a Bible-School Curriculum.* Chi-
                  cago: University of Chicago Press.

Peirce, Bradford K.
1868   *The Word of God Opened: Its Inspiration, Can-
                  on, and Interpretation Considered and Illustrat-
                  ed.* New York: Phillips and Hunt.

Rossi, Alice
1973   *Feminist Papers.* New York: Columbia University
                  Press. Pp. 401–6.

Russell, Charles T.
1897   *Studies in the Scriptures: A Helping Hand for
                  Bible Students.* 7 volumes. Allegheny, PA: n.p.

Schlesinger, Arthur M., Sr.
1967   *A Critical Period in American Religion.* Philadel-
                  phia: Fortress. Reprint of an article from the *Mas-
                  sachusetts Historical Society Proceedings* 64
                  (October 1930–June 1932). 523–46.

Schmucker, Samuel C.
1913   *The Meaning of Evolution.* Meadville, PA: Chau-
                  tauqua-Century Press.

Sims, P. Marion
1936   *The Bible in America.* New York: Wilson-
                  Erickson.

Steiner, Franklin
1924   *The Bible: Should It Be in the School Room?* Gir-
                  ard, KS: Haldeman-Julius Co.

Terry, M. S.
1881   *Man's Antiquity and Language.* New York: Phil-
                  lips and Hunt.

Townsend, Luther T.
1885   *The Bible and Other Ancient Literature in the
                        Nineteenth Century.* New York: Chautauqua
                        Press.

Unger, Daniel R.
1969   *The Use of the Bible in Pennsylvania Public
                        Schools: 1834–1963.* Unpublished doctoral disserta-
                        tion, University of Pittsburgh.

U.S. Bureau of the Census
1960   *Historical Statistics of the United States, Colonial
                        Times to 1957.* Washington, DC: U.S. Government
                        Printing Office.

U.S. Commissioner of Education
1887   *Report of the Commissioner of Education, 1885–
                        86.* Washington, DC: Government Printing Office.

1891   *Report of the Commissioner of Education, 1888–
                        89.* Washington, DC: Government Printing Office.
                        1:429–38, 622–34.

Vincent, John H.
1879   *Christian Evidences.* New York: Phillips and
                        Hunt.

1882   *Biblical Exploration, or How to Study the Bible.*
                        New York: Phillips and Hunt.

1886   *The Chautauqua Movement.* Boston: Chautauqua
                        Press.

1891   "Sunday Readings." *The Chautauquan* 14/1
                        (October): 31.

1910   "Bible Reading." *The Chautauquan* 60/1 (Septem-
                        ber): 122–23.

Vincent, Leon
n.d.   *John Heyl Vincent.* New York: Macmillan.

Weidner, R. F.
1889, 1890   "Recent Objections to the Bible Answered." *The
                        Chautauquan* 10/3 (December); 10/4 (January).

Wittmer, Paul W.
1969   *The Secularization of Geology Textbooks in the
                        United States in the Nineteenth Century.* ERIC
                        Document ED 022 684.

VII

New Interest in the Bible:
The Contexts of Bible Study Today

Boardman W. Kathan

The purpose of this essay is to examine the situation today regarding the study of the Bible in churches, synagogues, and their schools. Excluded from this survey are colleges, universities, and seminaries, where most of the biblical scholarship is done as well as the lion's share of the systematic, comprehensive instruction. Also omitted from scrutiny have been the public elementary and secondary schools, where a number of projects have been developed since the U.S. Supreme Court decisions of 1962 and 1963 in prayer and Bible reading. The focus of this article is on the use of the Bible in the private or religious sector, where legal and constitutional questions of church-state relations are not germane. Finally, the essay does not address the whole area of private, devotional, or inspirational uses of the Bible; it is a description of popular programs and widely distributed resources in churches and synagogues, set within the context of the struggle for the meaning, interpretation, and application of the Bible for problems in the world today.

Preliminary Observations

First, there continues to be a wide gap between biblical scholarship and Bible study, between the groves of academe and the churches and synagogues, between the clergy and laity. Local congregations cannot keep up with the rapid changes in biblical interpretation and exegesis. Just when the concepts of the "unfolding drama of the Bible," "biblical theology," and the historical-critical method were beginning to permeate the adult Bible classes, a new generation of scholars began to proclaim the lack of unity in the Bible, "the crisis of biblical theology," and the bankruptcy or the end of the historical-critical method. The situation is fluid and changing. No single book emerged in the 1970s that could express the spirit of the times or set the trend for the future as had Harry Emerson Fosdick's *A Guide to Understanding the Bible* in the 1930s or Bernhard Anderson's *Rediscovering the Bible* in the 1950s. Yet a number of voices announced the end of the old and the beginning of the new.

The second observation is that there continue to be lines of division among the various ideological schools of thought regarding the Bible. The modernist-fundamentalist controversy of the 1920s has been revived with new alliances and fresh arguments. Roman Catholic scholars have joined forces with Protestants on some cooperative enterprises, but resistance to Vatican II reforms lingers on. Many conservative Protestant scholars have embraced the historical-critical method, but they are divided over theories of the authority and inspiration of the Scriptures as well as other issues.

The third observation is that the Bible is an enormously popular book. It is estimated that more than eight million Bibles are purchased in the U.S. each year. *Publishers Weekly* for February 13, 1978, reported that more than twenty-three million copies of The Living Bible had been sold by 1977, more than ten million of the Good News Bible, and more than nine million of the New English Bible. Millions of the King James Version editions continue to be distributed as well as the Revised Standard Version. The Catholic Jerusalem Bible has gone over the million mark, and so has the evangelical Protestant New American Standard Bible. The most recent evangelical Bible, the New International Version, has already sold more than one million copies. These statistics prove that the Bible is purchased but do not demonstrate that the Bible is studied.

The fourth observation is that adult Bible study continues to be the most common form of adult education in the churches. One denomination, the United Presbyterian Church of the U.S.A., reported in 1978 through its research division, *Presbyterian Panel,* that a majority of the study groups in which its members and elders participated during the previous year focused on the Bible. What is true for the Presbyterians can be shown to be true for other denominations as well. Despite the lecture method, despite the idiosyncrasies of leaders and members, this type of Bible study has survived with its deep sense of class loyalty and its strong emphasis on fellowship. As Norman Langford has pointed out in the *Westminster Dictionary of Christian Education,* the adult Bible class has in many cases clung to the evangelistic, pietistic, and moralistic ideas of a former age. /1/

General Views About the Bible

Protestant

Since the Reformation of the sixteenth century Protestants have held the Bible in high regard. They have regarded it as the word of God, the essential guide for faith and practice, and the repository of everything necessary for salvation. In opposition to the medieval Roman Catholic Church's reliance on Tradition as the major source of faith and practice, Martin Luther established the principle of *sola scriptura:* the Bible was set in judgment over all traditions and institutions. At the same time, the reformers called for the right of each individual to read and interpret the

Scriptures for himself or herself under the guidance of the Holy Spirit. In the post-Reformation period a particular view of the Bible was established in specific creeds and confessions of faith that produced a literalistic approach to the Bible. Only after the Enlightenment and the development of the historical-critical method did Protestant views of the Bible begin to change (see chaps. IV and VI above).

Roman Catholic

In reaction to the Reformation, the Council of Trent proposed the authority of the church as the criterion for interpretation of the Scriptures. The supremacy of Tradition was further enhanced when the Vatican Council of 1870 affirmed the ultimate infallible authority of the Pope in matters of faith and morals. Without detracting from the authority of tradition or the church, Vatican II promoted the reading and study of the Bible. One of the most important decrees emanatimg from the Council was the "Dogmatic Constitution on Divine Revelation" (*Dei Verbum*), which was promulgated in 1965. Article 22 states: "Easy access to sacred Scripture should be provided for all the Christian faithful" (Abbott: 125). Commentators have suggested that this is the most innovative section in the entire constitution—not since the early centuries of the church has an official document from Rome urged the availability of the Scriptures to all. Other articles of the constitution encouraged the correct translation and exposition of the Scriptures by scholars and teachers as well as the careful and prayerful study of it by clergy, religious, deacons, catechists, and all the faithful. Ten years after the council Bible study in Catholic parishes was growing rapidly, in part because of the new Catholic translations and study materials available and in part because of the great enthusiasm generated by the charismatic movement.

Jewish

The Bible has always occupied the central place in Jewish life and learning. Study of Torah is a lifelong obligation for Jews. It is the supreme *mitzvah* (commandment), and setting aside a period each day for study is as sacred a religious duty for Jews as prayer. However, study of Torah involves much more than the Pentateuch—the first five books of the Bible. It includes also the monumental rabbinic compilations, such as the Mishnah and Talmud, as well as the more popular ethical and legendary commentaries. Maimonides, the revered medieval rabbi, instructed fathers to begin to teach their sons as soon as the children began to talk, beginning with passages in Deuteronomy, especially the Shema, "Hear O Israel, the Lord our God, the Lord is One." After his sixth or seventh birthday the child was to be enrolled in a class with a teacher. Adults were encouraged to join a synagogue study group, and clubs for the study of the different commentaries were formed (S. Greenberg).

Institutional Resources

Protestant

Without a doubt the most widely used material for Bible study in Protestant churches is the Uniform Series, also known as the International Sunday School Lessons or International Bible Lessons for Christian Teaching. Originally adopted by the American Sunday School Union at its convention in 1872, the lessons have been continued by successor organizations, the International Council of Religious Education (1922) and the Division of Christian Education of the National Council of Churches (1950). The lessons are prepared today on a six-year cycle by the Committee on Uniform Series made up of selected representatives from a number of denominations. Completed outlines are then sent to the various denominations and independent publishers for adaptation and development. Included in the outlines are course, unit, and lesson titles, devotional reading, background Scripture, key verse or verses, and suggested emphases for children, youth and adults. All printed Scripture and key verses are taken from the Revised Standard Version of the Bible, although denominational publishers are free to use other translations without violating the copyright of the Committee on the Uniform Series. With modification, the principle of uniformity underlying the entire series is that on any given Sunday, churches of many different denominations would be studying the same biblical material. It was reported to the 1974 consultation on the series that a total of seventeen denominations and many independent publishers had printed over ten million pieces of study material the previous year for Sunday and church school classes. Even allowing for some unsold stock or unused copies, it is clear that millions of people of all ages are involved in the weekly study of the Bible using the Uniform Series.

In view of the criticisms of the lesson materials through the years, it is a noteworthy achievement for the Uniform Series to celebrate its centennial and to show no signs of departure from the scene. In every generation there have been efforts to scrap or to transform radically the series. Before 1900 opposition had steadily mounted against its uncritical use of the Bible and its promulgation of the same Scripture passage and lessons for all age groups. Even after a graded approach was adopted, criticism focused on its choice of passages and its uncreative teaching methods. In 1925 Willard Uphaus completed a doctoral dissertation at Yale University, "A Critical Study of the International Sunday School Lesson System." Among his conclusions were the following: (1) that the lessons failed to give an adequate idea of the rich content of the Bible, with little attention to the prophets, wisdom literature, and poetry; (2) that they did not teach the Bible according to recognized principles of psychology and pedagogy, ignoring the age group differences; and (3) that they failed to give any impression of the progress in the development of religious ideas, conveying the notion instead that the whole body of truth was handed down once for all time (Uphaus: 233–35).

The Education Commission of the International Council worked on these criticisms of the Uniform Series in the late 1920s and the 1930s. By 1945 major changes in format and organization had appeared. In 1948 a handbook of principles and procedures was developed and it has been revised and updated continually. According to the handbook, the series is a plan for reading and studying the Bible, the purpose being to help persons to know the content of the Bible and to understand its message in the light of their own experiences and relationships. The courses are designed to study in a six-year cycle material from all the canonical books. In reaction to those who would like to see personal, social, and political topics covered, the view has been held consistently that such concerns should be dealt with only as they are clearly related to the Scripture passages being studied. At the 1974 consultation, Howard Colson of the Southern Baptist Convention spoke of the assumptions behind the series from its beginning: "that dedicated and qualified representatives of evangelical denominations can work together harmoniously and effectively around an open Bible to develop appropriate and educationally fruitful lesson outlines for meeting the Bible study needs of the rank and file of the people in the local church" (Colson: 17). According to Colson, the long history and continuing success of the lessons show the truth of the statement.

Various denominations have invested millions of dollars and years of work with competent staff people to produce the most attractive and up-to-date Church school curriculum materials. Studies in depth have been made of the Faith and Life Curriculum of the United Presbyterian Church of the U.S.A., the Seabury Series of the Episcopal Church, the United Church Curriculum, and the Covenant Life Curriculum of the Presbyterian Church, U.S., and other Reformed bodies. Each curriculum attempted to utilize the best of current biblical theology and scholarship, group dynamics and psychological understanding, creative methods and audio-visual aids. For example, in 1963 Raymond S. Wolfgang concluded in his Princeton Theological Seminary thesis "An Evaluation of the Use of the Bible in the Curriculum of the United Church of Christ":

> This is not a packaged Bible course with dogmatic interpretations of the scripture and specific instructions for the teacher at each stage of a precisely planned session. This is a Bible course in that the Bible is the main resource, and biblical materials are the foundation of every concept, and the main biblical concepts are lifted out and presented as a positive way of life for today. I believe the use of the Bible in the United Church Curriculum allows the message of God to come through with understanding for the pupils at every stage of their growth. (333)

Though receiving excellent evaluations, these new curricula are now largely unused. These denominations have joined together in a consortium called the Joint Educational Development in order to develop future materials as well as to carry out other projects in youth ministry, adult education, professional development, etc.

Out of this educational partnership of a number of Protestant denominations in the United States and Canada has come "Christian Education: Shared Approaches." There are four shared approaches for congregations to choose from or to mix and match as they feel appropriate or as determined by thoughtful surveys of congregational beliefs and attitudes. These four "tracks" occupy points on a continuum from the Bible-content "Knowing the Word," based on the Uniform Series on the youth through adult levels, to the issue-centered "Doing the Word," which is basically the "Shalom resources" of the United Church of Christ. In between these two points are "Interpreting the Word" and "Living the Word." One denomination has reported that on the adult level the "Knowing the Word" or Uniform Series is outselling the other materials by anywhere from a three-to-one to a five-to-one margin, depending on the particular quarter of the year. /2/

One of the more organized, highly centralized alternatives to the Uniform Series in churches is the Bethel Bible Series, written by Harley A. Swiggum and produced by the Adult Christian Education Foundation in Madison, Wisconsin. Since the publication of the series in 1960 it has been used in thousands of congregations by close to one million students. Unlike the Uniform Series, it features a highly organized four-year training program, two years for teachers and two years for congregations. Also, instead of six-year cycles that are constantly revised, the Bethel Series has a fixed body of forty lessons, accompanied by an instructional poster for each lesson. The first objective is to provide an overview of the contents of the Bible as a basis for future in-depth study. Other objectives are: to acquaint students with basic fundamentals of both the Old Testament and the New Testament narratives; to help students see the interrelationship of events and ideas; and to give students an appreciation of some principles of interpretation. Herbert W. Chilstrom in his doctoral dissertation at New York University on the Bethel Series concluded that congregations were quite satisfied with the series and felt its results were beneficial to their programs of adult education. The series was most successful among lay teachers, but the rigid demands, especially the large quantities of material to be memorized, tended to discourage some from completing the course. Chilstrom pointed out that no revisions had been made since its inception and that the visual materials were in need of revision.

If one were to judge by sales alone, the most popular Bible study tools in the more conservative churches seem to be *Halley's Bible Handbook*, the *Scofield Reference Bible* (new, 1967), and *What the Bible Is All About* by Henrietta Mears. The *Handbook* and the Mears book are outline guides to the entire Bible, while the Scofield Bible is in reality the King James Version with notes and comments emphasizing biblical prophecy, covenants and dispensations. There is a wealth of Bible-centered curriculum material available, published by denominational firms such as Concordia and by non-denominational companies such as Gospel Light, Scripture Press, David C. Cook, Moody Press and others.

The Moody Bible Institute carries out an extensive Bible correspondence course program and also reports hundreds of groups using its material. Inter Varsity Press, which specialized for years in college campus projects, is now providing resources for church and home use as well. Two "alumnae" of the Inter Varsity Christian Fellowship, Marilyn Kunz and Catherine Schell, desiring to provide Bible study beyond the college years, inaugurated Neighborhood Bible Studies (NBS) in 1960 with a central office in Dobbs Ferry, New York. Since that time they have prepared twenty study guides to the books of the Bible, and well over one million copies have been sold. Although more often initiated by people of more conservative Protestant convictions, the Bible study groups now include Catholics as well as people of little or no religious background. An emphasis of the NBS is on group discussion skills, but a key purpose is to use Bible study for evangelistic outreach. Consider, for example, statements of purpose in the introductory booklet: "to bring each person to consider God's invitation in Jesus Christ" and "to share the gospel of Christ with his neighbors." Alternatives to the geographical neighborhood are groups of work associates or colleagues. Regional coordinators serve to help start groups and to set up area meetings for leaders once or twice a year. One of the strengths of the program, besides the discussion technique, is the inductive method of studying the Bible. Participants are urged to bring any translation they choose and to approach the Bible with open minds and hearts. They are also urged to "bring a non-Christian friend."

It is clear that the Bible study movement is growing by leaps and bounds. Networks of groups are expanding around the country. One may obtain information about many of them through notices and newsletters at Christian bookstores. In some cases the networks are developed by the publishers. For example, the Harold Shaw Publishers in Wheaton, Illinois, offers a series of sixteen inductive Bible study books for neighborhood, student, and church groups called the "Fisherman Bible Study Guides." Another approach is exemplified by the Bible Study Fellowship directed by A. Weatherall-Johnson in Oakland, California. These groups tend to be more structured, including formal lectures, and are found generally in church buildings.

Roman Catholic

The rapidly growing phenomenon of Bible study in Roman Catholic parishes has already been mentioned; much of it is owing to the impetus of Vatican II and the earlier work of the Pontifical Biblical Institute and the Catholic Biblical Association. One of the earlier indications of the renewed interest in the Bible on the part of the laity was the tremendous sale of the series of pamphlets, New Testament and Old Testament Reading Guide Series, published by Liturgical Press beginning in 1960. At about the same time the Pamphlet Bible Series was distributed by Paulist Press, and many more books and texts have been developed since that time. According to a survey by the Catholic Biblical Apostolate of the U.S. Catholic Conference, the most widely used book in Catholic parishes and high schools is *Understanding the Bible* by Ronald J. Wilkins, published by William C. Brown Co. for the first time in 1972. The book was intended as an introductory course for senior high school youth and young adults to help them understand their "roots"—to know the foundation of their religious beliefs, worship, and way of life. Rather than beginning with dogmatic conclusions, the course starts with the doubts, difficulties, questions, and problems faced by adolescents. It presents the Bible as a guide or roadmap to help students know what the Judaic experience of God was in order to help them understand the meaning of Jesus in the world of the twentieth century. Knowing about the Bible is seen as a means to an end, helping students find a God in whom they can believe. Wilkins made clear in the guidebook that there are three ways of studying the Bible: literally, rationally, and with faith. He espouses the third way. Integral to the teacher manual are reprinted articles by Gregory Baum and Raymond E. Brown as well as an excerpt from the Dogmatic Constitution on Divine Revelation of Vatican II. This study material has been so well received that, even though planned originally for youth, it is the most frequently used course for adult study in Catholic parishes as well.

Two other books that are widely used in Catholic parishes and schools are *These Stones Will Shout* (Old Testament) and *The Seventh Trumpet* (New Testament), both by Mark Link and published by Argus Communications. These resources provide a combination of material from historical, archeological, and present-day sources with a rich variety of illustrations. According to the author, the purpose of Bible study is not only information or formation but also transformation or the recreating of the whole person. The first level of facts and the second level of values or life style lead to the third level of faith. "Here, Scripture is presented as the revealed word of God, calling each hearer to a response in faith to that word" (1978b:2). The Hebrew Scriptures were intended not as factual reports but as testimony in the first person, "I was there!", while the New Testament was to provide a faith encounter of the person with Jesus.

Unique among Catholics are the diocesan Bible study programs. For example, in the Diocese of Memphis parishes were led in a study of the Gospel of Matthew, out of which came a book, *A Commentary on the Gospel of Matthew*, by Albert Kirk and Robert E. Obach. This was followed by a study of the Gospel of John. In the Diocese of Oakland, Catholic couple Clarence and Edith Roberts started a small Bible study group in their home in 1970. Three years later it had grown into a group of over one hundred persons meeting in an unused seminary in the diocese for weekly classes. The program now is housed in fifteen different centers. Called "Sharing of Scripture" (S.O.S.), the program is designed for those who are ready to start a more meaningful relationship with God through the study of Scripture (Roberts: 5). It is planned as an ongoing weekly study program throughout the school year, and the emphasis is on "sharing" in small groups under the direction of a trained leader. This program has also been published by Paulist Press, and "mini-Scripture lessons" in capsule form are also printed in a Bible study column in the magazine, *Catholic Charismatic*.

Jewish

A variety of Bible study materials for all age groups has been developed for synagogues, including the highly recommended *A Child's Introduction to the Torah* and *A Child's Introduction to the Early Prophets*, both published by Behrman House. For older students there is the three-volume *Rabbi's Bible*, which includes selected passages from the Bible in the most recent translation from the Jewish Publication Society and also the popular commentaries called midrashim. In addition, the Jewish Publication Society has issued *Pathways Through the Bible* with introductions to the individual books. The book by Harry M. Orlinsky is widely used by Jewish high school sutdents; in addition, each branch of Judaism publishes materials on the Bible for various age groups.

The most ambitious Jewish program in Bible study is the Melton Research Center Series called "The Heritage of Biblical Israel." Founded in 1960 by the Jewish Theological Seminary of America in New York City with the help of Samuel Mendel Melton, the research center chose the Bible as the subject for which to develop and implement a currriculum for Jewish schools. Materials for teachers and students have been produced on the books of Genesis and Exodus, and the other books of the Torah are being prepared. In his introduction to the Series Simon Greenberg wrote:

> Precisely because the Bible has occupied so central a place in Jewish thought and life, it is the most difficult text to teach our children. Time and usage have bestowed upon many of the past generations' interpretation of the Bible a sanctity almost equal to that attached to the text itself. Moreover, the identification of the Book of Genesis in particular with stories told to six and seven year old children in both Christian and Jewish religious schools has left the widespread impression that this book was written primarily for the entertainment of youngsters. (Sarna: xiv)

The purpose of the series is "to make the Bible of Israel intelligible, relevant and hopefully inspiring to a sophisticated generation, possessed of intellectual curiosity and ethical sensitivity" (Sarna: xxii). The basic book, *Understanding Genesis*, was written by Nahum M. Sarna, and *Understanding Exodus*, by Moshe Greenberg. There are also pupils' books for eleven- and twelve-year-olds with activities and suggestions designed around the enquiry method. According to a doctoral dissertation written at Vanderbilt University in 1970 by Jerome Kestenbaum, the Melton Series succeeds in challenging students to find out what the Bible means. An experimental group using the materials, in fact, learned more than a control group, as measured by post-study tests. Kestenbaum recommended that the materials be used by other groups besides Jewish students because of their substantial and enduring value and contemporary relevance far beyond the American Jewish community and because of their emphasis on justice and equal and universal human rights.

From Book to Life

The second half of this chapter will discuss the context within which the struggle is going on for the meaning, interpretation, and application of the Scriptures (hermeneutics). The word "hermeneutics" comes from the Greek verb *hermēneuein*, which means "to interpret." H. Edward Everding, Jr., has written, "In ancient times these words were associated with the messenger-god Hermes whose function was to bring to human understanding the otherwise unintelligible messages of the gods" (41). For the purposes of this study the field of hermeneutics is taken to include the three related but very complex tasks of translation, interpretation, and expression or application to personal and social issues. In *The Strange Silence of the Bible in the Church,* James Smart called attention to the impressive gains in biblical scholarship in the twentieth century but noted little progress on the part of the church in showing the significance of these ancient texts for the contemporary world. Scholars like Smart have charged that the Scriptures are fading from the consciousness of the church and that people are not as frequently exposed to the Bible today as they were in past generations. The reason, according to Smart, is the confusion in hermeneutics. My research shows that Smart has failed to see the extent of Bible study, but he is probably correct about the hermeneutical problem.

Translation

Some groups in both churches and synagogues study the Scriptures in the original languages, but for others the choice of an English translation is an important decision. In the twentieth century there has been a proliferation of translations, much like the sixteenth century, which culminated in the Douay-Rheims version of 1582 (New Testament) and 1609–1610 (Old Testament) and the King James Version of 1611. For most of the intervening centuries there was little activity, except for the efforts of Bishop Challoner to revise the Douay-Rheims version in the mid-1700s. Finally a British committee undertook a revision of the King James Version and the entire Bible was completed in 1885. The American Standard Version was published in 1901. Even though these versions were more accurate, it was felt from the outset that they lost some of the beauty and power of the KJV. Subsequent developments pointed to the need for revision of the translations. The unearthing of many older manuscripts of the biblical books revealed errors accumulated through centuries of manuscript copying. Archeological discoveries gave scholars new knowledge of the language, history, culture, and geographical composition of the biblical lands. The English language itself had changed considerably since the Elizabethan period of King James; the meanings of many words had changed, and some were obscure or ambiguous.

In 1929 a committee of fifteen scholars was appointed by the International Council of Religious Education to revise the American Standard Version. Their final decision was to undertake a new translation but to stay as close to the Tyndale-King James tradition as possible. The result was the Revised Standard Version, the New Testament being completed in 1946 and the Old Testament in 1952. In many places the new translation was readily accepted and it became an instant best seller, but in other circles—especially among conservative Protestants—it was roundly denounced and condemned. (Luther Weigle, chairman of the RSV Committee, was fond of pointing out that the King James Version endured bitter attacks for seventy years after publication.) There had been other attempts by individual Protestant scholars and groups to translate the Bible into more contemporary English. Early in the century the Smith-Goodspeed and Moffatt translations were published. J. B. Phillips's translation of the New Testament into a modern idiom received praise and commendation. One of the most popular and widely distributed versions has been the Todays' English Version or Good News Bible, produced by the American Bible Society and completed in 1976. Another important work was the New English Bible, commissioned by the General Assembly of the Church of Scotland, the Church of England, and some of the free churches in Great Britain.

Motivated by the interest of evangelical leaders, the Lockman Foundation in California commissioned a group of scholars to revise the 1901 American Standard Version, and the result was the New American Standard Version (New Testament in 1963 and Old Testament in 1971). Another group of evangelical scholars, with the support of the New York Bible Society International, completed the New International Version of the entire Bible in 1978. But the most popular Bible, outselling all the rest, was not a translation at all but a paraphrase by Kenneth Taylor called The Living Bible, completed in 1971. John Ellington, a missionary of the Presbyterian Church (U.S.) in Zaire and a translation consultant with the United Bible Societies, has written an article, "Can We Trust The Living Bible?" in the May 1979 issue of A.D. magazine. According to him there are three tests of a Bible: readability, the textual basis of translation, and the accuracy of interpretation. Although high in readability, The Living Bible failed on the other two counts. It contains serious inaccuracies, i.e., whole sentences have no basis whatever in the original languages, and at places there is complete disregard for the clear intention of the original authors. Ellington wrote: "A translation of the Bible should be reliable as well as readable. The evidence clearly indicates that this paraphrase is not" (19). Yet, Christians by the millions have deserted their King James Versions for this new book, which has been endorsed by many leading evangelical groups, including the Billy Graham Evangelistic Association.

Renewed Catholic interest in translating the Scriptures is often traced to the encyclical *Divino Afflante Spiritu* by Pope Pius XII in 1943. Catholic scholars were directed by the Pope to use the original languages and the new scientific tools in translating and interpreting the Bible: "In like manner therefore ought we to explain the original text which, having been written by the inspired author himself, has more authority and greater weight than any, even the very best, translation, whether ancient or modern; this can be done all the more easily and fruitfully, if to the knowledge of languages be joined a real skill in literary criticism of the same text" (Gaul: 89). One of the fruits of this renewed interest was the Jerusalem Bible, which was originally translated from Hebrew and Greek into French under the direction of the Dominican Biblical School in Jerusalem and was then translated into English. Another result of twentieth-century Catholic scholarship is the New American Bible, sponsored by the Bishops Committee of the Confraternity of Christian Doctrine and carried out by members of the Catholic Biblical Association. The Vatican II Constitution on Divine Revelation had recommended that new translations be made in cooperation with the "separated brethren," and as a consequence four Protestant scholars were involved in this translation. At the same time the RSV Committee added Catholic (and Jewish) scholars to its team, and in 1965 the Oxford Annotated RSV Bible with the Apocrypha received the *imprimatur* of Richard Cardinal Cushing, Archbishop of Boston. It was the first edition of the English Bible to receive both Catholic and Protestant approval.

Important translations of the Hebrew Scriptures have also been done in the twentieth century. Isaac Leeser had translated the Scriptures into English in 1845, and this remained the standard American Jewish edition until the new translations by the Jewish Publication Society in 1917. In more recent years the society has commissioned several committees of biblical scholars, who completed the Torah in 1962, the Psalms in 1972, and the Prophets in 1978. They now are translating the Writings.

Any student of the Bible is confronted with a bewildering choice of translations, so much so that a flurry of articles and booklets has appeared on such subjects as "Why So Many Bibles?," "What Bible Can You Trust?," "Which Bible Should You Read?" A professor of English at Wheaton College, Leland Ryken, was asked to write an article on "The Literary Merit of the New International Version" for *Christianity Today*. He recommended the Revised Standard Version as the best modern translation because it retains the King James wording and phrasing wherever possible and is a superior literary achievement over the New International Version. Samuel Sandmel, the late Jewish biblical scholar at Hebrew Union College–Jewish Institute of Religion, recommended the Revised Standard Version and the New English Bible. In an article on "Translations and Interpretation" in

Interpretation, Lamar Williamson, Jr., recommended that Bible study groups use a variety of translations. It is clear that students of Scripture have the luxury of choosing from among the outstanding products of Protestant, Catholic, and Jewish scholarship.

Interpretation

The issue of hermeneutics—the meaning and interpretation of the Bible—is a more complicated one than the choice of translation. Of fundamental importance to hermeneutics is the historical-critical method, which has characterized the scholarly study of the Bible for the past two hundred years. At an Ecumenical Study Conference held in England in 1949 the essential steps in the historical-critical method were listed: (1) the determination of the text; (2) the literary form of the passage; (3) the historical situation, the *Sitz im Leben*; (4) the meaning which the words had for the original author and hearer or reader; (5) the understanding of the passage in the light of its total context and the background out of which it emerged (Richardson and Schweitzer: 241–42). Many commentators consider this method to be one of the great achievements of post-Reformation Protestantism, but it has not been without its critics and problems. Some spokespersons have remembered Luther's conviction that Scripture should be its own interpreter and have accused historical criticism of subjecting the Bible to outside or secular standards of judgment. Others have charged it with undermining the authority of the Bible or destroying faith.

A major battle over the authority and inerrancy of Scripture was fought in the Lutheran Church, Missouri Synod, after the election of J. A. O. Preus as President of the Synod in 1969. The controversy revolved around a 1932 doctrinal statement that said in part: "Since the Holy Scriptures are the Word of God, it goes without saying that they contain no errors or contradictions, but that they are in all their parts and words the infallible truth, also in those parts which treat of historical, geographical, and other secular matters" (Lindsell: 76). This statement was enforced by the synod's new president after 1969, and it led to the dismissal of the president of the synod's largest seminary, Concordia (St. Louis). Many faculty members and students joined the ousted president in a "seminary in exile." A split in the entire denomination resulted. The presidency of the Southern Baptist Convention was contested in 1979 on grounds of biblical authority and inerrancy. More than any other person, Harold Lindsell, the author of books like *The Battle for the Bible*, has made the inerrancy and verbal inspiration of the Scriptures part of a modern battle cry, but few responsible scholars seem ready to discard two hundred years of biblical scholarship.

Edgar Krentz, one of the Missouri Synod Lutherans who left Concordia Seminary, has written an introductory volume entitled *The Historical-Critical Method* for the series Guides to Biblical Scholarship. In this volume are listed some of the achievements of historical criticism, for example:

(1) research tools for Bible study have been provided, such as grammars, lexicons, concordances, dictionaries, commentaries, histories, translations; (2) the life and history of Israel, the early church, and the ancient Near Eastern and Graeco-Roman cultures have been clarified; (3) the original grammatical and historical sense of the Bible has been grasped; (4) the historical character of the Bible has been made evident (63–67). Krentz pointed out that all the problems have not been resolved, but the historical-critical methods have been self-correcting and have been at the service of the church and synagogue.

Nevertheless, there are responsible scholars who have raised serious questions about the historical-critical approach, and some of these are summarized by Gaylord Noyce in an article in *The Christian Century*, "How Shall We Use the Bible Now?" For example, David Kelsey has pointed to the variety of ways in which theologians find support in the Bible for their positions. James Barr has questioned whether the whole matter of the authority of Scripture should be abandoned. Walter Wink has claimed that the historical-critical method has become bankrupt, needs to come under new management, and has proposed a new paradigm influenced by a psychological, Jungian method. Noyce, in response, has suggested that if authority is no longer the most helpful concept we should focus on the Bible's functions—it provides the language for the church to carry on community building and decision making and supplies a symbol of transcendence. In addition to the scholars cited by Noyce, Brevard Childs in *Biblical Theology in Crisis* has written about the inadequacy of the historical-critical method for the theological task of the exegesis of Scripture. Childs has indicated that the canon of the Christian church is the most appropriate context within which to do biblical theology. The goal of this approach is to take seriously the responsibility of interpreting the Bible as the Scripture of the church and to develop the rigorous exegetical skills that can do the job. This would include drawing upon the so-called pre-critical exegesis in the long history of the church.

It is not possible in a short essay to do justice to the issues that have been raised regarding the interpretation of the Bible, except to suggest some of the possibilities and options. The historical-critical methods will continue to be used but along with the other theological and exegetical tools. The hermeneutical "circle" means that the interpreter approaches the text with all kinds of assumptions, presuppositions, and beliefs. As the text is studied new insights and interpretations will develop and influence the interpreter in the next round.

Application

In addition to translation and interpretation, Bible study also faces the issue of application or expression. How can one help people search the Scriptures so that they will have their consciousness raised regarding such problems as sexism, anti-Semitism, and racism? How can they become biblically-informed people regarding the life-and-death issues of human sexuality, war and peace, ecology, world hunger, technology, etc.? A model for the three-fold process of hermeneutics can be found in *The Liberating Word: A Guide to Nonsexist Interpretation of the Bible,* edited by Letty M. Russell. Its purpose is to involve Christians in the task of liberating the Bible from sexist bias, so that its translation, interpretation, and usage will be in inclusive language. It is clear that the Bible was written in a patriarchal society where women were considered little more than chattel or possessions and that it has been translated and interpreted through the centuries in a church that was male-dominated and controlled. The authors of the articles in this study guide point out passages in Scripture where women have acted responsibly on their own and have been treated with dignity and also passages that reflect the patriarchal or androcentric traditions of Hebrew culture. Besides calling for future scholarly efforts, the book provides practical suggestions for present liturgical and educational activity.

The issue of anti-Semitism in the New Testament cannot be avoided in the study of the Bible. Through the centuries the so-called rejection of Jesus by the Jews, the role allegedly played by the Jews in the crucifixion of Jesus, and the hostile references to the "Jews," especially in the Gospel of John, have molded Christian attitudes toward the Jewish people and have contributed to the persecution and massacre of Jews by Christians. A great French educator, Jules Isaac, called attention to these facts in his books, and he is generally credited with having influenced the decision of Pope John XXIII and Vatican II to drop the charge of deicide against the Jews. However, the problem of anti-Semitism in the New Testament has remained. The part it has played in church school materials has been researched by scholars like Bernhard Olson, and its theological implications have been explored by Gregory Baum, Rosemary Radford Ruether, and others. Olson and evangelical scholars generally deny that the Gospels are anti-Semitic in themselves, even though they were interpreted in this way later. However, Olson acknowledged that Jews consider the New Testament as a prime source of anti-Semitic teachings. One Jewish scholar concluded: "It is simply not correct to exempt the New Testament from anti-Semitism and to allocate it to later periods of history" (Sandmel, 1978:143–44). Samuel Sandmel rejected the notion that Christian theology is inherently and irrevocably anti-Semitic; he believed that a solution to the problem could be found if the facts were known and confronted.

The issue of racism and the black experience has been treated by James H. Cone in *A Black Theology of Liberation.* Cone rejects the notion that the Bible provides a perfect guide for discerning God's action in the world. He concedes that it is a valuable symbol for pointing to God's revelation in Christ, but it is not self-interpreting. From within the context of the black community the author lifts the motif of liberation from the Bible as the content of theology. For Cone the only theology consistent with the Gospel of Jesus is a black theology of liberation for oppressed people. Gustavo Gutierrez carries this a step farther in A Theology of Liberation: History, Politics and Salvation. In addition to traditional theologizing Gutierrez calls for critical reflection on the praxis (the presence and actions) of Christians who seek to improve the world. From the perspective of Latin America and the plight of politically and economically oppressed peoples, Gutierrez provides what some have called a "political hermeneutics." In this approach the creation of the world is seen as the first act of salvation, Christ is the great Liberator, and the struggle for a just society is a part of salvation history.

The issue of human sexuality has been the concern of much biblical exegesis and interpretation in the past. In recent years major studies have been done by the Catholic Theology Society (Kosnik, 1977) and the United Church of Christ (1977), with a surprising amount of common agreement. The intent of both studies was to further the process of study and dialogue within the respective church bodies. In the case of the United Church, an ad hoc group was formed that believed that the official study was limited in perspective and did not reflect the diversity in the denomination. Out of this was born the United Church People for Biblical Witness, which has also prepared and published a volume on sexual ethics and sent it to the local congregations for study (Duffy, 1979). Both studies quote the same biblical passages—for example on homosexuality—but interpret them differently. Not surprisingly, the subject of homosexuality has received much attention in the United Church and elsewhere. This issue has presented an example of Bible study on the front lines of church policy making, somewhat removed from cloistered halls or ivy-covered walls.

Other examples of issue-centered Bible study could be given, but these will suffice. A new era in hermeneutics has dawned, when group study of the Scripture must not only deal with the issues of historical, literary, and textual criticism but also with sexism, anti-Semitism, racism, oppression, human sexuality, and other problems. According to James Sanders, the Bible should be seen not as a historical document but as a theological and canonical document. For Sanders, the word "canonical" refers to the Bible's function in assisting ongoing believing communities to seek answers in their time to such questions as "Who are we?" and "What are we to do?" "The Torah is first and foremost adaptable, like a paradigm, to assist in properly conjugating the verbs of God's continuing presence and activity in this world" (382). This means that the church and synagogue are challenged to share the experience of God's activity and to work out the implications for their own lives. The biblical witnesses were not the last persons to experience God's activity but only the first. This can best be done in the context of a group, a class, a church, a synagogue, where there is a common commitment to discover the will of God for personal and corporate life.

Projections

When Robert M. Grant revised *A Short History of the Interpretation of the Bible* fifteen years after it first was published, he decided to refrain from prophecy and to set forth the basic principles of historical and theological interpretation. The business of crystal ball gazing and predicting future trends has become entirely too risky in the field of Bible study and interpretation, but some directions are clear. Small Bible study groups will continue to multiply, especially in homes and retreat centers, but there will be a greater emphasis on trained lay leadership through diocesan programs like the ones mentioned in this chapter as well as through other channels. One called to my attention is the Adult Biblical Learning Clinic set up by Eugene Trester in the Toronto area to train leaders in adult learning skills or "andragogy" as well as in biblical skills. A variation of the small group study is intergenerational learning, using the "family cluster" model pioneered by Margaret Sawin and utilizing resources being developed by church groups such as the Joint Educational Development consortium. Protestants and Catholics will join together in Bible study far more than they have in the past, and an exciting prospect for the future will be Christians and Jews studying the Hebrew Scriptures together and even looking at the "nodal events" or painful problem areas in postbiblical history that have contributed to misunderstanding, prejudice, and open hostility.

In the realm of hermeneutics, the gap between some liberals and conservatives can be bridged, if they are willing to accept both the accomplishments and the limitations of the historical-critical method. Samuel Sandmel pointed out that "Higher Criticism" is learned and scientific and thorough, but it is also dull and unimaginative. He did not say that it is not correct but only that it is just pedantic, unperceptive, and has recently turned "gushingly pious." The main thrust of biblical scholarship has not deepened the affective response to the great literature of the Bible or answered the critical questions of God's revelation or self-disclosure (Sandmel, 1972:4–5). One still needs to have the "eyes of faith" and to realize that the Bible was written "from faith to faith." The call for a canonical approach to the Bible is promising, because it seeks to interpret the Scriptures within the life and activity of the church. Not only can the preacher of the word help in this hermeneutical task, but the teacher can as well. Larry Richards has sought a "communication theology," which calls for a "communicator who incarnates the Word taught; a community established in family love as the fertile soil into which the Word is to fall; a teacher/learner relationship rich in love so that each feels free to talk about the realities of his daily life and to bring them under the scrutiny of the Word of God" (18). In passing, it might be added that the great popularity and wide acceptance of the Daily Study Bible series and other books by William Barclay have shown that groups need not always be divided along ideological lines. In the preface to his book, *Introducing the Bible*, Barclay wrote:

> Today we find a new sympathy between the conservative and the liberal, between the fundamentalist and the radical. It is not that either is willing to abandon his stance and his beliefs, but it is that both are willing to sit down together and talk, even if they do not agree with each other; and, when they do talk, it sometimes happens that they discover that they are not so far apart as once they thought they were. (9)

This holds great promise for the future of Bible study.

Bridges have already been built in the ecumenical study of the Bible by Protestants and Catholics. One of the outstanding Catholic scholars, Raymond E. Brown, wrote a book in 1975, *Biblical Reflections on Crises Facing the Church*. The issues discussed were: catechetics, Christology, the future of ecumenism, the ordination of women, the papacy, and the role of Mary. In the preface Brown acknowledged a debt to Protestant biblical scholarship:

> The Roman Catholic Church could not have made its advance in biblical criticism without Protestant aid. In the first third of the century the torch of biblical criticism was kept lighted by Protestant scholars; and when after 1943 Catholics lit their candles from it, they profited from the burnt fingers as well as the glowing insights of their Protestant confreres. It is no accident that Protestant and Catholic biblical scholars have been coming closer together ever since, to the point now of producing common studies of divisive problems. (ix)

Why the continuing popularity of Bible study? Probably for the same reasons that the Bible continues to be a runaway best seller in whatever translation it appears. There are those who may look upon it as something magical or mystical, a talisman or charm not so much to be read as to be possessed. For most people it represents something far more substantial. In an age when all the moorings seem to have come loose, when all values seem relative, when there is little confidence in government or in other public institutions, the Bible remains an anchor or a rock. Young and old are seeking something to believe in, something to hold on to, a sense of roots—so that knowing who they are and where they have been they will better know in which direction to go. The Scriptures seem to be the one norm, the one unchanging certainty in a time of flux.

NOTES

/1/   Though the adult Bible class is nominally a part of the church, structurally it parallels churchly functions: prayer, fellowship, exhortation, mutual support, worship. It also usually has a separate membership, with some of its members not attending the church services.

/2/   Interview with Dr. Robert Koenig, United Church of Christ Board for Homeland Ministries, August 1979.

WORKS CONSULTED

Abbott, Walter M., S.J., ed.
1966   *The Documents of Vatican II.* New York: America Press. Pp. 111–28.

Barclay, William
1979   *Introducing the Bible.* Nashville: Abingdon Press.

Brown, Raymond E., S.S.
1975   *Biblical Reflections on Crises Facing the Church.* New York: Paulist Press.

Childs, Brevard S.
1970   *Biblical Theology in Crisis.* Philadelphia: Westminster Press.

Chilstrom, Herbert W.
1976   "The Bethel Bible Series: A Critical Investigation of an Adult Education Program for Christian Churches." Unpublished Ed.D. Dissertation, New York University.

Colson, Howard P.
1974   "Presuppositions Underlying the Uniform Series." *Report: Consultation of Issues Facing the Committee on the Uniform Series.* New York: National Council of Churches.

Cone, James H.
1970   *A Black Theology of Liberation.* Philadelphia: J. B. Lippincott Co.

Duffy, Martin
1979   *Issues in Sexual Ethics.* Souderton, PA: United Church People for Biblical Witness.

Ellington, John
1979   "Can We Trust the Living Bible?" *A.D. 1979* 8/5: 17–19.

Everding, H. Edward, Jr.
1976   "A Hermeneutical Approach to Educational Theory." *Foundations for Christian Education in an Era of Change,* ed. Marvin J. Taylor. Nashville: Abingdon Press.

Gaul, Cyril, and Louis, Conrad, O.S.B., eds.
1953   *Rome and the Study of Scripture.* St. Meinrad, IN: St. Meinrad's Abbey.

Grant, Robert M.
1963   *A Short History of the Interpretation of the Bible.* New York: Macmillan.

Greenberg, Moshe
1969   *Understanding Exodus.* New York: Behrman House.

Greenberg, Simon
1973   "Lifetime Education as Conceived and Practiced in the Jewish Tradition." *Religious Education* 68: 339–47.

Gutierrez, Gustavo
1973   *A Theology of Liberation: History, Politics and Salvation.* Maryknoll, NY: Orbis Books.

Kestenbaum, Jerome
1970   "The Melton Research Center in American Jewish Education." Unpublished D.Div. Dissertation, Vanderbilt University.

Kosnik, Anthony, et al.
1977   *Human Sexuality: New Directions in American Catholic Thought.* New York: Paulist Press.

Krentz, Edgar
1975   *The Historical-Critical Method.* Philadelphia: Fortress.

Kunz, Marilyn, and Schell, Catherine
1966   *How To Start A Neighborhood Bible Study.* Wheaton, IL: Tyndale House.

Langford, Norman F.
1963   *The Westminster Dictionary of Christian Education,* ed. Kendig B. Cully. Philadelphia: Westminster. Pp. 50–52.

Lindsell, Harold
1976   *The Battle for the Bible.* Grand Rapids, MI: Zondervan.

Link, Mark, S.J.
    1975   *These Stones Will Shout: A New Voice for the Old Testament*. Niles, IL: Argus Communications.
    1978a   *The Seventh Trumpet: The Good News Proclaimed*. Niles, IL: Argus Communications.
    1978b   "The Three Levels of Bible Study." Unpublished paper presented at the 75th Anniversary Convention, The Religious Education Association, 20 November 1978.

Noyce, Gaylord
    1979   "How Shall We Use the Bible Now?" *The Christian Century* 96/12: 370–73.

Olson, Bernhard
    1963   *Faith and Prejudice: Intergroup Problems in Protestant Curricula*. New Haven: Yale University Press.

Richards, Larry
    1977   "Church Teaching: Content Without Context." *Christianity Today* 21/14: 16–18.

Richardson, A., and Schweitzer, W.
    1951   *Biblical Authority for Today*. London: SCM Press.

Roberts, Clarence, and Roberts, Edith
    1978   *Sharing of Scripture*. New York: Paulist Press.

Russell, Letty M., ed.
    1976   *The Liberating Word: A Guide to Nonsexist Interpretation of the Bible*. Philadelphia: Westminster.

Ryken, Leland
    1978   "The Literary Merit of the New International Version." *Christianity Today* 23/2: 16–17.

Sanders, James
    1975   "Torah and Christ." *Interpretation* 29/4: 372–90.

Sandmel, Samuel
    1972   *The Enjoyment of Scripture: The Law, The Prophets, and The Writings*. New York: Oxford University Press.
    1978   *Anti-Semitism in the New Testament*. Philadelphia: Fortress Press.

Sarna, Nahum
    1966   *Understanding Genesis.* New York: McGraw Hill.

Smart, James D.
    1970   *The Strange Silence of the Bible in the Church.*
                            Philadelphia: Westminster.

United Church Board for Homeland Ministries
    1977   *Human Sexuality: A Preliminary Study.* Philadel-
                            phia: United Church Press.

Uphaus, Willard
    1925   "A Critical Study of the International Sunday
                            School Lesson System." Unpublished Ph.D. Disser-
                            tation, Yale University.

Weigle, Luther A.
    1976   *The Glory Days: From the Life of Luther Allan
                            Weigle,* ed. Richard D. Weigle. New York:
                            Friendship Press. Pp. 62–74.

Wilkins, Ronald J.
    1972   *Understanding the Bible: Teacher Manual.*
                            Dubuque, IA: Wm. C. Brown Co.

Williamson, Lamar J.
    1978   "Translations and Interpretation: New Testament."
                            Interpretation 32/2: 158–70.

Wink, Walter
    1973   *The Bible in Human Transformation: Toward a
                            New Paradigm for Bible Study.* Philadelphia:
                            Fortress Press.

Wolfgang, Raymond S.
    1963   "An Evaluation of the Use of the Bible in the Cur-
                            riculum of the United Church of Christ." Unpub-
                            lished Th.M. Dissertation, Princeton Theological
                            Seminary.

VIII

The Bible is Worthy of Secular Study:
The Bible in Public Education Today

Peter S. Bracher and David L. Barr

The place of the Bible in public education is today more clearly defined than at any other time since it lost its status as the core of colonial education. Although its new role is not widely understood and although several issues remain to be solved, real progress in defining a role for the Bible in contemporary public education has been achieved in the last few decades. This essay seeks to explore that new role, to provide some analysis of the current situation, and to discuss the social, legal, and intellectual issues that now shape teaching about the Bible in public schools. The chief thrust of this essay concerns secondary education, though much that is said here can also be applied to higher education.

The New Place of the Bible in Public Education Today

Historically, the dominant movement of our culture—a movement strongly reflected in the public schools—has been toward cultural integration. Most strikingly embodied in the image of the melting pot, this conception encouraged Americans to view the United States as a commingling of ethnic and religious groups unified by a common core of shared values (see Herberg: 21–23). From the first immigrations in colonial days to the latest influxes of Asian and Cuban boat people, American citizens have come from many places, have carried with them many cultures, have spoken many languages. Yet this diversity was largely transformed into a distinctively American culture, dominated by the English language and permeated by Anglo-Saxon values and customs. Until the middle of the twentieth century the country's greatest need was to prevent that diversity from fragmenting society. The need was for unity, and intense energy was invested in creating the appearance of that unity.

The very success of this drive toward a common culture allowed the opposite impulse slowly to surface. Although cultural diversity has existed in the United States from colonial times, through most of our history it has not been valued. However, American history is the record of the gradual extension of

political and economic power. For reasons too complex to be analyzed here
(Littell: 129–69; Marty: 1–5), this process ultimately not only forced recognition of the real diversity of American culture but also encouraged a growing
acceptance of cultural pluralism. This shift in attitude became increasingly
obvious about the middle of the twentieth century. The Supreme Court's
decision in 1954 to outlaw racial segregation in the public schools as
"inherently unequal" in the famous case of *Brown* v. *Board of Education of
Topeka* is an early indicator of this change. During the next two decades the
civil rights movement, the emergence of the so-called counter culture,
women's liberation, the gay rights movement, and a new ethnic awareness
that shattered the image of the melting pot all emphasized the fact that
American society consists of many minorities. Only half aware, the nation
seemed to undertake an experiment to test the long-established drive toward
cultural integration and consensus values. And as greater and greater cultural diversity was acknowledged, the core of shared values had to be corre-
spondingly reduced (see Chapter II above).

These patterns of cultural change had their effect in the public schools.
The Bible, which had once functioned in public education as a sign of the
core of shared values, was reduced to a largely symbolic role by the middle
of the twentieth century. Perfunctory readings of a biblical passage without
comment began each school day in thousands of classrooms across the
nation. This practice reflected both the impulse toward unity and the
impulse toward diversity. There was widespread agreement that the Bible
was important (hence it was read), but everyone explained and interpreted
it differently (hence it was read without comment). Inevitably the Bible in
the public school became the focus for dispute between those who approved
current practice and those who did not. There were problems about which
version of the Bible should be read (Michaelsen, 1970:89–98), and eventually, as the pressures for acknowledging diversity grew stronger, there were
objections to reading the Bible at all.

Sooner or later this ferment had to have an impact on the place of the
Bible in public education. That impact was embodied in a series of Supreme
Court rulings in the early 1960s: the 1962 prayer decision (*Engle* v. *Vitale*,
370 U.S. 421) and the 1963 Bible reading decision (*Murray* v. *Curlett* and
Abington v. *Schempp*, 374 U.S. 203, hereafter referred to as *Schempp*). The
historic *Schempp* decision could not have been written had not two important cultural changes affecting the role of the Bible in public education
occurred. One was sociological—the explicit affirmation of the value of
cultural diversity, which already has been discussed. The two 1963 cases
asserted the rights of minority religious positions—that of an atheist, Mada-
lyn Murray O'Hare, and that of Unitarians, the Schempp family of German-
town, Pennsylvania. The other change was legal—the application of the
Fourteenth Amendment to public education. Rulings about religion in the
public schools depended upon establishing the relevance of the First

Amendment to the Constitution ("Congress shall make no law respecting an establishment of religion, or prohibiting the free exercise thereof. . . .") to state law and thence to laws governing the public schools (Boles, 1961:30–31; Warshaw, 1979: 7–8). The mechanism for this change was the Fourteenth Amendment, passed in 1868 to protect the rights of the newly emancipated black citizens. A series of court decisions only gradually defined the impact of this amendment on state law, and it was not until 1940 that the Supreme Court ruled that the religious restrictions of the First Amendment were legally binding upon the states.

A broadened view of the role of minorities in American culture and of the legal applicability of the First Amendment made it possible for the Supreme Court to rule in 1963 that the practice of reading the Bible without comment in public schools was unconstitutional because the schools, as agencies of the state, were thereby establishing an official practice of religion, however diluted it might be. The rights of minorities were affirmed, but a storm of public outcry was unleashed. Such decisive removal of a public symbol can cause both concern and outrage; both quickly surfaced in the wake of the *Schempp* ruling. Partly to forestall the outcry and partly to clarify the place of the Bible in public education, both majority and minority opinions of the Court made a special effort to spell out what constituted legal use of the Bible in public education. The key points are embodied in two widely quoted dicta:

> It might well be said that one's education is not complete without a study of comparative religion or the history of religion and its relationship to the advancement for civilization. It certainly may be said that the Bible is worthy of study for its literary and historic qualities. Nothing we have said here indicates that such study of the Bible or of religion, when presented objectively as part of a secular program of education, may not be effected consistently with the First Amendment. (Justice Clark, for the majority)

> The holding of the Court today plainly does not foreclose teaching *about* the Holy Scriptures or about the differences between religious sects in classes in literature or history. Indeed, whether or not the Bible is involved, it would be impossible to teach meaningfully many subjects in the social sciences or the humanities without some mention of religion. (Justice Brennan, concurring)

One key distinction concerns the difference between teaching religion and teaching *about* religion. In effect the Court upheld teaching *about* the Bible rather than the direct presentation of the Bible as in the Bible reading practices. More basic, however, is the distinction that rejects a devotional and religious use of the Bible in the public schools and affirms an educational and secular use of it. It is not surprising that the crucial term in Clark's statement is the word *study*. Study is, after all, what public education is all about, and it is reasonable that the Bible, like any other religious or secular literature, may form a part of the curriculum of the schools. But to secularize the Bible in this fashion is to affirm explicitly a crucial symbolic shift in the Bible's place in public education. The Bible, instead of functioning as a symbol of common values, becomes one of the many things that may be studied—another piece of curricular material like *Huckleberry Finn* or the periodic table. While the Court did not clarify the principle of studying the Bible "objectively as part of a secular program of education," the implications of this principle are important. In fact, they undergird the whole dynamic of the educational community's response to the *Schempp* decision. Since 1963 the idea of a secular study of a sacred book has spurred thought, created controversy, and elicited experimentation. But a growing consensus about the principles that ought to govern the use of the Bible in public education has taken shape. In an effort to define and elaborate those principles, some of that history must now be sketched.

The Bible Goes to School:
The New Activity after Schempp

The opportunities for introducing the Bible into the public school curriculum opened up by the *Schempp* decision almost immediately created ripples of response among professional educators, among biblical and religion scholars, and among a wide variety of lay people and clergy members with diverse confessional and evangelical motives. Interest came from the Protestant and Roman Catholic as well as the Jewish communities. In 1964 the American Association of School Administrators committed itself to the view that as an integral part of human culture, the study of religion must be included in the public school curriculum (55–56). The same year, Thayer S. Warshaw, then a high school English teacher in a Boston suburb, published an article called "Studying the Bible in Public School" (1964), which described his experimental nine-week unit on the Bible. Its timely appearance earned him national attention and even was reported by United Press International. Other articles began appearing in the *English Journal*, the principal professional publication for secondary English teachers, with titles like "The Bible in the English Program" (Hogan, 1965), "We Study the Bible as Literature" (Hildebrand, 1966), and "A Realistic Approach to Biblical Literature" (Capps, 1969). The Nebraska Curriculum Development Center was spurred to add units on the Bible to the English curriculum it was developing. In Fort Wayne, Indiana, a grant from the Lilly Endowment allowed James V. Panoch to expand the work of the Religious Instruction Association, founded in 1964, to serve as a clearing house for information and materials on the teaching of the Bible and religion generally in the public schools. In 1965 the Florida State Department of Education formed a "State Committee on Study about Religion in the Public Schools." Also in 1965 the Broward County (Florida) Board of Education formed a committee of teachers to prepare a course in biblical literature in response to the Court's decision. In December 1965 the General Assembly of the

Commonwealth of Pennsylvania amended the Public School Code to allow the introduction of courses "in the literature of the Bible and other religious writings," an action that culminated in the publication of a textbook, *The Religious Literature of the West* (Whitney and Howe, 1971). The cultural diversity that had made possible the *Schempp* decision was immediately evident in these responses to it.

Such signs of interest in teaching about the Bible in secular educational programs eventually led to efforts on a national scale to bring together those who shared an interest in the opportunities for biblical education that the *Schempp* decision made possible. In April 1969 fifty educators, business people, and religious leaders gathered in Rye, New York, for the Wainwright House Conference on the Bible in the Public Schools under the sponsorship of the Laymen's National Bible Committee. The conference was notable for several reasons. First, it reflected the diversity of motives that lay behind public interest in teaching the Bible and that, inevitably, made strange bedfellows. The conference included scholars committed to academic objectivity, business leaders whose interests were evangelical and primarily conservative, proponents of cultural pluralism, and as the keynote speaker a United States senator who spoke with almost revivalistic fervor and a rather confused understanding of the distinctions the Court was trying to establish. The conference had some trouble separating its nominal topic, the Bible in the public schools, from teaching about religion generally. Nevertheless and second, it did formulate many of the issues that would preoccupy those professionally involved in teaching the Bible in the public schools. Among those issues were the definition of "religion"; the proper training of public school teachers; the issue of sensitivity to personal religious beliefs; and the relation of the Bible to literature, history, and ethics. The conference struggled with the place of the Bible in the curriculum: "There are implications here that the Bible may be taught as literature, as part of history, in the study of comparative religions, or be related to the study of culture or of societies or even in sociology, anthropology, or human psychology," said the Committee on Legal Aspects (Wainwright Report, 1969:47). Finally, the conference brought together two men—James Ackerman, a biblical scholar from Connecticut College, and Thayer Warshaw, the English teacher from Massachusetts, mentioned above—whose fruitful collaboration over the next decade would do much to direct and shape the successful movement of the Bible into the English classrooms of public high schools during the 1970s. For it was in the literature program that the Bible found its chief home within public education.

Although the Wainwright Conference pointed out that the Bible fit naturally into a wide range of the humanities and social studies subjects that are taught in the public schools, little happened in the succeeding decade to encourage teachers of history and social science to make the Bible a significant component of their courses. In language arts, on the other hand, the

Bible as literature seemed a natural addition to the curriculum. And the time was ripe for such changes. The late 1960s saw a development in high school education that made the introduction of new courses in world religions or the Bible both feasible and attractive. In response to social pressures that affected education generally and reflected the new emphasis on cultural diversity, high schools in many areas abandoned the old curricular patterns of required year-long courses based on mammoth textbooks or anthologies. Instead they began instituting elective systems and introducing shorter courses—nine week mini-courses, for example. Such developments made far more room in most high school curricula for special courses than had previously been possible. Venturesome teachers were not slow to take up the challenge of the *Schempp* decision and introduce courses on biblical literature in their schools. There was no lack of response to the opportunities the Court created (for a listing of some of the more prominent courses see Panoch and Barr, 1968).

Legal Requirements, Pluralism, and Teaching the Bible: The Issues Take Shape

The issues that the Wainwright Conference brought into focus were observable in many quarters. Evangelical Protestants often saw *Schempp* as a legal means of introducing the "good news" into the public schools. They seemed unaware of the degree of confessional bias and the lack of objectivity in their courses and materials. Professional educators and many scholars, on the other hand, found the issue of objectivity a crucial starting point. This in turn raised the issue of expertise. The context for an objective study of the Bible was the academic study of religion as it had evolved in American universities, especially those supported by public funds. This rigorous academic discipline and methodology offered a way of achieving objectivity. And so the training of teachers who could bring expertise to their work became a major concern. This emphasis on objectivity also forced educators to take into account the growing sense of American pluralism. This required a new sensitivity to the special concerns of believers and nonbelievers, of Protestant and Roman Catholic, of Christian and Jew, of conservative and liberal and to the biases of teachers and students. Awareness of such problems as these also made educators acutely conscious of the need for appropriate methods and materials in order to implement the *Schempp* decision in the classroom.

Resolving these issues proved difficult and time consuming. It has preoccupied those who have been active in the years since the *Schempp* decision—teachers, their supervisors, and scholars. With few exceptions the public schools do not have trained teachers of religion or the Bible. So the teaching of the Bible has generally fallen to certified English or social studies teachers who do not have professional training in religion studies comparable to the training in their major fields. The issues of expertise, sensitivity, and objectivity thus remain central problems for the Bible in public education today.

Objectivity

At the same time that the Court offered a legal rationale for teaching the Bible in the public schools it also established an important condition: that the teaching of the Bible—and religion generally—must be done objectively. The Court thus underscored the importance of treating religion and the Bible as academic subjects like mathematics, English, or biology. The Bible was not to be used as a source of religious inculcation or a vehicle for a narrowly conceived values education. The Bible was to be kept squarely in a broad cultural context for believers and nonbelievers alike.

The Court's choice of the term "objectively" has stimulated a good deal of discussion about what the term means and how, in fact, objectivity is to be achieved (Michaelsen, 1977). The quest for objectivity has led some to feel that in dealing with the Bible as literature, for example, it was essential to "leave religion out." Such a view has produced efforts to teach the Bible without reference to its religious content and significance. While this may sidestep theological debate—or at least provide a means of cutting it off—it is an unrealistic way of approaching the Bible, as unrealistic as reading Milton's *Paradise Lost* and ignoring its religious content or Shakespeare's history plays and ignoring their political content. Few experts would advocate such a timid approach to objectivity.

The religious content of the Bible is a part of its literary interest. The problem is finding a suitably objective framework for dealing with it. Philip Phenix has spoken of "disciplined intersubjectivity" as a key to an academic and objective approach to religion. It means to "enter into the subjectivity of persons other than oneself in a disciplined way. . . . This is the fundamental mark of human intelligence" (1967:86–88). No one can be totally empathetic nor totally objective about material, but it seems evident that objectivity requires bringing all biases into the open and giving them a sympathetic hearing, whether they are the biases of teacher or student. Ideally, a skilled teacher can turn them into teaching tools that, in the case of the Bible, not only reveal its richness of meaning as literature but also enlarge students' awareness of other people and their points of view. Such pluralistic openness is likely to help maintain a distinction between the study about religion and the practice and propagation of religion, which is an ever-present danger when the Bible becomes a school text.

Two other and opposite dangers must also be avoided, the danger of taking a Sunday school approach to the Bible and the danger of courting controversy. Many public school teachers have been exposed to the Bible only within the context of their religious communities and may, in their inexperience, tend to treat their classes as extensions of their Sunday schools.

The original Broward County (Florida) material is a good example. But experience, openness, the use of expert outside consultants, and the leadership of dedicated teachers like Julia Chandler reversed the situation, demonstrating that materials can be greatly improved and that teachers can grow into the challenge of presenting the Bible objectively (Broward County). In contrast, the Chattanooga Bible program, a more recent example of a nonobjective course in biblical literature, refused to conform to the dictates of the *Schempp* decision until forced to by court action. The program had been funded and controlled by a private corporation, and the teachers were not regular literature teachers but were privately hired. More seriously, the material being taught was decidedly biased toward a Christian and conservative, even fundamentalist, understanding of the Bible. In fact, the stated goals for the course included the Christian development of the students. Not surprisingly, a recent court challenge to this program has been successful (*Wiley* v. *Franklin* 468F supp 133 [1979] and 474F supp 525), so that it will have to be radically changed or abandoned.

It is the essence of objectivity that multiple viewpoints and multiple interpretations be considered (Phenix, 1967:89). But this very multiplicity can lead to unsettling problems when the classroom is turned into a debating society. Such an atmosphere of controversy can as effectively eliminate a truly literary and objective approach to the Bible as the confessional approach referred to above. A pluralistic, nonconfessional, objective approach requires a certain openness on the part of the teacher and also the ability to create an open environment in the classroom.

Sensitivity

Defined this way, objectivity is a function of a certain kind of sensitivity. The Bible is a living book, even for nonbelievers. It is a sacred text for three major religious groups. As the Wainwright Conference noted, "The Bible is not just literature but *sacred* literature, and it is offensive to some religious people even to present it in a lesser context" (Wainwright Report: 48). But quite apart from doctrinal differences, religious feelings, and what may be objected to as a secularization of the Bible, Christians and Jews do not share a common Bible in either content or organization. And even when their Bibles do overlap, they use different translations and find different meanings. Moreover, among biblical scholars there are reasonably well-defined conservative and liberal orientations to biblical scholarship and interpretation, often closely related to particular confessional positions. Thus even among the Christian community there are widely differing conceptions about the origins and nature of the Bible as well as different interpretations of it. And, of course, sincere and highly motivated believers are not always able to transcend their evangelical concerns when dealing with the Bible and when discussing religion. The relationship of the Bible to nonbiblical mythologies and to the mythologies of our culture generally is also a sensitive issue. And nonbelievers sometimes make it a point of honor to be contentious. Thus a teacher must be prepared to deal with a wide range of sensitivities and concerns. It can even be argued that a primary objective of the study of the Bible in public schools should be the development of sensitivity to such wide-ranging points of view. Certainly a concern with sensitivity is an effective counter to the pressure toward classroom dogmatism generated by religious biases that encourage readers to look for one "right" reading of a biblical text. Such sensitivity may also help overcome the easy assumption made by many English teachers that there is one "right" reading of any literary text.

The many ways in which bias can crop up and the ease with which it can color approaches to the Bible is nowhere more apparent than in the materials that have been developed in the last decade for use in the public schools in teaching the Bible as literature. This bias—or simply, perhaps, a lack of sensitivity—may be reflected in the failure to distinguish clearly between the Hebrew and Christian Bibles, as when students are asked to discuss what the parables of Jesus tell about the "religion of the Bible" (Ryken, 1977:37; see also Lee and Lee, 1973a, 1973b). Or it may occur in the widespread use of the term "Christ" as a synonym for the name "Jesus," a common imprecision in our culture that may reflect a confessional bias (Capps, 1971; Vedral; Brown; Ryken and others). More serious is the Christian typological interpretation implicit in a study question for the Song of Songs that asks students "How does Christ feel about his church?" when there is no explicit mention of Jesus or the Christian church in the text (Vedral). A more sophisticated but still Christian orientation can be found in texts influenced by archetypal literary criticism (Lee and Lee 1973a and b). The biases of biblical scholarship can also color a book's point of view. A bibliography that lists no work by Jewish or Roman Catholic scholars and lists twelve works of a conservative Protestant orientation out of a total of nineteen items does not reasonably reflect the range of established biblical scholarship and suggests a questionable weighting in favor of one tradition (Vedral). The casual use of the term "legendary" or the assertion that the first eleven chapters of Genesis "cannot, properly speaking, be regarded as history in the way that much of the Old Testament can be understood" betrays the perspective of critical scholarship (Brown: 3, 77). In fact, judged against a rigorous standard of objectivity, no textbooks prepared for classroom use seem completely free of bias. They must be used with care by knowledgeable teachers if the goal of objectivity is to be met.

Teacher Training and Resource Materials

Awareness of sensitivity is obviously intimately related to expertise. The more thorough a teacher's preparation in biblical scholarship, the greater that teacher's awareness of the problems raised by the diversity of viewpoints brought to bear upon the Bible and the better prepared that teacher is for dealing with them. In addition, the academic study of the Bible, even at the secondary level, requires some knowledge and discussion of biblical scholarship. But knowledge of the Bible learned in a specifically confessional setting—in Sunday school or Hebrew school or a denominational college classroom—does not provide the kind of objective expertise essential to informed teaching of the Bible. Thus, teacher training and the development of resource material for teachers became a major concern of those with a professional interest in the teaching of the Bible in the public schools. No public school teacher can be expected to become an expert biblical scholar, but much can be done to eliminate the most obvious kinds of ignorance and to enable the teacher to respond sensitively to cultural pluralism.

The most important and influential response to these needs was the Indiana University Summer Institute on teaching the Bible in public schools (1970–1978). The institute was the joint effort of James S. Ackerman, whose book *On Teaching the Bible as Literature* (1967) provided background on the Old Testament for high school teachers of the Bible as literature, and Thayer Warshaw, who had turned his early acclaim as a teacher of the Bible in the public schools into a widely acknowledged expertise on the problems and techniques of teaching the Bible on the secondary school level. The largest and most elaborate of a number of teacher-training efforts under-taken in the 1970s, the month-long Indiana Institutes were intensive and mind-stretching experiences for participants. They provided a unique combination of extraordinarily rich and diverse substance and materials, consistently high quality, an intellectually stimulating level of biblical and literary scholarship, and an appealingly down-to-earth pedagogical practicality. From these resources the institute evolved solutions to the need for training in biblical content and background and teaching methods as well as for the development of curricular and reference resources.

Although the 1960s and the early 1970s were characterized by wide-spread efforts to develop model public school curricula in many subject fields, the Indiana Institute chose an alternative approach, one that re-sponded to cultural diversity. Instead of developing an "Indiana curricu-lum," it provided background and resources to individual participants and encouraged them to create their own courses and units and to develop their own materials and methods (Ackerman, 1971:4; 1972:458). From the beginning the Institute tried to accommodate a wide range of individual backgrounds, interests, needs, and teaching situations. The regular program of eighty hours of formal lectures (four a day) covered four broad areas: "historical and critical study of Scripture, sensitivity to problems of teaching the Bible in the public schools . . . of an open society, critical analyses of literature that depends on the Bible . . . , and the Bible as literature" (Gros Louis: 7). Optional supplementary sessions considerably broadened the scope of the institute and placed a strong emphasis on how to teach the Bible. This wide-ranging smorgasbord of background, methodology, resources, and media materials was complemented by an individualized project. Each participant created a curricular unit or set of teaching materials designed for use in the home school. Participants emerged from this regimen as more self-conscious and better-informed teachers of the Bible, thoroughly introduced to the subject areas with which they needed to be conversant.

Because it undertook to meet a diversity of needs and interests, the institute was careful to maintain an objective, nondoctrinaire stance. In fact, if there were defining characteristics of the institute, they were its emphasis on pluralism and its awareness of the sensitivity issue. Although the lectures on biblical history and scholarship reflected the viewpoint of contemporary critical scholarship, the institute was careful not to neglect more traditional approaches and to advocate the greatest possible openness in dealing with the Bible in the classroom. Thus institute participants were exposed to the views of visiting experts, including representatives of the Jewish and the conservative Christian traditions. The emphasis on alternative and interfaith perspectives and an almost painful self-consciousness about bias are evident in many of the materials developed by the institute. For example, the introduction to Ackerman's expanded revision of his book on Old Testament backgrounds notes the book's attempt to represent a "general consensus" of Protestant, Catholic, and Jewish scholarship and warns readers to be alert to "the writers' bias." The book begins with a lengthy footnote to the first sentence carefully explaining the authors' use of terms like "Old Testament" and "B.C." and why these terms are offensive to the Jewish community. The notes also "incorporate various interpretations of the biblical narratives" (Ackerman and others: xi, xiii).

This over-riding concern with pluralism helped to define classroom methodology and even the objectives of teaching the Bible itself. Teachers are advised, in the introduction to Ackerman's book, "to make certain that a full range of interpretations of a specific narrative or passage is given by various students" so that they will understand that "almost every man approaches the Old Testament with a particular point of view that is neither right nor wrong but is based on the sum of his experience." Students, by examining each other's biases, will become more tolerant and understanding of one another (Ackerman and others: xvi). The introduction to the Ackerman-Warshaw student text, *The Bible in/as Literature,* states that study of the Bible as literature "provides a common ground for people of all traditions and attitudes to examine and appreciate the Bible in the same classroom." Thus, the problems of dealing with the Bible in a pluralistic society should not be viewed as "barriers" but as "welcome reminders that teachers and students must be aware of the sensibilities of other people" (Ackerman and Warshaw: 1).

The institute stressed the importance of protecting those sensibilities. The textbook disclaims any "intent to ignore or diminish [the Bible's] cultural,

historical, moral, and religious content" (Ackerman and Warshaw: 1), and
Ackerman's introduction to the Old Testament notes that its purpose is not
to deny "religious faith" (Ackerman and others: xiii). Warshaw, in his *Handbook*, cautions teachers against constructing a kind of biblical house-that-
Jack-built, which will crush religious sensibilities: "Teachers need not, nor
should they, completely avoid explicit or implicit ideas in biblical stories and
teachings, especially when students raise questions about them. What teachers must keep in mind is that ideas involve meaning, meaning involves interpretation, interpretation involves clashing religious sensibilities, and the
clashing of religious sensibilities worketh suffering" (1978:29). In an open
classroom, the teacher seems little more than a referee—a fair-minded but
neutral party who should "refrain from *initiating* a discussion and evaluation of those ideas" but who should not restrain students from asking questions. When they do, the teacher has an "*obligation*" to make sure that "as
many denominational, as well as non-religious, points of view are fairly
presented as is practical" (Warshaw, 1978a:21). Thus the institute's stance on
pluralism in effect defines a methodology for teaching the Bible.

The institute thus sought to make pluralism not merely an ideal but a
working classroom approach. The institute also adopted a traditional definition of religion—as a "set of beliefs, of cultic practices, or of codes of behavior"—rather than the broader view of religion as "ultimate concern" because
it made it easier to distinguish the religious from the nonreligious in teaching about the Bible (Warshaw, 1972:116; Ackerman, 1972:473). Finally, the
institute found in a clearly delineated literary approach to the Bible (to be
discussed later in this essay) another way of steering safely through the
shoals of theological controversy and confessional sensitivity. Given the social
and legal pressures of the 1960s and 1970s, the institute was both a natural
product of its time and the appropriate response to its time. And though the
institute's gingerly approach seems at times a little too objectively antiseptic,
the Indiana Institute remains a model training program that embodies the
best solutions yet found to the problems facing teachers who must cope with
the Bible in the classroom.

As important as the need for developing pre- or in-service programs for
teachers has been the need for teacher resource materials. The directors of
the Indiana Institute discovered after one summer that they could not even
refer teachers to a convenient bibliography. And so the institute broadened
its original scope to include the preparation of materials to help teachers
with the full range of problems confronting them (Warshaw, 1972:111). The
result has been a noteworthy set of books that provides the single most valuable resource available for teachers of the Bible in the English classroom.
These books include the student textbook *The Bible in/as Literature* (Ackerman and Warshaw, 1976), two books of biblical backgrounds and scholarship (Ackerman, 1973; Juel, 1978), two anthologies of essays dealing with the
Bible as literature (Gros Louis, 1974) and with biblical images in literature

(Bartel, 1975), and a number of more practical aids including a bibliography of Bible-related curriculum materials (Warshaw and Miller, 1976), Warshaw's invaluable *Handbook* (1978a), a book on legal issues (Warshaw, 1979) and one on religious terms (Warshaw, 1978b). *The Bible Reader* (Abbott, 1969) with its interfaith annotations and Leland Ryken's discussion of the Bible as literature from an archetypal literary point of view and a theologically conservative stance (1974) help to round out the range of viewpoints a teacher needs to be prepared to bring into the classroom. Today no teacher should avoid opportunities to teach the Bible for want of resource materials. What is now available makes it possible for teachers to undertake a self-study course that will more than prepare them for the challenge of teaching the Bible as literature.

Curricular Materials

In courses on the Bible, the basic text is obvious. But in the secondary schools, teachers often find using a textbook—perhaps an anthology of biblical selections or a book that combines biblical with nonbiblical literature or one that provides supplementary materials of some kind—preferable to an unabridged edition of one of the many available translations of the Bible. In the years immediately following *Schempp*, curricular materials of this kind were almost nonexistent, but as publishers interested in cashing in on the new market created by elective courses in the high schools began to develop Bible and Bible-related textbooks, it soon became obvious that authors, editors, and publishers were as much in need of help as teachers. The concerns that shaped teacher training needed to be translated into guidelines and standards that could be applied to curricular materials. The observations in the section on sensitivity about the elements of bias found in so many textbooks illustrate the problem. A pluralistic approach demands standards that are not easy to meet, but in the later 1960s two projects pointed the direction, blazing the way toward a high standard of excellence for curricular materials.

The Bible Reader: An Interfaith Interpretation (Abbott and others, 1969) was the result of a project that pre-dated the *Schempp* decision. One Roman Catholic, one Jewish, and two Protestant scholars spent eight years preparing a book that would acquaint ordinary readers with those parts of the Bible that "best contribute to an understanding of our history, our literature, [and] our culture." The book is elaborately annotated and contains other valuable apparatus as well. The interfaith element of the book was reflected not merely in the background and training of the editors but also in their stated intention to help people understand passages related to the "religious observances and beliefs" of one another's faiths and that have "produced varied denominational emphases." The whole orientation of the project reflects the ideals of a pluralistic society coupled with a desire to emphasize "what we have in common" so that people can "live together in harmony" (ix). An invaluable resource to teachers, the book sets standards for academic responsibility, sensitivity to pluralism, interfaith perspectives, and meeting legal limits that are a model for other works.

A second project pointed in a different direction. In 1966 the Pennsylvania State University contracted to produce a course "in the literature of the Bible and other religious writings" that had been mandated by state law. Under the leadership of senior author John Whitney, a group of scholars and numerous other consultants created a course of study eventually published as *Religious Literature of the West* (Whitney and Howe, 1971). A collection of extracts from the Old and New Testaments, the Apocrypha, the rabbinic writings, and the *Qur'an*, the course was given extensive prepublication field-testing by certified English teachers throughout the state of Pennsylvania. The initial material was significantly revised in the process so as to stress "open inquiry," objectivity, and "various interpretive approaches" (15–16). The result is a fine textbook for teaching the Bible as religious literature but not for teaching the Bible as literature. The focus of the work is on meaning and interpretation of texts rather than on their formal or artistic qualities. It is thus better suited to a social studies course than to a literature course.

Works like these helped scholars and educators to set the direction that evaluation of curricular materials had to go. A widely used standard was developed by the Public Education Religion Studies Center (PERSC), which established six criteria: (1) Is the material educationally sound and pedagogically effective? (2) Does the material reflect an academically responsible approach? (3) Is the material sensitive to the religious and political problems of America's pluralistic society? (4) Does the material reflect a nonconfessional and interfaith perspective? (5) Does the material reflect and has it been written within the parameters of the major Supreme Court decisions? (6) Has the material been field-tested? Material must be suitable to both the teachers and students who will use it and to their levels of competence; it must reflect sound scholarship presented in a balanced and objective way; and it must reflect pluralistic values and encourage sensitivity to various positions and religious commitments (Bracher and others: 12–14; Warshaw, 1978a: 105–6; Collie). Guidelines like these not only enable teachers to evaluate curricular materials but also help them see where and how to compensate for the inadequacies of material they choose to use in the classroom.

In the nearly two decades since the *Schempp* decision, experience with the practical realities of taking the Bible to school has produced considerable clarification of what the Court required of those who undertook to teach the Bible in the public schools. The pluralism that brought about the decision itself became one of the key principles shaping teaching about the Bible in public education. It shaped teacher training and the development of curricular and resource materials. It shaped classroom approaches, emphases, and methodologies. And it shaped the evaluation of materials to be used in the classroom. It made objectivity and sensitivity central concerns of the classroom teacher.

The Impact on the Curriculum

When Justice Clark declared the Bible to be "worthy of study for its literary and historic qualities," he was pointing to the fact that the Bible has become an integral part of Western culture. Thus an education that ignored the Bible would be incomplete and inaccurate. The Bible provides the foundation stories of the three major Western religions—Judaism, Christianity, and Islam. It has shaped American social organization, institutions, economic practices, and sexual morality. It has provided crucial images for the United States in its times of crisis, from the New Exodus of the New England Puritans to the Civil War with its competing notions of the kingdom of God. Western art, music, and literature are permeated with biblical resonances; the very way we speak the language reflects biblical cadences. John Livingston Lowes called the King James Version of the Bible "the noblest monument of English prose" (1936). Not only is literature (and daily life) replete with biblical allusions, Northrop Frye has described the Christian Bible as the most complete form of the myth that underlies Western culture, the myth of creation and redemption, of progress and the kingdom of God (1957:314–26; 1964:110–11). As such, the Bible lies at the imaginative center of our literary tradition.

Theoretically then the Bible ought to receive major consideration in such divisions of the public school curriculum as literature and social studies as well as in interdisciplinary humanities courses. Probably the least has been done with the Bible in the humanities, particularly in terms of recognizable projects, courses, or curricular materials. The possibilities, however, are rich and varied. Where such courses include art and music, there are almost endless resources for lessons or units that focus on the Bible. The Bible can be incorporated also into the study of mythology (for sample texts see Leeming, 1973, and Jewkes, 1973). Popular culture provides still another humanities framework for dealing with the wealth of cultural artifacts— from editorial cartoons to popular songs to comic strips—that are biblically related. But in most sections of the country humanities courses are not a growing component of the curriculum. Despite an exciting potential they have seldom provided an important locus for the Bible in public education.

The Bible as a Social Force: Ignoring the Bible

Little has been done with the Bible in social studies. When the social studies have responded to the *Schempp* decision, they have been primarily concerned with a study of world or American religions or with the general area of religion and culture (for a summary and analysis of these developments, see Piediscalzi and Collie, 1972, and Will, 1981). This is as it should be, yet the major impact of the Bible on Western culture deserves some study from a social science perspective. The social studies—an amalgamation of psychology, sociology, history, and anthropology—attempt to understand the human person in society. This approach has never included philosophy or the relatively new discipline of religion studies, a discipline that has only reached full development in the past fifty years. It has thus excluded an important dimension of human social behavior from the purview of the social studies curriculum.

Religion studies seeks to understand human religious behavior and intention. People engage in religious behavior because they find it meaningful. Religion studies seeks to uncover that meaning. It seeks to make *religious* sense out of human behavior. One of the most useful definitions of religion is that of Clifford Geertz, who sees religion as the interlocking of life style and world view: "a religion is: (1) a system of symbols which act to (2) establish powerful pervasive, and long-lasting moods and motivations in men by (3) formulating conceptions of a general order of existence and (4) clothing these conceptions with such an aura of factuality that (5) the moods and motivations seem uniquely realistic" (4). Such a definition of religion recognizes that human action is never random or piecemeal. It fits into some conception of a unified whole—what Geertz calls a "general order of existence" and what the sociologist Peter Berger calls the "sacred canopy," which provides the overarching protection for mundane existence. Religion studies seeks to discover the relationship between human actions and this posited order.

The academic study of religion proceeds concretely from the description to functional analysis to systematic interpretation. Taking a phenomenon like the Ten Commandments, religion studies begins with descriptive analysis: What do they actually say? What was their context in ancient Near Eastern law? What was their setting in the ritual worship of Israel? What is the significance of their unique absolute form? Such questions lead to functional analysis: What functions of social organization, control, or modification did they perform? What was the relation of monotheism to monarchy? the nature of theocracy? the economic implications of Sabbath observance? All the explanations generated by such questions are valuable, but religion studies seeks to move beyond such explanations to find an overall interpretation of these data—one, for example, that explores the relation of these commandments to the covenant in Israel. For the covenant and the Exodus are the central symbols in Israel's picture of the cosmos and thus provide a general order of existence, a sacred canopy. Only when the relation between Sabbath observance and the Israelite notion of their special covenant with God is understood can the meaning of the Fourth Commandment be grasped.

Thus religion studies offers the teacher of social studies a workable approach to dealing with the Bible. Since very few social studies teachers are trained in either biblical or religion studies, few attempts to study the social and religious meaning of the Bible in its ancient contexts have been made. Nor are they likely to be. The few courses offered—"The Bible as History," for example—have usually been rather naive in their understanding of both the Bible and history. But this lack of past success should not prevent future development. Teachers trained in social studies methodologies should be encouraged to apply them to the Bible. And they may, in fact, feel more comfortable with a second option—analyzing the Bible in more recent cultural settings. The same kinds of descriptive, functional, and interpretive questions can be applied to topics like those dealt with in earlier chapters of this book or to the role of the Bible in such current phenomena as the abortion controversy, the women's and gay rights movements, and the involvement of evangelical Christians in the political process. In this way the social studies teacher, while not making a direct study of the Bible, can examine its cultural uses in American society.

One problem is that few suitable curricular materials exist to help guide the teacher in such a difficult undertaking. Two books discussed above would be of some use. *Religious Literature of the West* could be used in a class examining the original context of the Bible, and the *Bible Reader* points out many connections between the Bible and contemporary culture. In fact, *The Bible Reader's Guide*, a manual to help teachers develop units, includes a substantial section on social studies (Allen and others: 47–92). A second problem is that there is little professional support of Bible-related study in social studies. As both the Religion Studies Special Interest Group in the National Council for the Social Studies and a recent special issue of *Social Education* (45/1, January 1981) devoted to religion studies indicate, current professional interest centers on world religions rather than the Bible. In the public schools the primary study of the Bible has been and probably will continue to be in literature rather than social studies programs.

The Bible as Literature: Secularizing the Bible

Moving the Bible into the classroom requires finding an essentially secular way of dealing with it "as part of a program of secular education." A rationale tied to our American heritage and to democratic principles or to the formulation of moral and spiritual values in society becomes so entangled in the dogmas of what has been called America's civil religion that it blurs the distinctions the Court was attempting to make. The Bible must be kept within the broad cultural context and as free as possible of values-laden approaches. This objective can be most easily accomplished by perceiving the Bible as a document that fits naturally into a well-defined academic discipline with clear objectives and a methodology of its own. The strongly literary nature of the Bible's cultural role and the presence of a well-established language arts program in the public schools quite naturally suggested the solution of treating the Bible as literature. During the later 1960s courses appeared all over the country with titles like "Literary Genres of the Bible," "Literature from the Bible," "Hebrew Literature," and "Appreciation of Biblical Literature." Spurred by the newly competitive atmosphere of the elective curriculum, a venturesome teacher occasionally tried a title like "Man in Search of God." And the articles that began appearing in professional and church magazines were usually written by English teachers describing their fears: "Hey, it's against the law to have a Bible in school!" (Bagger: 6) and their successes: "I think I got more out of that unit than anything else I had in high school" (Stainer: 19). Thus the history of the Bible in the public schools becomes in its most recent phase an account of dealing with the Bible from a literary point of view. With this emergence of the Bible as a part of the English curriculum came a special set of problems that had little to do with legalities or with biblical scholarship.

Like Thayer Warshaw, whose first effort to teach the Bible was a course on "biblical knowledge" designed to overcome students' biblical illiteracy (1964), many English teachers traced their first impulses to teach the Bible as an "English" subject to their students' inability to field biblical allusions in literature. Ruth Hallman, a suburban Dayton, Ohio, high school teacher, has recounted how her frustrations in dealing in a senior English class with the parallel between Joseph and Potiphar's wife and Henry Fielding's Lady Booby and Joseph Andrews led her to propose a nine-week elective course to familiarize students with frequently encountered Bible stories, characters, symbols, and quotations (1974:80). Her frustration and her success were duplicated across the country. But as experience with new courses accumulated, it became evident that various approaches and emphases—more or less literary—were being employed. Behind often innocuous sounding and loosely differentiated titles like "Biblical Literature" and "The Bible as Literature" things were happening that were not very accurately reflected in the titles being used and that betrayed rather dissimiliar objectives.

It has become conventional to distinguish several common approaches to teaching the Bible in English classes (e.g. Warshaw, 1978a:30–31). The Bible *for* literature surveys those parts of the Bible that most readily enable students to understand biblical allusions in English and American literature: for example, Keats's allusion to Ruth "amid the alien corn" in "Ode to a Nightingale" or the Jacob-Esau relationship employed in Robert Louis Stevenson's *The Master of Ballantrae*. Although a course or unit taking this approach offers little more than instruction in footnoting great (and not so great) literature, biblical literacy is an important teaching objective. Many biblical allusions are crucial to understanding the works in which they appear. The Bible *for* literature also provides a comfortable refuge for teachers hoping to escape religious controversy by avoiding discussion of the "meaning" of biblical texts. But the approach, by concentrating upon factual content, is a severely limited one.

The Bible *in* literature refers to studying the Bible in conjunction with nonbiblical literature that makes extensive or significant use of biblical materials or that adapts or amplifies biblical stories. Ernest Hemingway's *The Old Man and the Sea*, for example, makes important use of the Christ figure, and Archibald MacLeish's *J. B.* is a widely used retelling of Job

(Hallman, 1972; Bracher, 1972). The Bible *and* literature suggests a still looser relationship between biblical and nonbiblical literature based on parallels in theme or form rather than on the use of biblical content. Stephen Vincent Benét's story "By the Waters of Babylon" might be read with the Garden of Eden story, or some seventeenth-century religious poems might be read with Psalms. Archetypal relationships between biblical and secular literature might be examined in D. H. Lawrence's story "The Horse Dealer's Daughter," with the pattern of symbolic death and rebirth. Courses or units on the Bible *and* literature, like those on the Bible *in* literature, often devote more time to studying nonbiblical than biblical materials. And because courses of this kind are often organized thematically, attention to the content and artistry of a biblical text may be limited. But studying the Bible *in* literature, particularly, offers an understanding of how writers have used the Bible and of its continuing impact upon our culture. It also can illuminate a biblical text by revealing an author's imaginative response to it. But both approaches risk giving more attention than deserved to nonbiblical literature of an inferior order simply because it has a discernible relationship to the Bible.

Those who want to keep the Bible at the center of a course find the ideal approach to be the Bible *as* literature. This approach concentrates on reading biblical texts in the same way that a text by Homer, Milton, Whitman, or Steinbeck would be read in the classroom. Thus, English teachers are encouraged to deal with the Bible in terms of the "usual categories of their discipline" rather than in terms of biblical scholarship or relationship to other literature. The Bible *as* literature is usually explained as the study of a biblical narrative in terms of the traditional elements of fiction (plot, character, setting, theme) or of a poem in terms of imagery and figures of speech, for example. The emphasis is usually placed on the "formal literary aspects" of the work, artistry, technical considerations, and style. Literature understood in this way allows for a classroom treatment of biblical texts that emphasizes content and how it is expressed, analysis but not interpretation and evaluation.

These distinctions can be summarized by adapting Thayer Warshaw's typology and using the book of Job as its illustration:

(1) The Bible *for* literature asks students to get firmly in mind the story and arguments in the book of Job as well as its famous lines so that their later examinations of literature—or of music or art—can then call upon their knowledge.

(2) The Bible *in* literature asks students to read and analyze Job and MacLeish's *J. B.*, perhaps emphasizing the latter, in order to see how a modern writer uses the Bible story and to discuss the relationship between the two selections.

(3) The Bible *and* literature asks students to read the book of Job and *The Bridge of San Luis Rey* or *Candide* to see how the theme of unmerited suffering is treated in each book.

(4) The Bible *as* literature asks students to examine the artistry of the book of Job: its structure and the framing, characterization, dialogue, use of irony—verbal and situational—its recurring images and motifs, and the sweep of its language.

To this list, Warshaw adds a fifth possibility: the Bible and *its contexts* asks students to read Job and relate it to the historical and cultural climate of postexilic Israel (1975; 1978a:30–31). While this is not a basically literary approach, it is an almost essential adjunct to any presentation of older literature in the classroom, whether it is *The Odyssey* or *Pride and Prejudice.* English teachers, who are used to dealing with old texts and to recreating their contexts, will recognize such cultural and historical concerns as a familiar type of activity. Neither Greek nor Elizabethan drama, for example, can be taught without helping students understand the theaters of those periods. Thus, there is a point at which biblical scholarship and the literary study of the Bible come together.

Despite the fact that the curricular materials developed during the last decade have placed a good deal of emphasis on the Bible *in* literature and the Bible *and* literature, it is the Bible *as* literature—the direct, literary examination of the biblical text by the same means that are used to interpret secular literature—that has most dramatically shaped the treatment of the Bible in public education in the last decade. Such serious treatment of the Bible as literature is a relatively new development. As recently as 1970 the directors of the Indiana Institute found very little true literary analysis among either the voluminous work of biblical critics or the occasional efforts of literary critics. To fill this void the institute produced a series of "innovative lectures," some of which have found their way into print in *Literary Interpretations of Biblical Narratives* (Gros Louis, 1974).

Whatever the ultimate impact of such efforts on biblical studies generally, treating the Bible as literature provides a suitably secular classroom approach to the Bible, which effectively distances it from theological and religious controversy. The Indiana Institute has evolved a well-defined way of dealing with the Bible as literature that meets these objectives. It starts by drawing a distinction between human and literary goals in teaching literature. The latter focus on "craftsmanship" and the "formal literary aspects" of a work of literature, and these are the aspects—including such familiar matters as plot, characterization, point of view, setting, and imagery—to be emphasized in dealing with the Bible as literature. The focus, in short, is on form, conventions, techniques, and literary devices. Institute materials repeatedly stress the importance of examining the artistry of the Bible in these terms and then relating it to content. Thus a kind of methodology evolves. The class begins with an analytical examination of the details of content and of the occurrence of literary techniques and devices. The second stage is to uncover structures of detail and device and to consider how form, thus perceived, relates to content and how form and content work together to produce meaning.

The methodology is the familiar one of close reading, which under the influence of new critical theory has been the dominant pedagogical technique in literature classrooms for more than a generation. A more sophisticated statement of this approach is found in the published work of Kenneth Gros Louis, the principal lecturer on the Bible as Literature at the Indiana Institute. By his own admission a "formalist," Gros Louis is strongly influenced by new critical methodology. Biblical narratives, he suggests, should be studied "as worlds of their own apart from all of these concerns" of context. The critic should analyze "internal dynamics, ironies and paradoxes, interaction among the characters and among scenes, narrational intrusion, settings, development of thematic and imagistic patterns, transformations of character, formal structure." "The text is best understood," he concludes, "when taken as a whole and when the questions raised center on literary craftsmanship" (13). The level of literary analysis can become, Gros Louis seems to suggest, quite sophisticated.

The institute's emphasis on literary elements and on meaning arrived at inductively provides a safely circumspect and indirect way of approaching the ideas of the Bible. The institute does not suggest that a teacher avoid discussing the religious themes of the Bible and their "relevance to the reader's own experience and values" (Ackerman and Warshaw: 1; Warshaw, 1978a:20–21). But by subordinating human goals and making literary goals the central concern of the classroom, the teacher can carve out a large neutral ground in which the Bible can effectively be distanced from the difficult interpretations of church and synagogue. "It seems advisable," suggests Warshaw, "that teachers should not focus students' attention, especially at the outset, on the religious ideas expressed or implied by the stories" (1978a:28). Matter and manner, then, are most important—not values and issues. Matter and manner *and* the classroom experience itself: "The answers are less important than the process of arriving at them. Students have to consider both what the text says and how it is said. The invitation to use their imaginations does not come out of the blue; it is tied to what the students have been digging out of the text" (Warshaw, 1978a:37).

Leland Ryken has argued that controversial religious issues cannot be sidestepped this easily. Noting the essentially religious nature of biblical literature, he observes that "this religious identity manifests itself in the purpose of the writers, who display a strong didactic impulse. Probably no work of literature in the Bible exists only for the sake of artistic pleasure or entertainment" (1974:16). Furthermore, says Ryken, the Bible tends to engage its reader in a special way:

> The concept of encounter goes far to explain what happens to the reader of biblical literature. There is an important sense in which the reader of biblical literature is its subject and center of reference. Biblical writers, motivated by a consciously didactic purpose, intend to tell the reader something about himself. From this perspective, biblical literature exhibits two patterns—the reader's humiliation and his education. . . . The reader who

assimilates this twofold lesson will have participated in something more than a literary
experience. In the final analysis the reading of biblical literature is an encounter with
God. (21)

These are not the only problems that arise from treating the Bible *as*
literature as a matter of artistry. The method of close reading is a fairly
sophisticated one, and it assumes a sophisticated text. Applying it to the
Bible applies it to a text to which it is not, in many cases, ideally suited.
Much biblical literature has more in common with myth, folk material, and
popular literature than with the literary texts usually studied in the classroom (Robertson: 16–32). It is, moreover, often explicitly didactic. Such
considerations—even granting the artistry of biblical passages and putting
aside the problems of attempting close readings of materials in translation—
limit the effectiveness and appropriateness of the method. The results often
yield something that might better be called rhetorical than literary analysis,
and there is the danger—as with all close reading—of over-reading the text,
of being too ingenious. Nevertheless the effort to test the assumptions of
artistic worth, of careful fashioning, of the Bible's susceptibility to close
reading has produced a valuable attempt to understand the literary nature
of the Bible. The long-range value of these efforts is still to be determined,
but in the meantime the approach provides a valid solution to the problem
of presenting the Bible in a secular educational setting.

Even if one regards examination of technical nuances and of sophisticated relationships between form and content as appropriate objectives for
the secondary classroom, restricting the arena of literary analysis and discussion to the world of the text itself tends to restrict the depth of thematic discussion and may not necessarily bring to light the most significant literary
facts about the Bible. Teachers of the Bible, like any literature teachers,
eventually may wish to go beyond the text itself. One option is to turn to the
"human goals" of literary study, to the world of values and personal experience, and thus to the world of belief and religious commitment. But there
are at least two literary means of moving away from the text itself and still
maintaining a check upon the troublesome area of values and issues. Both
involve relating biblical texts to other literature and to broader categories of
literature. One of these is the generic approach; the other is the archetypal
approach.

The oldest approach to the Bible as literature—and one that has not yet
lost its vitality—is the generic approach (Moulton; Gardiner; Chase; Ryken,
1974; and Warshaw, 1978a:65–67). Often, in an effort to treat the Bible as
one does other literary texts, one attempts to fit the Bible into the framework of the established pattern of genres—fiction, poetry, drama, and their
complex categories of sub-genres. Thus, one finds discussion of biblical literature as short story or epithalamion or tragedy. But because the Bible does
not always fit easily into these familiar categories, the list of generic labels
attached to biblical literature is widely diverse, ranging from epic, satire,

and pastoral on the one hand to prophecy, gospel, epistle, oratory, and apocalypse on the other. In between stand such terms as saga, legend, encomium, proverb, riddle, and parable. Such terms come from several sources—modern historical criticism, classical literature, oral and folk literature, and biblical form criticism among them. This bewildering multiplicity of categories only partially overlaps the familiar categories of classroom literary genre study. Thus, the generic approach to the Bible draws the student into a confusing world of unfamiliar categories and of literature that doesn't conform to the expectation aroused by the familiar labels attached to it. Generic study can also lead to a proliferation of sub-genres that can be as pointlessly unproductive as over-ingenious close readings.

The generic approach poses two special problems. One is the danger of imposing inappropriate forms of biblical literature—like Richard Moulton, who found sonnets in the Bible (306–15) or like Alton Capps, who in his generically organized textbook distinguished six kinds of lyric poetry including odes, elegies, dramatic lyrics, and the lyric idyl (1971). The fact remains that Esther, although a piece of fiction, is not a novella, and Job, although making extensive use of dialogue, is not a play. And it is doubtful if anything is gained by labeling the familiar thirteenth chapter of 1 Corinthians a "hymn to love" (Juel: 321). Generic classification can lead to distortions that no responsible literary critic or scholar would countenance. The second problem relates to dividing the biblical text. What constitutes a legitimate and independent unit of material in the Bible, one that can reasonably be identified by a generic label? Should books of the Bible be treated as independent units? Can the testing of Abraham or the story of Joseph and his brothers be separated from the rest of Genesis? Can the great story of the Exodus, scattered through four different books, be treated as a unit? And in the New Testament, should the teacher of literature follow the current fashion among biblical scholars and treat each Gospel as an independent unit rather than fragmenting them or amalgamating them?

The answers to these questions are not easy. On the one hand, Howard Mumford Jones has labeled the Bible "a huge and colorful mosaic" (50), and T. R. Henn, failing to find "literary" unity in the Bible, notes that its "units . . . are relatively small" (21–31). On the other hand, while pointing out that the word "Bible" means "little books," Leland Ryken observes "Because individual parts of biblical literature are interdependent, no single work can be regarded as a totally self-contained unit. The meaning of individual works is deepened and modified by other works" (1974:14–15). He notes too that there is a unity of plot provided by the "great spiritual conflict between good and evil" that provides the framework of the Bible (26–27). The Bible turns out to be much like Homer and Chaucer—a work that is at once a mosaic of pieces that can have an independent status (and may even have a separate generic identity) and a work in which we seek unity without a guarantee that we will find it.

Although a sense of the genres of biblical literature is part of such recent discussions of the Bible as literature as those of T. R. Henn and Leland Ryken, problems like these militate against organizing courses or units around a generic approach. But generic classifications and parallels, if not insisted upon too rigidly and categorically, are valuable ways of dealing with biblical literature. Genre is one way of relating the Bible to the already familiar, and it is also a way of imposing some order on the unfamiliar. Definition and comparison and contrast are essential modes of learning. It is interesting to point out that the story of Joseph has parallels with legendary material from other cultures. It can be helpful in studying the story of Saul to point out similarities in his character to the characteristics of the Greek tragic hero. And the story of the Exodus certainly has "epic sweep," even if this use of the term is little more than metaphorical. Most teachers will find the generic approach an essential component of any good course on biblical literature. Genres are a useful way of organizing treatment of literary techniques and conventions, and the generic approach is a valuable way of helping students understand biblical literature by relating it to the larger world of literature with which they already have experience.

Another interesting kind of parallel that can be made with the story of Joseph is to point out its similarities to the fairy tale of Cinderella and to the Horatio Alger stories. Such parallels point to a second way of analyzing and then reaching beyond a literary text. Biblical literature can be related to secular literature and even to nonliterary material through an archetypal approach. In its way, archetypal criticism also deals with the rudiments of literature, with the basic building blocks of convention and form and content. Archetypal critics, however, are especially concerned with the connections created by the recurrence of similar units in numerous works of literature. They propose that the significant literary structures are those that emerge from a careful study of these similarities. Patterns of recurring archetypes— images, character types, symbols, and narrative patterns—not only provide essential insight into the form and content of individual literary works but also provide the means of relating those works to each other and, ultimately, of perceiving the structural unity of all literature. Northrop Frye, the leading proponent of archetypal criticism, has argued persuasively that archetypes also provide the raw materials as well as the shaping principles of human imaginative experience. Hence archetypes undergird all literary creativity, and a study of archetypes in literature becomes an essential process of educating the imagination (1957; 1964).

There are several ways in which the Bible can be fruitfully related to archetypal criticism. Northrop Frye has called the Bible "the major informing influence on literary symbolism" (1957:316). The Bible is a major source (though not the only one) of archetypal images in Western culture, and thus it is a major source of the basic building blocks of literature. To have some knowledge of biblical narratives and their archetypal nature is thus a first step in a student's literary education. But such knowledge also helps one to understand the form and content of biblical narratives themselves by placing them within the system of archetypal images and patterns. Beyond this the Christian Bible, says Frye, contains the "most complete form" of the basic myth of our culture (1964:110; 1957:314–16). Myths stick together and "the containing framework of the mythology takes the shape of a feeling of lost identity which we had once and may have again" (1964:111). Thus the Bible embodies a kind of monomyth of central cultural significance. It follows a pattern of loss and recovery that is articulated in the Christian Bible in the sweep of the whole story from the Garden of Eden to Revelation. Another archetypally significant pattern of most of the Bible is the dialectical pattern that depicts opposition of two worlds: the ideal and the unideal worlds, paradise and hell. These patterns not only offer a way of seeing a continuity to the narrative portions of the Bible but also unify the Bible itself. As Ryken put it, "Although biblical literature appears at first glance to be a heterogeneous collection of fragments, it turns out to be a single, composite whole" (1974:25). Goals like these have been implemented in two series of textbooks for use in secondary English classes: the three volumes in the Uses of the Imagination series (Lee and Lee, 1973a; 1973b; 1974) and the six booklets in the Literature of the Bible series (Ryken and others).

Archetypal criticism with its interest in uncovering literary megastructures is a highly systematized endeavor. Teachers making use of it will always be plugging into an elaborate scheme of terms, categories, and relationships. Both teacher and student may need initiation into these mysteries before they can make biblical applications (although the Uses of the Imagination series undertakes the initiation process inductively). Like the generic approach, archetypal criticism runs the risk of distorting literary works by forcing too inflexible an application of its categories. Finally, it is a comparative method and unless used in relationship to other literature may lose much of its point. Nevertheless, some attempt to deal with biblical literature from this perspective is illuminating. It helps students understand how biblical literature works, what its appeal and continuing interest are, and how it relates to other literature and even to nonliterary aspects of their culture and experience. The methodology of archetypal criticism takes the reader beyond the text, but its essentially secular orientation assures that movement of being broadly cultural and not religious.

Summary

Today the Bible appears most often in the public school curriculum by virtue of its status as one of our chief cultural legacies. This standing has earned it a place in the high school English program. There, within the constraints of objectivity established by the Supreme Court and the need for sensitivity imposed by a pluralistic society, the Bible, as part of the canon of classic works that have become the standard fare of literary study, is taught for its impact on other literature and for its literary artistry. English teachers have found ways of presenting the Bible that enable them to treat it as they would any other piece of literature and in essentially the same terms. In so doing, they have found a way of distancing the Bible from the touchy problems of theological controversy and personal commitment. The Bible can be dealt with in an essentially secular context, which in an open classroom allows sufficient latitude for students to experience the diversity of each other's beliefs while coming to appreciate the richness of biblical literature. Much has been accomplished in the years since the *Schempp* decision. Models, guidelines, and resources are now available for teachers who wish to offer instruction in biblical literature.

Unfortunately, these achievements are not as widely known as they should be. Although more than a decade of experience has proven that the Bible can be studied in the public schools legally, responsibly, and effectively, confusion still surrounds the place of the Bible in public education. This confusion stems from a faulty understanding of the role of the public schools in American life, from distortions of the Supreme Court's decisions about the Bible and public education, and from a failure to distinguish between religious and academic approaches to the Bible. Nearly twenty years after *Schempp* many schools, especially in the South, still carry on devotional Bible readings much like those the Court found unconstitutional. These schools seldom have academic courses on the Bible (Dierenfield, 1967). In other schools formal courses on the Bible are offered, but because of confusion and misunderstanding they are often taught from a religious (usually conservative Christian) perspective. This evangelical approach to the Bible confuses students, raises the suspicions of religious minorities, and disconcerts school administrators wary of controversy. In short, the impact of two decades of debate over the legal, intellectual, and cultural issues raised by the *Schempp* decision is yet to be felt in all quarters.

The varied achievements of the post-*Schempp* years have not been as widely utilized as had been expected. The momentum of the early 1970s, when dozens of new courses appeared each year and publishers were eager to issue textbooks for them, has slowed, and a recent development—the decisive shift "back to basics"—has begun to limit the study of the Bible in public schools. The fad of optionality has given way to the fad of basics, which has discouraged electives and novel courses and encouraged a more traditional curriculum. That traditional curriculum, unfortunately, never made much provision for study of the Bible. While the new priorities have not entirely eradicated biblical courses and units, it is difficult to tell how many of the gains of the 1970s have been transferred to the more standard courses that have been reappearing in high schools in recent years. Curricular surveys seem to suggest an increase in public school study of the Bible over the earlier period but little continued growth (*PERSC Newsletter* 7/1

[1979]:4–5). At this point, the future expansion of study of the Bible in public education looks uncertain.

Dwindling opportunities for study of the Bible in the schools in turn shrink the market for textbooks. Already some of the books published in the late 1960s and early 1970s have gone out of print, decreasing the resources available to teachers. If this seems an ominous note, it is good to remember that the old adage is probably true: teachers teach what they have been taught. Thus, the classroom teacher remains the key to the future of the Bible in the public school. Many classroom teachers are still teaching the Bible, but few of them have learned anything about the Bible as part of their own pre-service education. They are self-educated or the products of the in-service programs of the 1970s. Actually, many teachers still work without benefit of the developments of the last decade: without knowledge of biblical scholarship, without knowledge of the literary analysis of biblical texts, without an understanding of the issue of sensitivity. There is a real need for appropriate teacher-training opportunities for pre-service and especially in-service education in the Bible. In addition to the dramatic success of the Indiana Institute discussed above, modest programs have also been attempted by other universities including the University of Kansas, Wright State University, Southwest Missouri State University, and Harvard University. Unfortunately, no permanent legacy of training programs has survived from the high point of activity in the early 1970s. Thus, the continued inclusion of the Bible as a notable component of the public school curriculum will depend largely upon the development of a sustained program of teacher training.

Teacher training, however, is not the only item for the agenda of the future. The study of the Bible must be extended beyond the English curriculum. Imaginative approaches to integrating the Bible into social studies and humanities programs are an obvious need. Thus, the agenda should include also new models for studying the Bible and other sacred literature in a pluralistic and secular context. In this respect the future is wide open. More than a decade and a half of activity has shown the climate in the schools to be receptive, not hostile. The pluralism characteristic of our society has already encouraged not one voice but many voices. Out of it has come a healthy diversity. And from this variety of activities and views has emerged a clearer sense of what is appropriate, of what is workable, of what is interesting—of what it means to include the Bible in a secular program of education.

WORKS CONSULTED

Abbott, Walter M.; Gilbert, Arthur; Hunt, Rolfe Lanier; and Swaim, J. Carter
1969   *The Bible Reader: An Interfaith Interpretation.*
                New York: Bruce.

Ackerman, James S.
1967   *On Teaching the Bible as Literature: A Guide to*
                Selected Biblical Narratives for Secondary
                Schools. Bloomington: Indiana University Press.
1971   "Religion in the Public Schools." *PTA Magazine*
                65/9: 2–5.
1972   "The Indiana University Summer Institute on
                Teaching the Bible in Secondary English." *Journal*
                of Church and State 14: 457–74.

Ackerman, James S.; Jenks, Alan Wilkin; Jenkinson, Edward B.; and Blough, Jan.
1973   *Teaching the Old Testament in English Classes.*
                Bloomington: Indiana University Press.

Ackerman, James S., and Warshaw, Thayer S.
1976   *The Bible as/in Literature.* Glenview, IL: Scott,
                Foresman.

Allen, Rodney F.; Barr, David L.; Panoch, James V.; and Spivey, Robert A.
1970   *The Bible Reader's Guide.* New York: Bruce.

American Association of School Administrators
1965   *Religion in the Public Schools.* A Report by the
                Commission on Religion in the Public Schools,
                American Association of School Administrators.
                New York: Harper & Row.

Bagger, Elizabeth R.
1972   "I Teach Bible in Public School." *The Lutheran*
                10/2: 6–9.

Bartel, Roland, ed.
1975   *Biblical Images in Literature.* Nashville: Abing-
                don.

Berger, Peter
1967   *The Sacred Canopy: Elements of a Sociological
                           Theory of Religion.* Garden City, NY: Doubleday.

Boles, Donald E.
1961   *The Bible, Religion, and the Public Schools.* New
                           York: Collier Books.
1967   *The Two Swords: Commentaries and Cases in
                           Religion and Education.* Ames: Iowa State Univer-
                           sity Press.

Bracher, Peter
1972   "The Bible *and* Literature." *English Journal* 61:
                           1170–75.

Bracher, Peter; Panoch, James V.; Piediscalzi, Nicholas;
and Uphoff, James K.
1974   *PERSC Guidebook: Public Education Religion
                           Studies, Questions and Answers.* Dayton: Public
                           Education Religion Studies Center, Wright State
                           University.

Broward County (Florida) School Board
1971   *The Bible As Literature.* School Board of Broward
                           County, Florida.

Brown, Douglas C.
1975   *The Enduring Legacy: Biblical Dimensions in
                           Modern Literature.* New York: Scribner's.

Capps, Alton C.
1969   "A Realistic Approach to Biblical Literature."
                           English Journal 58: 230–35.
1971   *The Bible as Literature.* New York: McGraw-Hill.

Chase, Mary Ellen
1952   *The Bible and the Common Reader.* Rev. ed. New
                           York: Macmillan.

Collie, William
1976   "PERSC Evaluation of Curriculum Materials: The
                           Problems, the Procedures and the Process." *PERSC
                           Newsletter* 3/3: 5–6.

Dierenfield, R. B.
      1967   "The Impact of the Supreme Court Decisions on
                                    Religion in Public Schools." *Religious Education*
                                    62: 445–51.
      1973   "Religion in Public Schools: Its Current Status."
                                    Religious Education 68: 96–114.

Frye, Northrop
      1957   *Anatomy of Criticism: Four Essays*. Princeton:
                                    Princeton University Press.
      1964   *The Educated Imagination*. Bloomington: Indiana
                                    University Press.

Gardiner, J. H.
      1907   *The Bible as English Literature*. New York:
                                    Scribner's.

Geertz, Clifford
      1966   "Religion as a Cultural Symbol." In *Anthropological
                                    Approaches to the Study of Religion*, ed. M. Ban-
                                    ton. London: Tavistock Publications. Pp. 1–46.

Gros Louis, Kenneth R. R., ed.
      1974   *Literary Interpretations of Biblical Narratives*.
                                    Nashville: Abingdon.

Hallman, Ruth D.
      1972   "Teaching *Job* and *J. B.*" *English Journal* 61: 658–
                                    62.
      1974   "Bible Literature in the Curriculum." *Today's
                                    Education* 63/1: 80–82.

Henn, T. R.
      1970   *The Bible as Literature*. New York: Oxford Uni-
                                    versity Press.

Herberg, Will
      1960   *Protestant-Catholic-Jew: An Essay in American
                                    Religious Sociology*. Garden City, NY: Doubleday.

Hildebrand, R. Paul
      1966   "We Study the Bible as Literature." *English Jour-
                                    nal* 55: 1022–29.

Hogan, Robert
      1965   "The Bible in the English Program." *English Jour-
                                    nal* 5: 488–94.

Jewkes, W. T.
1973   *Man the Myth-Maker*. New York: Harcourt Brace
                           Jovanovich.

Jones, Howard Mumford
1960   "The Bible from a Literary Point of View." In *Five
                           Essays on the Bible: Papers Read at the 1960
                           Annual Meeting of the American Council of
                           Learned Societies*. Erwin R. Goodenough and oth-
                           ers. New York: American Council of Learned Soci-
                           eties. Pp. 45–59.

Juel, Donald
1978   *An Introduction to New Testament Literature*.
                           Nashville: Abingdon.

Lee, Alvin A., and Lee, Hope Arnott
1973a   *The Garden and the Wilderness*. New York: Har-
                           court Brace Jovanovich.
1973b   *The Temple and the Ruin*. New York: Harcourt
                           Brace Jovanovich.
1974   *The Peaceable Kingdom*. New York: Harcourt
                           Brace Jovanovich.

Leeming, David Adams
1973   *Mythology: The Voyage of the Hero*. Philadel-
                           phia: Lippincott.

Littell, Franklin
1962   *From State Church to Pluralism: A Protestant
                           Interpretation of Religion in American History*.
                           Garden City, NY: Doubleday.

Lowes, John Livingston
1936   "The Noblest Monument of English Prose." In
                           Essays in Appreciation. Port Washington, NY:
                           Kennikat, reprint 1967. Pp. 3–31.

Marty, Martin
1959   *The New Shape of American Religion*. New York:
                           Harper and Row.

Michaelsen, Robert
1970   *Piety in the Public Schools*. New York: Macmillan.

1977   "Constitution, Courts and The Study of Religion."
                Journal of the American Academy of Religion
                45/3: 291–308.

Moulton, Richard G.
    1899   *The Literary Study of the Bible: An Account of
                    the Leading Forms of Literature Represented in
                    the Sacred Writings, Intended for English Read-
                    ers.* Rev. ed. Boston: Heath.

Panoch, James V., and Barr, David L.
    1968   *Religion Goes to School: A Practical Handbook
                    for Teachers.* New York: Harper & Row.

Phenix, Philip H.
    1967   "Religion in American Public Schools," *Religion
                    and the Public Order.* Chicago: University of Chi-
                    cago Press.

    1969   "Religion in Public Education: Principles and
                    Issues." *Religion and Public School Curriculum:
                    Proceedings of the National Council on Religion
                    and Public Education,* ed. Richard U. Smith. *Reli-
                    gious Education* 67/4 (Pt. 2): 11–24.

Piediscalzi, Nicholas, and Collie, William E., eds.
    1977   *Teaching About Religion in Public Schools.* Niles,
                    IL: Argus Communications.

Robertson, David
    1977   *The Old Testament and The Literary Critic.* Phil-
                    adelphia: Fortress.

Ryken, Leland
    1974   *The Literature of the Bible.* Grand Rapids: Zon-
                    dervan.

    1977   *A Teacher's Guide to Parables and Portraits of
                    the Bible.* Chicago: Literature of the Bible.

Ryken, Leland, and others
    1977   The Literature of the Bible Series (booklets with
                    teacher's guides): *Heroes of Genesis,* ed. Leland
                    Ryken; *Heroines of the Bible,* ed. Leland Ryken
                    and Mary Ryken; *Poetry of the Bible,* ed. Vernon
                    Boerman; *The Garden and the City,* ed. Dan Van-
                    der Ark; *The Epic of Exodus,* ed. Dan Vander
                    Ark; *Parables and Portraits of the Bible,* ed.
                    Leland Ryken. Chicago: Literature of the Bible.

Stainer, Betty
  1967   "Don't Forget to Bring Your Bible to Class." *Minnesota Journal of Education* 48/4: 16–19.

Vedral, Joyce
  1973   *A Literary Survey of the Bible.* Plainfield, NJ: Logos International.

Wainwright Report
  1969   "Report of the Wainwright House Conference on the Bible in the Public Schools, Rye, New York, April 15–16, 1969." New York: Laymen's National Bible Committee.

Warshaw, Thayer S.
  1964   "Studying the Bible in Public School." *English Journal* 53: 91–100.

  1972   "Teaching English Teachers to Teach the Bible: The Indiana University Model." *Indiana Social Studies Quarterly* 25/1: 110–18.

  1975   "Approaches to the Bible in Literature Classes." *PERSC Newsletter* 2/2: 2.

  1978a   *Handbook for Teaching the Bible in Literature Classes.* Nashville: Abingdon.

  1978b   *Abingdon Glossary of Religious Terms.* Nashville: Abingdon.

  1979   *Religion, Education, and the Supreme Court.* Nashville: Abingdon.

Warshaw, Thayer S., and Miller, Betty Lou, eds.
  1976   *Bible-Related Curriculum Materials: A Bibliography.* Nashville: Abingdon.

Whitney, John R., and Howe, Susan W.
  1971   *Religious Literature of the West.* Minneapolis: Augsburg.

Will, Paul; with Piediscalzi, Nicholas, and Swyhart, Barbara, eds.
  1981   *Public Education Religion Studies: An Overview.* Chico, CA: Scholars Press.

INDEX

Abbot, Ezra, 104
Abbott, Walter M., S.J., 1b1, 145, 192
Abingdon v. *Schempp*, 62, 126, 166
Abott, Lyman, 131, 137, 138
Ackerman, James S., 169, 174, 175, 192
Adler, Cyrus, 51, 68
Allen, Rodney F., 192
American Association of Christian Schools, 62
American Association of School Administrators, 168, 192
American Bible League, 124
American Institute of Sacred Literature, 126
American Sunday School Union, 26, 82, 94, 146
Anderson, Bernhard, 143
Andover Seminary, 42
Anglicans, 15
Archaeology, 132
Archetypal literary criticism, 173, 188
Arnold, C. Harvey, 113, 117
Arthur, William, 122, 138
Asbury, Francis, 78
Association of Christian Schools, 68
Association of Christian Schools International, 62
Auburn Seminary, 67
Augustine, 9

Bacon, Benjamin W., 110–13, 117
Bagger, Elizabeth R., 182, 192
Bailyn, Bernard, 6, 20
Bainton, Roland H., 117
Baldwin, Lewis, 81
Bancroft, George, 103
Baptist, 13
Baptist Missionary Training School for Women, 53
Barclay, William, 159, 161
Bar Mitzvah, 61, 67
Baronius, 128
Barr, James, 156
Bartel, Roland, ed., 192
Bates, Katharine Lee, 135, 138
Bat Mitzvah, 61
Baum, Gregory, 150, 157
Baxter, Richard, 20
Bayly, Lewis, 10, 20
Beecher, Lyman, 79
Benderly, Samuel, 67
Ben-Horin, Meir, 48, 68
Berger, Peter, 193

Bernard Revel Graduate School of Yeshiva, 59
Bertrand, M., 65, 69
Bible,
   attitudes toward, 54, 122
   authority of, 8, 11, 97, 122, 127, 156
   memorization of, 80, 81
   proper interpretations of, 46, 64, 84, 115, 143, 145, 152, 155
   role of in colonial education, 19
   social functions of, 19, 47, 55, 79, 94, 129, 157, 179
Bible and nationalism, 31
Bible and piety, 12, 113, 128, 167
Bible as literature, 57, 131, 181
Bible in Public Schools, 124, 126, 129, 131, 138, 165–91
   bias, 173, 175
   criteria for curricula, 178
   curricula, 177
   objectivity, 170, 171
   sensitivity, 172
   social studies, 179, 181
   teacher training, 170, 173–77
Bible institutes, 54, 63
Bible Reader, 181
Bible reading, 17, 27, 45, 166
   Edgerton, Wisconsin, court decision banning, 127. See also *Abingdon* v. *Schempp*
Bible Schools, 52
Bible School Curricula, 149, 152, 173
Bible study,
   goals of, 63, 81, 82, 84, 98, 125, 149, 181–84
   methods of, 83, 85, 89, 90, 92, 93, 97, 99, 104, 125, 135, 146, 176, 184, 186, 188
   and sociology, 114. See also Bible, social functions of
Bible Study Fellowship, 149
Bible Student and Teacher, The, 124
Bible Study in Public Schools, 167. See also: Bible in Public Schools
Bible Today, The, 65
Bible translation, 16, 41, 64, 125, 132, 152
Biblical ethnocentricism, 31
Biblical renewal (Protestant) in 19th century, 52ff
Bierbower, Austin, 128
Blackstone, W. E., 52
Blair, John, 18
Blake, J., 32, 40
Blodgett, H., 138
Boles, Donald E., 126, 131, 138, 167, 193

Boston Latin School, 15
Boville, Robert G., 125
Boyer, Anne M., 79
Boyer, Paul, 94
Boylan, Anne M., 94
Bracher, Peter, 193
Brauer, Jerald C., 9, 20
Bray, F. Chaplin, 134, 138
Bray, Thomas, 17
Brennan, Justice William, 67
Briggs, Charles, 105, 107–9, 117, 124
Broward County (Florida) Board of Educa-
    tion, 168, 172, 193
Brown, Daniel, 65, 69
Brown, Douglas C., 173, 193
Brown, Jerry W., 101, 103, 104, 117
Brown, Raymond E., S.S., 150, 160, 161
Brown v. Board of Education, 166
Bruce, F. F., 5, 20
Buckle, Emory Stevens, 78, 80, 94
Buckminster, Joseph Stevens, 103
Burton, Ernest D., 113, 114
Byrd, William, 7

Calvin, John, 8, 10
Capps, Alton C., 187, 193
Carey, Matthew, 78
Carpenter, Joel, 68, 69
Carper, James C., 69
Carroll, John, Bishop, 6
Cassidy, Francis P., 48, 69
Catholic, see Roman Catholicism
Catholic Biblical Association of America, 65,
    149
Catholic Bible Movement, The, 64
Catholic Theological Society, 158
Ceroke, Christian P., 65, 69
Chandler, Julia, 172
Chase, Mary Ellen, 193
Chatanooga Bible program, 172
Chautauqua, 52, 53, 121, 133, 137
Chautauqua Literary and Scientific Circle,
    121
Cherry, Conrad, ed., 20
Childs, Brevard S., 100, 118, 156, 161
Chilstrom, Herbert W., 148, 161
Chomsky, William, 59, 60, 61, 69, 70
Christian Advocate and Journal, The, 80
Christian Day Schools, 62
Christian Schools International, 62
Civil Religion, 2
Clark, Justice Tom, 179
Clarke, James Freeman, 122
Classical learning, 9
Cobb, Lyman, 27
Cocceius, Johannes, 11
Cohon, Samuel S., 51, 70
Cole, Stewart, 138
College of Philadelphia, 16

College of Rhode Island, 16
Collie, William, 179, 193
Colonial education, 5
    at home, 16
    controls of, 15
    goals, 6–8, 13, 14
    role of Bible in, 19
Colson, Howard P., 147, 161
Commager, Henry Steele, 27, 40, 122, 138
Cone, James H., 128, 157, 161
Confraternity Revision, 65
Constitution on Sacred Liturgy, 65
Conversion, 8, 9, 10, 12, 38, 84f
Cope, Henry Frederick, 78, 94
Cotton, John, 11
Council of Trent, 145
Cox, Richard, 5
Cranmer, Thomas, Archbishop, 5
Cremin, Lawrence A., 6, 16, 18, 20
Crenshaw, Thomas, 78
Curti, Merle, 13, 15, 20

Daily vacation Bible School, 125
Damm, John Silber, 42, 70
Darby, John, 52
Darwin, Charles, 32
Day, George E., 110
Day schools, 1940–present, 58ff
Deists, 14
Dei Verbum, 145
Dell, William, 20
DePasquale, Leonard, 65, 70
De Vries, S. J., 122, 139
Dierenfield, R. B., 194
Dispensationalism, 52, 56
Divino Afflante Spiritu, 64, 154
Division of Christian Education of the Na-
    tional Council of Churches, 146
Dodge, William E., 79
Doherty, John T., 65, 70
Dowey, Edward A., 8, 21
Duffy, Martin, 161
Duker, Sam, 67, 70
Dunker, 13
Durrell, J. M., 139
Dushkin, Alexander, 48, 49, 50, 58, 59, 61, 62,
    68, 70
Dutch Reformed, 13, 15
Dwight, Timothy, 110

Education, Purpose of in Puritan theology,
    8–9, 12
Edwards, Jonathan, 8, 11
Eggleston, Edward, 88, 89
Eliot, John, 11
Ellington, John, 161
Elliott, William, 78
Empiricism, 97
Engel v. Vitale, 62, 166

Episcopal Sunday and Adult School Union of Philadelphia, 26
Episcopalian, 13, 42
Evangelism, 55
Everding, H. Edward, Jr., 152, 161
Everett, Edward, 104
Evolution, 32, 122
Ewing, William, 80, 94

First Amendment, 166–67
Fiske, John, 122
Flood, Theodore, 122, 134, 139
Florida State Department of Education, 168
Forbes, Allyn B., and Mitchell, Steward, eds., 8, 9, 21
Fosdick, Harry Emerson, 143
Fourteenth Amendment, 166
Franklin, Benjamin, 7, 13, 14, 18, 21
Frazer, James, 134
Freeman, James M., 134, 139
Frei, Hans W., 11, 21
Frost, Shimon, 60, 71
Frye, Northrop, 188, 194
Fundamentalism, 54, 68
Funk, Robert W., 113, 118

Gaebelein, Frank E., 63, 71
Gamoran, Emanuel, 58, 60, 61, 71
Gardiner, J. H., 194
Gartner, Lloyd P., 48, 49, 67, 68, 71, 125, 136, 139
Gaul, Cyril, 162
Gaustad, Edwin Scott, 6, 21
Geertz, Clifford, 180, 194
German Baptist Brethren, 13
German Reformed, 13
Gewehr, Wesley M., 16, 18, 21
Gibbs, Willard, 110
Gilmour, Richard, 46, 71
Giltner, John H., 118
Gladden, Washington, 124, 128
Goodrich, Samuel, 30, 32, 40
Goren, Arthur A., 71
Gourary S., 71
Grant, Robert, 133, 139, 159, 162
Gratz College, 59
Gray, James M., 55, 57, 71
Great Awakening, 12, 18
Green, William Henry, 97, 98–101, 118
Greenberg, Moshe, 61, 71, 151, 162
Greenberg, Simon, 145, 151, 161
Grimkee, Thomas, 30
Grinstein, Hyman B., 44, 71
Gros Louis, Kenneth R. R., 174, 184, 194
Gutierrez, Gaustad, 158, 162

Hadarim, 49
Haldeman-Julius, E., 131
Hallman, Ruth D., 182, 194

Handy, Robert, 122, 138, 139
Harkness, Robert, 68, 71
Haroutunian, Joseph, 21
Harper, William Rainey, 52, 53, 110, 113, 126, 134, 139
Harris, William T., 129, 139
Harrisville, Roy A., 110, 118
Hartman, Louis F., 65, 72
Harvard College, 15
Hautt, William David, 62, 72
Hebrew Union College, 50
Heder, 48
Hegelian idealism, 97
Heimert, Alan, and Miller, Perry, eds., 12, 21
Heinz, H. J., 88
Henn, T. R., 187, 194
Herberg, Will, 165, 194
Herbert, George, 21
Higher criticism, 99–116, 122, 128, 133. See historical-critical method
Hildebrand, R. Paul, 194
Hillard, George, 27
Historical-critical method, 53, 99, 145, 155. See also: Higher criticism
Historical Jesus, 111
Hodge, A. A., 66
Hodge, Charles, 83, 95, 98, 122
Hogan, Robert, 194
Holocaust, 61
Honor, Leo L., 48, 72
Hudson, Winthrop, 122, 138, 139
Huit, Ephraim, 21
Huntingdon, F. D., 95
Hurlbut, Jesse L., 123, 127, 135, 139
Hurst, John, 133, 140

Imitation of Christ, The, 47
Immigration, 13, 129
Indiana University Summer Institute, 174–76, 184
Indians, 11, 32
Ingersoll, Mrs. Robert, 130
International Council of Religious Education, 146
International Lesson System, 90
International lessons, aim of, 89
Isaac, Jules, 157
Israel and America, 11

Jacobs, B. F., 88, 89
Jefferson, Thomas, 14
Jewish Day Schools, 43
Jewish day schools, progressive, 62
Jewish education, 58
Jewish Theological Seminary, 50, 59
Jewkes, W. T., 179, 195
Johnson, Frank, ed., 136, 140
Jones, Howard Mumford, 187, 195
Judaism, 44, 50
    anti-Jewish attitudes, 31

Judd, Orange, 87
Judson, Albert, 81
Juel, Donald, 195
Kaminetsky, Joseph, 49, 72
Kane, John Joseph, 136, 140
Kaplan, Louis L., 60, 72
Katzoff, Louis, 48, 50, 72
Keane, John J., 129
Kelsey, David, 156
Kestenbaum, Jerome, 151, 162
Kevane, Eugene, 65, 72
Kirk, Albert, 150
Kittredge, J. E., 140
Klaperman, Gilbert, 51, 67, 72
Knappen, M. M., 9, 21
Knight, Edward W., ed., 15, 17, 22
Knoff, Gerald E., 95
Koenig, Robert, 160
Kohler, Kaufmann, 136
Kosnik, Anthony, et. al., 158, 162
Krentz, Edgar, 155, 162
Kubo, Sakae, 140
Kunz, Marilyn, and Schell, Catherine, 149,
    162

Langford, Norman, 144, 162
Lankard, Frank Glenn, 87, 91, 95, 132, 140
Laquer, Thomas Walter, 95
Laymen's National Bible Committee, 169
Lee, Alvin A., 195
Leeming, David Adams, 179, 195
Leeser, Isaac, 43, 154
Leibman, Morris, 50, 51, 72
Libraries, 17
Liebman, Charles S., 59, 61, 72
Lilly Endowment, Inc., 67, 168
Lindsell, Harold, S.J., 155, 162
Link, Mark, S.J., 150, 163
Littell, Franklin, 166, 194
Lloyd, W. F., 83, 95
Locke, John, 13
Loetscher, Lefferts A., 118
Lossing, B. J., 40
Lotz, Philip H., 125, 140
Lowes, John Livingston, 195
Loyola, Mother, 47
Lubavitcher Yeshiva, 62
Luther, Martin, 144
Lutheran, 13, 15, 42
Lynn, Robert W., 88, 95, 125, 140

Magnes, Judah, 67
Maly, Eugene S., 65, 73
Mann, Horace, 27
Marble, A. P., 131
Maring, N. H., 136, 140
Marsden, George M., 68, 73
Marty, Martin, 166, 195

Massachusetts Sabbath School Society, 87
Mather, Cotton, 16, 17, 22
Mather, Richard, 22
Mathews, Shailer, 113–16, 118, 134, 136, 140
Maxson, Charles H., 22
Mayhew, Jonathan, 7
McGiffert, A. C., 127, 128, 140
McGuffey, William Holmes, 27, 40
McGuffey's Eclectic Readers, 27–40, 121
    Biblical content of, 32–57
    worldview of, 28–30
McSweeney, P. L., 66, 72
Mead, Sidney E., 18, 22
Melton Research Center Series, 151
Memorization, 125
Mennonite, 13
Metcalf, Edith E., 56, 68, 73
Methodists, 17
Methodist Sunday School Union, 80
Michaelsen, Robert, 166, 171, 195
Millenarian exegesis, 11
Moody Bible Institute, 55, 56
Moody, Dwight L., 88
Moore, Joseph, 65, 73
Moore, LeRoy, Jr., 73
Moravian, 13
Morison, Samuel Eliot, 22
Morris, G. P., 30
Morris, Samuel, 18
Moulton, Richard G., 187, 196
Muhlenberg, Henry, 7
Murdock, Kenneth B., 22
Murray, Lindley, 27

Nagel, Paul C., 88, 95
Nardi, Noah, 49, 62, 73
National Association of Christian Schools, 73
National Union of Christian Schools, 64, 73
Nebraska Curriculum Development Center,
    168
Neighborhood Bible Studies, 149
Neill, Stephen, 133, 141
New Englands First Fruits, 22
New York Catholic School Board, 73
New York Sunday School Union, 81
New York Sunday School Union Society, 95
"Niagara Bible Conferences", 52
Nichols, James, 141
Norton, Andrews, 104
Noyce, Gaylord, 156, 163
Nuttall, Geoffrey F., 10, 22

Obach, Robert E., 150
Olbricht, Thomas H., 118
Olson, Bernhard, 157, 163
Orlinsky, Harry M., 151

Palfrey, John Gorham, 104
Parmele, Truman, 81

Panoch, James V., 168, 170, 196
Parochial Schools, 26, 42, 129, 136
  Catholic, 46
  Jewish, 44
  Lutheran, 42
Pease, George W., 136, 141
Phenix, Philip H., 171, 172, 196
Philadelphia First-Day Society, 78
Philadelphia School of the Bible, 57
Piediscalzi, Nicholas, 179, 196
Pierce, Bradford K., 130, 141
Pilch, Judah, 61, 67, 73
Pluralism, 18, 38, 165, 175
Pollard, Alfred W., ed., 5, 22
Pontifical Biblical Institute, 149
Pope, H. W., 74
Pope John XXIII, 157
Pope Leo XIII, 124
Pope Pius XII, 64
Pray, Lewis G., 78, 79, 95
Presbyterian, 13, 15
Preston, John, 8, 22
Preus, J. A. O., 155
Private Schools, 42
Providentissimus Deus, 124
Public Education Religion Studies Center, 178
Public Schools and Religion, 27. See *Bible in Public Schools*
Puritans, 7
Puritan exegetical methods, 11
Puritan theology and purpose of education, 8–9, 12

Quaker, 13
Quincy, Samuel, 13
Qur'an, 122, 178

Rabbi Isaac Elchanan Theological Seminary, 50, 51, 59
Raikes, Robert, 77
Rashi, 44
Rationalism, 13
Religious Education Association, 126, 134, 136
Religious Instruction Association, 168
Religious Literature of the West, 169, 178, 181
Revel, Bernard, 51
Rice, Edwin Wilbur, 81, 95
Richards, Larry, 159, 163
Richards, Zalmon, 128
Richardson, A., 155, 163
Roan, John, 18
Roberts, Clarence, 150, 151, 163
Robertson, David, 196
Robinson, Edward, 107, 119
Robinson, William, 18
Roman Catholicism, 13, 16
  Anti-Roman Catholic attitudes, 16, 31
  Bible in school curricula, 47

dissatisfaction with the common schools, 45
  parochial schools, 46
Rossi, Alice, 130, 141
Rousseau, Jean, 30
Ruether, Rosemary Radford, 157
Rush, Benjamin, 78
Russell, Charles T., 125, 141
Russell, Father, 47
Russell, Letty M., ed., 157, 163
Russell, W. H., 64, 74
Ryken, Leland, 154, 163, 185, 187, 196

Sabbath, 10
Sampey, John R., 89, 96
Sandeen, Ernest R., 68, 74
Sanders, Charles, 27
Sanders, James W., 74, 158, 163
Sandmel, Samuel, 154, 157, 159, 163
Sarna, Nahum, 151, 164
Sawin, Margaret, 159
Scharfstein, Zvi, 61, 74
Schempp,
  See *Abingdon v. Schempp*
Schiff, Alvin I., 49, 62, 74
Schlesinger, Arthur M., Sr., 122, 141
Schmucker, Samuel C., 124, 141
Schools, Colonial, 14–19
  and National Identity, 25
  nineteenth century, 25
Schulman, Moses I., 50
Schweitzer, Albert, 134
Secularization, 28
Scofield, C. I., 52
Second great awakening, 98
Secularism, 62
Septuagint, 103
Selton, S. W., 81
Sewall, Judge Samuel, 18
"Sharing of the Scripture", 150
Sherrill, Lewis Joseph, 42, 74
Showers, Renald, 58, 74
Shulman, Moses I., 75
Shurtleff, Nathaniel B., ed., 8, 23
Simms, P. Marion, 23, 123, 130, 141
Slaves, 7
  education of, 7, 19, 78
Smart, James D., 152, 164
Smith, Gerald Birney, 113, 119
Smith, H. Shelton, 12, 13, 14, 23
Smith, Henry P., 124
Smith, Julia E., 130
Smith, Wilson, ed., 23
Smith, W. Robertson, 110
Society for the Propagation of the Gospel, 7, 12, 15, 17
Soviv, Aaron, 60, 75
Spotts, Leon H., 75
Stainer, Betty, 182, 197
Stanton, Elizabeth Cady, 130

Steiner, Franklin, 126, 131, 141
Stuart, Moses, 107
Sunday School, 26, 44
  "Babel" period of, 88
  curricula, 80, 86, 87, 88, 105, 147, 149
  denominational, 80
  English, 78
  interdenominational, 78f
  interdenominational conflict with denomi-
    national, 84
  Jewish, 44
  19th century, 77–94
Sunday School Spelling Book, 26, 40
Sunday School Teacher's Quarterly, 88
Sutherland, David, 80
Sweet, William Warren, 7, 13, 16, 23
Swiggum, Harley A., 148

Talmud, 44
Talmud Torahs, 48, 49
Tappan, Arthur and Lewis, 79
Teachers College, 68
Tennent, Gilbert, 12
Teresita, M., 65, 75
Terry, M. S., 130, 141
Textbooks, theology of in nineteenth century,
  37
Thayer, Joseph Henry, 101–3, 119
Todd, John, 83, 84, 96
Todes, David U., 43, 75
Torah, 43
Tos, Aldo J., 65, 75
Town, Salem, 27
Townsend, Luther T., 122, 126, 133, 142
Toy, Crawford Howell, 103–7, 119
Tresler, Eugene, 159
Trinterud, Leonard J., 23
Turretine, Francis, 98
Tyndale, William, 5
Tyng, Stephen H., 31, 85, 96
Typological interpretation, 11, 46, 173

Unger, Daniel R., 126, 142
Uniform Series, 146
United Church Board for Homeland Minis-
  tries, 164
University of Chicago, 52
Uphaus, Willard, 146, 164
U.S. Bureau of the Census, 142
U.S. Commissioner of Education, 142

Vatican II, 65
Vedral Joyce, 197
Vincent, John H., Bishop, 52, 88, 91, 93, 96,
  123, 125, 128, 130, 133, 135, 137, 142
Vincent, Leon, 142

Wainwright House Conference on the Bible
  in Public Schools, 169, 172

Wainwright Report, 197
Wanamaker, John, 88
Warshaw, Thayer S., 167, 168, 169, 174, 182,
  197
Watts, Isaac, 13
Weatherall-Johnson, A., 149
Weekday religious education, 44
Weidner, R. F., 123, 127, 136, 142
Weigle, Luther A., 164
Wenger, Robert Elwood, 68, 75
Westerhoff, John H., 40
White, William, 78
Whitney, John R., 169, 178, 197
Wiley v. Franklin, 172
Wilkins, Ronald J., 150, 164
Will, Paul, 179, 197
William and Mary, College of, 15
Williams, George Huntston, 119
Williams, Roger, 11
Williamson, Lamar J., 155, 164
Wink, Walter, 156, 164
Winthrop, John, 8, 9, 14
Wise, John, 13
Wittmer, Paul W., 142
Wolfgang, Raymond S., 147, 164
Wood, Samuel, 27
Woodbridge, William, 40
Wright, Louis B., 15, 23

"Ye Olde Deluder Satan Act", 1
Yeshiva, 48, 49, 61f
Yeshiva College, 51
Yeshivah Etz Hayim, 50
Yeshiva University, 50